Understanding

Also by David Byrne

Complexity Theory and the Social Sciences
Social Exclusion
Beyond the Inner City

Understanding the Urban

David Byrne

palgrave

First published 2001
PALGRAVE
Houndmills, Basingstoke, Hampshire RG21 6XS
and
175 Fifth Avenue, New York, N.Y. 10010
Companies and representatives throughout the world

PALGRAVE was formerly Macmillan Press Ltd and
St. Martin's Press Scholarly and Reference Division.

ISBN 0-333–72428–3 hardback
ISBN 0-333–72429–1 paperback

This book is printed on paper suitable for recycling and made from fully managed and sustained forest sources.

A catalogue record for this book is available from the British Library.

Library of Congress Cataloging-in-Publication Data
Byrne, D. S. (David S.), 1947-
   Understanding the urban / David Byrne.
      p. cm.
   Includes bibliographical references and index.
   ISBN 0–333–72428–3
      1. Cities and towns.   2. Metropolitan areas.   3. City and town life.
   I. Title.

HT119 .B96 2000
307.76–dc21

00-062599

10 9 8 7 6 5 4 3 2 1
10 09 08 07 06 05 04 03 02 01

Printed in China

Contents

Acknowledgements

A lot of people have helped me in thinking about the issues covered in this book. Tim Blackman encouraged me to develop ideas about cities as complex systems. Mary Corcoran and her colleagues at the National University of Maynooth in Ireland gave me the opportunity to argue about the nature of metropolises at a crucial stage in my thinking. Kazimiera Wodz and her colleagues at the Silesian University, Katowice, Poland gave me the opportunity to make several visits to their city region and provided me with both intellectual stimulation and much information about that important and fascinating place. Fred Robinson, my colleague at Durham, has provided a 'keep your feet on the ground' background grumbling which I hope has served its purpose. Paul Cilliers really made me think more about complex systems and offered a version of the postmodernist programme I can live with, although I don't think it will please many postmodernists! Several cohorts of Masters and undergraduate students at Durham have discussed this material with me and their contribution has been considerable. Catherine Gray has been an exemplary editor and her advice is much appreciated. Sally, Clare and Alissa paid the usual domestic price of having a workaholic about the place but, mostly, put up with it. Whenever I write about urban issues I always draw on the experiences of the people of Tyneside where I lead my non-academic life. The late Gordon Brown of Sunderland, a Makkem rather than a Geordie, provided me with much information, stimulating discussion, and a model of what a good citizen of a polis should be. The people of industrial cities have had a lot to cope with in recent years. I hope that the unregenerate engagement of my version of understanding the urban might help to do something about that.

DAVID BYRNE

Introduction

This book is about understanding 'the urban'. Whenever we attempt to understand anything, there are two aspects of the process of understanding which have to be understood themselves. The first is: what are we trying to understand? The second is: how are we to understand? We have to define both the object of our understanding and the ways – the plural is absolutely deliberate – in which we understand it. In this book we are going to engage with the scientific understanding of urban places. We need to get the nature of science sorted out. Here the word 'science' will not be used in its common English sense which is specific to a programme which began in the seventeenth century, employs as a prime method the controlled experiment,[1] and explains by a process of analysis in which things are broken up into component parts and single causes are identified so that a mechanical model of causation can be constructed. Ideally such models are represented as a set of mathematical equations.

The word in Polish and Russian usually translated into English as 'science' is *nauk*. However, *nauk* is not specific in the same way as the English term 'science'. Instead it includes all organised knowledge, whatever the method used to obtain it, whether it involves simple description, the construction of typologies, the establishment of either single causes or of complex causation – the conduct of a process of interpretation which is quite distinctive from the establishment of cause or any possible combination of any or all of these modes of understanding. In this book, unless specifically instructed otherwise, when you read the word 'science', think *nauk*. When I want to talk about the more limited version I will call it 'scientism'.

We will consider epistemological issues, the questions about how we understand, in the second part of this chapter and throughout the book. First, I want to specify what it is we are trying to understand – to make a preliminary ontological statement. I want to define 'the urban' by a process of negation through contrasting two different places in the middle of the nineteenth century. One place was the

1

antithesis of urban. The other place at the same time was absolutely urban. We will then consider how these places changed as the world became industrial and urban. That is to say we will deal in history, with change through time and across space. Moreover, we will deal in a particular sort of history. To use the language of chaos and complexity theory, we will deal with changes which involve phase shifts. What matters are changes in quality, in type, in the whole character of the social systems within which people lead their lives. There have been plenty of discontinuities in the last two hundred years but the transformation of the human social world from one in which most people lived as subsistence farmers into one in which most people live as wage workers in towns and cities was the first and most important of them. Those of us in the advanced industrial world are currently living through another – the transition from an industrial society, in which the basis of most people's livelihoods was waged work making material things-to a postindustrial society in which most of us still work for wages but more and more of us are now making immaterial services and signs.

The townland and the town: from the rural to the urban

Only one of my great-grandparents was born into the urban world. The others, all born in the 1840s and 1850s, were country people. I want to say something about the place one of my great-grandparents was born in. This will establish the nature of the urban by negative contrast, by a comparison with what the urban is not. It will also give us a sense of the scale of change in people's lives through the last one hundred and fifty years, across just two human lifetimes.

My great-grandfather Patrick Gannon was born in the district of Leyny in County Sligo in Ireland in 1848. In 1841 Leyny had a population of roughly 37 000 spread through an area of 120 000 acres. Only one settlement had as many as 750 people. Ireland's population had grown enormously since the seventeenth century when the country had been virtually depopulated by the conduct of a mixture of English colonial and civil wars in the island of Ireland. The basis of this increase was the potato. Most people in Ireland lived by growing potatoes which they ate boiled. They were not, in any real sense of the word, farmers. They were gardeners who grew potatoes with spade labour, fertilising them with their own dung, their animals' dung, and seaweed (wrack) if they lived close enough to the seashore to get it. A family of healthy and strong children could be fed on the product of a quarter acre.

People married young and got land by converting the blanket bog, the product of ecological change three thousand years before, into potato ground. All this land was owned, usually by Protestant landlords descended from English colonisers. The peasants had to pay money rent which they raised by selling butter, rearing calves which were sold on for fattening, or illegal distillation and sale of crude whisky (poiteen), but otherwise they were not much engaged in a cash economy. They were subsistence gardeners in a world where spades were wealth and domestic equipment was usually one iron pot. In the west of Ireland very few people lived in anything resembling a town. Instead they lived in townlands. A townland is an area in which people interact and have mutual obligations, but they live apart, spread through the countryside, on their own land.

The potato famine of the 1840s changed this dramatically. The population of Leyny crashed by 1851 to 25 000. Thousands died. Thousands, including my great-grandfather and his family, emigrated. Over the next fifty years Leyny became, as it had been for three thousand years before the introduction of the potato, a country of empty bogs and lowland farms on which people raised cattle on standing grass. It is now moving into a 'post' future based on global tourism which draws on the musical component of its traditions and its 'heritage'.

For the hundred years before the famine the people of Leyny, materially very poor but with a rich oral and musical culture and tradition, lived by digging the ground. They had minimal urban contact. At the time of first contact with the global system in the 1930s, their lives were closer to those of the people of Highland New Guinea – also subsistence gardeners growing high-calorie carbohydrate crops – than they were to those of the people who lived in the new industrial world to which so many Leyny people were forced to emigrate. Their only urban connection was through their landlords, who spent some of their rental income in Dublin and London.

Let us compare Leyny in Sligo in Ireland with Gateshead on Tyneside in England where I live at the end of the twentieth century, in the conurbation to which my great-grandfather came to work, first as a navvy and then as a coalminer. In 1850 Gateshead had a population of some 25 000, an increase of 5000 since the census of

1841. It comprised some 3000 acres of which 80 per cent was still farm land. Most of the people lived in the urban part. Pipewellgate, a street 330 yards long and eight feet wide (yes, feet) housed more than 2000 people. The property tax valuation was just under £40 000 or a third more than that of Leyny which had much the same population but was forty times as big in terms of area.

The people of Gateshead and its surrounding area were industrial proletarians, not peasants. Less than 600 occupied males from a total of 13 000 were either farm labourers or farmers and they worked on large modern capitalist farms, not on peasant smallholdings. There were 1600 coal miners, 1100 iron makers, and more than a thousand workers in each of engine making, construction, and marine transport. Most women in this zone of heavy carboniferous capitalism were wives or domestic servants, although there were dressmakers, milliners and glass makers. In a textile or clothing town there would have been many more female industrial workers.

Coal mined on Tyneside was by 1850 being exported on a global scale around the world as were people to the new territories of settler colonialism. Three of my great-grandfather's English brothers-in-law emigrated to Australia where one ended up as Prime Minister of South Australia! The towns of the new industrial capitalism were the driving force of the whole global system and were replicated in form and function in the colonies. Newcastle, New South Wales, was settled by people from the north east of England, developed by capital from the north east of England, and reproduced the industrial and social relations of coal mining and coal export on the other side of the world.

Gateshead was a typical industrial hell-hole of the middle nineteenth century. There were repeated outbreaks of cholera in the town in 1833, 1834 and 1849 although the most serious episode of excess mortality had been in 1847 when 'fearful increase is in a measure caused by the famine and fever stricken Irish who came over on the failure of the potato crop' (Rawlinson, 1850: 21). The lodging houses in which the Irish lived were appallingly overcrowded, with walls impregnated with the filth that soaked into them from the dunghills (human dung) in the streets, in a town which lacked adequate sewerage. In an earlier period, farmers used to come into the town and cart dung away as fertiliser but by 1850, urban growth had made this activity uneconomic. The carters would simply have had too far to travel. The symbiotic ecological relationship between the town and its countryside had broken down in this new industrial era. There was a crucial problem of public health and of the physical reproduction of an urban industrial proletariat because mid-nineteenth century industrial towns were human ecological disasters with massive death rates in childhood and adult life from infectious diseases. The population of places like Gateshead grew dramatically but only through immigration from rural areas – the urban / rural transition which is the foundation of our urban world. By the end of the nineteenth century, Gateshead's population had grown four fold and the property tax valuation had grown seven fold. Its population was then the same as that of the whole Irish county of Sligo of which Leyny was just one quarter, and it was worth much more than Sligo in terms of land values.

It is worth thinking about the extraordinary transition which would have been the experience of someone like my great-grandfather coming to Gateshead in the 1840s. People born and brought up in a Leyny townland would have known every other inhabitant of that townland. They would have known them not by differentiated role and in a partial way, but totally in terms of all their social relationships. They would know the exact genealogical relationship (to themselves) of almost every individual they met and much of the family background and cousinage of everyone else they knew. Although there would be people with special skills, all these skills would have been supplementary to the basic activity of growing potatoes. The only people with specialised roles would be the tiny numbers of outsiders – what modern rural Ireland calls 'blow ins' – priests, police, landlord's agent.

Leyny's townlands constituted a set of classic spatially bounded 'communities'. Community is an important word for our project of 'understanding the urban'. It is often used as a direct translation of Töennies' theoretical expression *Gemeinschaft*. Relationships which form part of the complex which constitutes *Gemeinschaft* are long-term, 'affective', that is, motivated by feeling and degree of mutual identification, reflect and reinforce social status, and usually exist in a context of cultural homogeneity and within specific spatial boundaries. They are holistic rather than differentiated. People know each other and regard each other as part of the same social unit.

Social relationships in Gateshead in the mid-nineteenth century were very different from those in Leyny. Töennies contrasted the *Gemeinschaft* of the rural community with the *Gesellschaft* of urban life. The word *Gesellschaft* is usually translated as 'association' but can be best understood as describing relationships which are partial and instrumental rather than holistic and affective. Human relationships under urban industrial condition were for Töennies founded around a complex and segmented division of labour, centred on contract rather than on mutual obligation derived from identity, and marked by the partial and specific roles through which people related to each other. People in the urban world did not know the whole of most of those they had dealings with. They knew them only in their role as shopkeeper, foreman, employee and so on. Moreover, there would be many they would see in passing whom they would not know at all.

The key economic relationship of mid-nineteenth century Gateshead was not that of landowner to peasant but of capitalist employer to wage worker. There were certainly landlords in Gateshead because the private ownership of land and the payment of rent, including the capitalised rents of purchase prices, are always extremely important in urban societies. However, the dominant economic relationship was one in which capitalists paid workers money wages which those workers used to purchase the things which they needed in order to be able to continue to work, to maintain the wives who cooked and cleaned for them, and to bring up their children as future workers. Labour power was reproduced through wages. One of the commodities which the workers purchased was accommodation paid for through rents, part of which went directly or indirectly to the owners of landed estates.

There is something extremely important which needs to be said now. In the world as a whole until the year 1996, more people lived in the way in which the people of Leyny lived and live than lived in the way in which the people of Gateshead lived and live. Only in 1996 did the proportion of the world's population living in towns and cities reach 50 per cent (Clark, 1996: 1). In 1950, less than 30 per cent of the world's population was urban (Clark, 1996: 48). Even in Britain, the world's first urbanised society, 1861 was the first year in which the majority of the population was urban. In 1890, less than 3 per cent of the world's population was urban.

Since the agricultural revolution some 6000 years ago most people have lived in rural settlements which had far more in common with Irish townlands than with anything we would recognise as towns. Most people lived in the country and lived by agricultural work.

Now, most do not. The processes by which that changed began with the development of capitalism as a world system (see Wallerstein, 1974) through the operations of the European seaborne empires of the sixteenth century. A system originating in the bourgeois free towns of European feudalism became global. In this process the period of massive acceleration was that of the industrial revolution when capitalism became a system of production as well as a system of exchange. The basis of this was the creation of the industrial town. This book is about the urban consequences of those changes and of subsequent changes in the internal form of capitalism itself as we enter a new millennium.

The point of the contrast

The first part of this chapter had two purposes. First, it was about the object of study. It showed by contrast the difference between urban and rural places in order to establish the nature of 'the urban' and began to examine the divergent trajectories of urban and rural places through time. That was explicit. Note, by the way, that we must deal not only with the trajectories of places but with the actual trajectories of people across space in time as they intersect with the trajectories of places among which they move. People move around the world from rural to urban places and among urban places. They also move within particular urban places which themselves are changing character. All these trajectories of people and places are embedded in the large scale trajectory of the world system as a whole.

There was also an implicit purpose which I am now going to make explicit. I wanted to illustrate the methods of 'understanding the urban' by using them before delineating them. Intellectual activity in the academic world has traditionally been organised around the frame of the 'discipline' which is constituted by the combination of specified object of interest and distinctive methodological programme. Sociology, Geography, Economics, History, Statistics, Demography, Politics, Biology – all are disciplines. All were used in the story of the divergent development of Leyny and Gateshead. However, they were not used in isolation the one from the other. The theoretical sociological concepts of *Gemeinschaft* and *Gesellschaft* were used in association with geographical information about the actual patterns and scales of settlement. These were tied to quantitative descriptions based on 'secondary data analysis', a technique from social statistics. A key element in that quantitative description was the use of data about births, deaths, immigration and the structure of populations – the very essence of demography. This was all related to the character of production and the nature of social relations in production, which are central concerns of the classical tradition of political economy. Reference was made to the significance of the potato as food, of the potato famine, and of the importance of infectious disease in the cities of the nineteenth century – themes of ecology and of applied biology in the form of public health. The story used history, in the classic form of history as a research project, by drawing from documents and drew on secondary interpretation by historians of non-cited historical sources. An account was given of administrative change and of people's responses to the relations of domination and exploitation which they experienced – the domain of politics.

The disciplines were not used separately. Rather they were brought together in a synthesis which used all of them in interaction to give an account of the urban and rural as they were and as they became. Becoming does not stop. We will look forward as well as backwards.

There are other accounts besides those which derive from the disciplines of social science. In this book, novels and films will play a part in our project of understanding. They will not be presented as objects for critical analysis although of course they will be interpreted. They will stand as representations of the real.

The description of urban studies as a multi- or interdisciplinary field is quite conventional. However, I want to prescribe a strong programme of interdisciplinarity as the basis of 'understanding the urban'. It will help here if multi-disciplinary approaches are distinguished from interdisciplinarity. In multi-disciplinary approaches work is done within the tradition of a variety of disciplines which investigate a particular problem or field of problems. In interdisciplinary work, the boundaries of disciplines are broken down and the intellectual approach is defined not by discipline as such but by what emerges from the interaction among them.

This cannot be described by using the name of a discipline as an adjective. Instead it is a book about 'the urban' and it will attempt to understand 'the urban' in an interdisciplinary way. Moreover it will do so in terms of a very strong programme of interdisciplinarity. That very strong programme is founded around the linked philosophical and scientific meta-theoretical programme of complex realism proposed by Reed and Harvey (1992).[2]

Cities as complex systems

Meta-theories are theories about the nature of theories. Meta-theories have two components, epistemology and ontology. Epistemology deals with the way in which that scientific programme understands. Ontology specifies the nature of what is being understood. Reed and Harvey link the programme of philosophical realism proposed by Bhaskar (1986) with the scientific account of complex systems to form a general approach to understanding in science as a whole. I think they are right and will follow that approach in this book. This is important, even if it seems somewhat abstract at this stage.

Social science as a science, as science understood as *nauk*, must be more than just a series of specific stories – it cannot be merely ideographic. However, claims for a universal law-based story of the social which attempts, like physics, to generate a universal theory from which everything can be derived, do not stand up. Such a nomothetic programme cannot deliver because in the emergent world where the social and the natural interact we cannot derive our explanations from general reductionist principles (see Williams, 1999). However, this does not mean that we have no way of understanding the world as it is. The issue is not about the logical foundations of our approaches to understanding – the epistemological turn of postmodernism. Rather it is about how the world works – it is ontological.

We need to get a clear view of this in general terms before proceeding. The combination of realism and complexity theory provides us with a way of understanding which takes account of the specificity of unique local context whilst providing a general story of how the world works and how human beings work in that world, even if that general story is itself local, in time as opposed to space. It is the general story of a phase in the character of the global system, not something which holds for all time.

The ontological essence of philosophical realism lies in the way it understands causal relations in the world. For positivism, causes are simple, single and directly accessible. For realism, causes are complex, multiple, contingent and take the form of mechanisms which are not directly observable. A full account of the realist position is given in Sayer (2000). Dear (2000) argues for the postmodernist alternative.

In this book the implications of realism will be developed in relation to specific issues as we go through them in general discussion, but there are three important consequences of the realist account which we need to note now. The first is that the causal mechanisms are real, long-lasting, but not necessarily permanent. The second is that they generate structures, a term which refers both to ongoing patterns of social interaction and to the social relations which derive from the material products of those interactions. These structures are primarily the product of human agency which both made them in the first place and keeps them in existence, but they are still 'caused'. The third is that the real is not simply both social and natural, but is the complex product of the interaction of the social and the natural. This is of profound importance for understanding of the urban. Likewise the real is not simply the material or the immaterial. It is neither just the world of things nor just the world of ideas, beliefs, identities, culture. It is the product of the interaction of both of these domains.

Chaos and complexity theory is an account of the character and development through time of complex systems. Complex systems are dissipative far from equilibric systems (see Prigogine and Stengers 1984). The dominant perspective in scientism since Newton has been that of mechanics, which describes the movement of objects through space under the influence of forces. The basic tool of applied mathematics, the differential calculus, was invented by Newton precisely to handle the description of the trajectories of objects moving in this way. In Newtonian mechanics things change incrementally and all change is reversible. We can describe any system in terms of the aggregate properties of the objects which make it up. Analysis, the breaking of systems up into bits, is therefore the appropriate mode of understanding. We reduce systems to the parts they are made of and explain the character of the system in terms of the properties of the parts.

Thermo-dynamics, developed in the nineteenth century to formalize the understanding of heat engines, is very different. It deals not with the objects which compose a system but with the system as a whole. Moreover the system cannot be described by simple aggregation of the properties of its discrete components. Interaction among components means that the system has emergent properties which cannot be derived from the properties of those components. The whole is greater than the sum of its parts. In consequence, such systems are not time reversible. They are evolutionary. They have unique histories and futures which must flow from those histories, although they are not absolutely fixed by them. Marx summed it up rather well in a phrase which I will paraphrase for our gender-aware times: People make history but not in circumstances of their own choosing. There are different possible futures but they start from the present we have now.

In social science, systems have traditionally been understood to be equilibric and homeostatic. If disturbed, they return, through processes of negative feedback, to something close to their original state. The whole elaborate programme of Talcott Parsons was founded on this model. Far from equilibric, systems are not homeostatic. They constantly test their own boundaries and have the capacity to evolve into something very different. In them, feedback can be positive, reinforcing change rather than damping it out. We can see the transformation of quantity into quality. Such systems are dissipative. That means that they are not self-contained but must interact with the environment of which they are a part. They receive energy from it and must dispose of waste products to it.

Cities are plainly dissipative complex systems with emergent properties and an evolutionary history. The identification of cities as dissipative systems matters a great deal because it describes the relationship between urban places, the 'unnatural' location of contemporary life within a 'built' environment and the natural systems of this planet. Cities are indeed complex systems but complex systems embedded within both the complex system of global economic and cultural relations, and the complex systems which compose the natural world.

This book will be in the realist tradition, as that has developed in interaction with ideas derived from chaos and complexity theory. Certainly our knowledge is socially constructed and thereby reflects the social context of that construction. However, it is not made out of nothing. Critical realism works with a notion of the emergent real. It sees the production of knowledge as a social process but asserts that there is a real foundation for that production – we make our knowledge out of something which exists, however much we transform as we make the knowledge. Moreover, we make the world as well, not just the immaterial social world of culture, but also all our material products, perhaps the most important of which is the built environment of the urban world. At the same time, we must never forget the significance of the natural world for the social world and vice versa. Cities may be built environments, the material products of human agency, but those built environments exist in relation to a world of nature transformed by human agency.

Taking things further

The processes of urbanisation through which peasants become urban industrial workers remain enormously important in the world, but urban places themselves continue to change as well. The older urban areas of industrial capitalism have been transformed in the last quarter of the twentieth century. The transition variously described as being from the industrial to the postindustrial, from the Fordist to the postFordist, from the modern to the postmodern, has generated a fundamental qualitative change in the character of the urban as we move into a new millennium. Grasping the nature and character of this continuing dynamic development of the urban, of the evolutionary changes in the far from equilibric systems which are cities, will be crucial for our efforts to understand what the urban is becoming. The idea of dynamic transformation is central to everything we will consider here.

It is worth considering the character of recent transformations, the transformations of the last quarter of the twentieth century, before we go forward. In scale, the largest transformation has been the product of exactly the process by which places like Gateshead became industrial towns in the nineteenth century. Industrial urbanisation has never stopped even while older industrial places have been transformed into a postindustrial form. Throughout the past one hundred and fifty years, there has been a constant creation and growth of industrial cities. Pittsburgh, Detroit, Birmingham Alabama, Katowice in Poland, Ekatarinaburg (Sverdlovsk) in the Urals and Krasnoyarsk in Siberia, Shenzan in the new economic zone over the border from Hong Kong, São Paulo (the world's second biggest city), Medellin in Columbia – these are primarily the product of industrialisation, whatever the original basis of their foundation. Krasnoyarsk, for example, was originally a Cossack encampment established in the conquest of Siberia in pursuit of the 'soft gold' of furs, but it is the place it is today – a metropolis of more than two million people – because it is industrial, with the largest aluminium smelter in the world.

São Paulo – a metropolis of more than twenty million – was originally a settlement of slavers raiding the Guarani settlements of Paraguay established by the Jesuits. Now it is the largest single industrial metropolis in the world. The cities of Japan, South Korea, Taiwan and the new China are overwhelmingly the product of this kind of industrial urbanisation and in many cases pure products, as much creations of industrialism from virtually nothing as Middlesbrough in the north of England, Katowice in Upper Silesia in Poland, Magnitogorsk in the Urals, or Gary, Indiana. Industrialisation is still the most important basis of urbanisation in the world because it is the basis of urbanisation in China, India and Indonesia which together contain most of what is left of the world's rural populations.

Fundamental though industrialisation was, it has never been the only process through which towns have been established. The Ireland of which Leyny is a part was the world's first colonial society in the modern sense and Dublin was the world's first modern colonial city – an urban territory established inside a pale (originally, literally a fence) – in which colonial laws and social relations were the basis of colonial conquest and expropriation. The cities of Latin America, Australia, and of colonial empires in Africa had exactly this function as did the treaty ports of China (notably, Shanghai re-emerging as one of the most important cities of the globalised world). In India, Calcutta and Mumbai (Bombay) were created in precisely this way. Ireland's two metropolises, Dublin the colonial city and Belfast the virtually pure product of industrial capitalism, are very good contrasting examples of these two different processes of city formation.

However, all cities industrialise and their industrial character always matters. Peter the Great created St Petersburg as the 'window on Europe' of Russia, as a capital and port through which European influences could transform an Asiatic country, but it was industrial Petrograd which made the 1917 revolution which shook the world in ten days. Calcutta and Mumbai were founded around 'factories' in the original sense of the word, warehouses, in which the East India Company collected goods from the Indian countryside, but they became the locations of enormous factories in the modern sense in which material products were made by industrial proletarians. Mumbai is undergoing a postindustrial transformation to which we will pay particular attention, but for a long time it was predominantly an industrial city. Shanghai was created as an entryport to extract wealth from the Chinese countryside but it rapidly became and still remains the largest industrial city in China and one of the largest in the world. London was the colonial entryport of the Roman Empire in Britain and the capital of the monarchies which replaced that Empire. It was and is one of the great trading cities of first the world and now the global system. However, it was and is a great industrial city, although one which has experienced profound deindustrialisation in the last quarter of the twentieth century. The same is true of New York, Tokyo, Paris, Los Angeles, Sydney and Melbourne.

Having noted the importance of industrialism, people of my age (fifties) have to recognise that students in advanced industrial countries at the beginning of the twenty-first century often have no real experience of the character of an industrial society because they were born into a world which was already postindustrial. Their parents were not; so at the risk of seriously annoying young adults, their teachers should always urge them to talk to their parents and grandparents about the world those generations grew up in and the changes those people have seen. Much of this book will be about exactly those changes – the transformation of industrial cities concerned with the making of material commodities, and colonial cities concerned with the export of material commodities into postindustrial cities based around economies of services and signs rather than material things.

This is an appropriate point to identify a set of themes. These themes will run through the whole of this book. Some will provide the organising principle of chapters but all of them are important. These themes are:

1. *The co-evolution of the urban and the industrial world and the significance of material production as part of the urban system.* The modern urban world became the dominant way of living because people worked in factories and made things. The industrial revolution was and is also the urban revolution. Young adults in China today are making exactly the same transition that my young-adult child's great-great-grandparents made more than one hundred and fifty years ago, from being rural subsistence peasants who lived on what they could grow, to urban

industrial proletarians working in factories. That mattered, and it still matters both because it is an essential part of urban history and because the transition is still going on.

2. *The contingent character of human physical reproduction in urban systems.* Cities are unnatural places and in consequence unhealthy places. Without elaborate and mostly unseen systems of public health, water delivery, and dung and urine removal, infectious diseases would kill nearly half of our children before the age of five and many of us in adult life. Without the delivery of food we would starve to death and without the delivery of energy many of us would freeze to death – something which is a real issue in northern Russian cities today. It takes effort to keep cities going. We cannot take urban life for granted. Indeed unless we get our cities into a sustainable form, the demands our urban systems make on the natural eco-systems, within which they are embedded and on which they depend, may become impossible to meet.

3. *The significance of immigration in the constitution of differentiated and multi-ethnic urban populations.* Cities grow by attracting people from the countryside. In the nineteenth century this was necessary because of the horrendous infant mortality rates in urban areas. As we go into the twenty-first century, it matters because urban people in the advanced industrial world, particularly in Europe, have virtually stopped having children because they cost too much to bring up, particularly in consequence of the foregone earnings of women. The countryside from which people come can be a countryside a long way away. It can be the hills of Laos in Southern California or Australia, Turkish Annatolia in Berlin, Pakistani Mirpur in Bradford, Mali in Paris. Sometimes people are political refugees. Sometimes they are economic migrants, a term which covers both the miserably poor Africans working in the filthy jobs of Paris and Brussels, and the highly qualified and highly paid Indian software engineers who are such a vital component of the labour force of Silicon Valley. People move for a better life for themselves and their children. Often of course both motives – political fear and economic improvement – are present at once.

4. *The importance of the forms of governance of urban space.* In general, democracy and urban life have developed together.

The United States was founded in a revolution which drew as much on free farmers as on urban dwellers and the Mexican revolution was rural but it is in the urban world that democratic processes have been established as the normal form of politics. The legitimacy of the capitalist social order is essentially founded on exactly this democracy and the very word is inherently urban in its origins. However, we shall find that in the governance of contemporary cities, democracy is in trouble, both because many of the crucial decisions affecting the futures of cities and their people are being taken by non-accountable and unelected elites, and because people, perhaps in part in consequence of this, are no longer participating in the traditional political forms and processes through which democracy has been maintained. An additional complicating factor here is the role of 'expertise' – the expertise of the planners – in determining the future of urban life.

5. *The significance of the actual processes by which the built environment is constituted.* Cities are built and the building of them is planned. We need to understand how material resources, land and labour are brought together to get things built. We need to understand the role of money and technical expertise in getting things built and in determining what happens to them when they are built. We need to see how the processes of urban governance and construction come together in shaping urban development, the future of cities, into the new millennium.

6. *The formation of collective social relations based on spatial association – the genesis of 'community'.* There is an enormous amount of urban ethnography and history which shows us that people do create 'communities' in urban contexts, communities which have their origins in complex mixtures of ethnic and other identities and, above all else, in class positions. Communities have traditionally been seen as inherently spatial, based on day to day contact in the same place. We shall see that, in postindustrial society, communal relations can be maintained across very large distances and indeed may exist in the virtual as opposed to material world. However, spatial propinquity – living and working together – still matters and much urban social politics has its foundation in communal identities and communal interests.

7. *The way in which the multiple and partial social relations inherent in urban life engender a mentality* which is different from that of small-scale rural 'communities' – what Wirth (1938) called 'Urbanism as a way of life'. Culture is a word with a variety of meanings and we need to explore all of them here. We might think for a moment about the word 'cosmopolitan' which plainly has a root in common with the word 'metropolitan'. The cosmopolitan person is in some sense rootless, belongs everywhere and nowhere, has a highly individual view of the world and of what matters to them as individuals. Comopolitans always live in metropolises. The style is inherently urban. Often the cosmopolitan is committed to high art, to culture understood in a general and global sense. We shall find that this is not just a matter of personal sensibility but that cultural industries with an essentially cosmopolitan form are a crucial part of the new economy of signs in postindustrial capitalism.

8. *The importance of the global interconnectedness of urban spaces as part of a whole world system.* Here we are dealing with what Castells (1998) calls the networked society. There is nothing new about global interconnectedness. The seaborne empires of the sixteenth century linked everywhere in the world which could be reached on tidewater and the invention of the railway opened up interiors by connecting them to tidewater ports and hence to the world. However, the new instantaneous telecommunications coupled with the ease of personal mobility through air travel makes the global much more accessible and present in our everyday lives. Specialists (like my grandfather, a merchant seaman) were very widely travelled even a hundred years ago, but now the global is encountered on a daily basis. This is particularly significant for immigrants. Their original world remains accessible to them, through telephone calls to friends and family and regular visits home. Of special economic significance are the global financial markets and their virtually instantaneous interconnection.

There is an ninth theme which did not play much part in the story of the contrasting trajectory of Leyny and Gateshead but which does matter and will be addressed where appropriate, although it will not have the significance of the other themes,[3] and that is: the way in which gender relations are expressed in urban space. Underlying all of the discrete themes will be a kind of meta-theme, the idea that urban spaces are evolving and changing complex systems, although this will be developed primarily in the conclusion to the book as a whole. In order to develop these themes, this book will be organised as follows.

Chapter 1 will be concerned with the nature of the urban in the late twentieth century. It will consider how we distinguish the present nature of places from their previous nature by using the word 'post': modern becomes postmodern; industrial becomes postindustrial; Fordist becomes postFordist. The chapter will explain these terms and consider the implications of their application to 'the urban'. This chapter will be a preliminary working through of the terms and their implications – a kind of first pass to get the ideas into play. We will keep coming back to them in relation to the substantive concerns of subsequent chapters.

Chapter 2 will consider the spatial reconstitution of the world system of production and circulation. It will examine the extent of deindustrialisation in metropolitan capitalism and review the accounts given from political economy and economic geography of the reasons for the massive decline in industrial employment in old capitalist economies. We will consider the role of space in the changing relations of capitalist production through the new international division of labour and the forms of capital export related to that division. The emphasis will be on changes in the geography of production but these will be related to the changes in the world financial system from being global over slow times, the time of a ship's voyage, to the instantaneously global of the electronic era. The chapter will conclude by reviewing the processes of development and underdevelopment and their implications for urban social orders.

Chapter 3 deals with the geographical and sociological concepts which order and describe space in the global system – locality and community. Locality is an essentially structural concept set in an economistically deterministic programme. The second half of the chapter will argue that the concept of 'community', although complex and contradictory, remains useful in understanding urban life. The implications of an understanding of the social in terms of community will be contrasted with the structuralist implications of conventional usage of the more spatial concept of locality.

Chapter 4 will develop the idea of a hierarchy of spatial elements begun in Chapter 3 and suggest that there is a related, but separate, hierarchy of actual cities ordered by the role that cities have in connecting real spaces and the world system as a whole. The first part of this chapter will develop the conceptual framework and relate it to efforts to establish 'city trajectories' through specific urban development policies which are intended to position cities at a higher level within this hierarchy.

In the second half of the chapter, attention will move to the internal characteristics of 'world cities'. This will be related to their global function and their openness to immigration at the ends of the social hierarchy, that is, to the mobile higher-service classes and to the immigrant poor. The nature of the resulting social polarisation will be considered in a preliminary way as a lead-in to Chapter 5. In the last section, the cultural themes which will be the subject of Chapter 6 will be examined in 'global' terms.

Chapter 5 will develop the account of the internal order of cities / localities. It will begin with an outline of the classic models of the Chicago school, relating these to earlier accounts of urban differentiation. There has been a revival of interest in 'urban social polarisation', which is closely related to the general debate about the so-called 'underclass' in advanced industrial societies. It is in this chapter that issues of gender will be introduced in relation to issues of class and ethnicity. The 'underclass' (the inverted commas are meant to indicate my rejection of this formulation) debate provides a good framework for beginning a discussion of the complex inter-action among these in the urban context.

Chapter 6 will begin with a review of the classical accounts of urban culture presented by Wirth and Simmel with particular attention given to Simmel's conception of the character of mental life in the modern metropolis, precisely because it provides such a good lead into a review of contemporary postmodernist accounts of the urban. The chapter will proceed with a development of the postmodernist account of the differentiated and fragmented city as a cultural form and locale of cultural processes. A consideration of the sociology of consumption will lead into an account of the role of cities in the production of culture in both its 'high' and its 'popular' forms. The placed culturalism and interpretative approach particularly associated with the recent work of Shields will be considered here.

Chapter 7 will deal with the production of the built environment. It will draw on three main bodies of literature. One is the 1970s' discussion of the role of professionals – 'evangelistic bureaucrats' – in planning, architectural design and construction processes. Another is a structuralist marxist account derived from political economy which analyses the production and circulation relations of land rent and construction. The last is an action-centred account derived from empirical investigations of actual situations. In the best empirically founded work (for example, Zukin's *Loft Living*, 1988) these themes are drawn together to show how cities are made and remade. This becomes ever more important in global terms, given the significance for finance capital of investments in capitalised rents in the form of real property. This chapter will pick up themes of urban fragmentation and relate these to the way in which the built environment structures and is structured by consumption-organised lifestyles.

The subject of Chapter 8 will be the governance of the urban. The chapter will relate the realist conception of a hierarchy of spatial levels outlined in Chapter 3 to the 'structural necessity' argument for levels of governance which correspond to those levels of space. This structuralist account will be complemented by a review of urban regime theory which places considerable emphasis on agency. Here we will refer back both to the discussion of the production of the built environment in Chapter 7 and to the discussion of the relation of cities with the global system in Chapter 4. The general character of urban governance will be illustrated by reference to recent use made of the development process (including here, developments both in the built environment and in culture) as the basis for bids for relocation of places in the hierarchy of global connectedness. The relationship between and among these levels, and local / regional social action is not simply dependent on global factors. On the contrary, local action constitutes the global framework, just as much as the global framework bounds local action.

The second half of the chapter will examine contemporary 'postmodernist' accounts of the sources of collective social action in urban life. Typically, these 'deprivilege' class and assert the equal significance of gender and ethnicity. More sophisticated accounts take up the idea that the main source of collective actions in contemporary society will be based on culturally founded choices and take the form of volitionally based social movements. We will consider the likely forms of collective urban social action in the future and the relationship of such action to the processes of governance of cities as complex systems.

The book will conclude with a consideration of the future, of the urban in the next millennium. The form will deliberately not be that of a tight conclusion but instead a number of themes, particularly that of posturbanism and / or edge city, and a number of modes of representation, will be taken up as a way of seeing what trajectories may be available for cities in the next century. Here I will draw on a literature which itself draws on the literatures reviewed in the text so far, but is seldom referenced in return – the revived formal modelling accounts of the urban as a complex social system. It is precisely the availability of complexity theory which has permitted a revival of systemic thinking and this is extremely important. I will also consider in this chapter what might be considered to be the absolute antithesis of such systemic approaches – ideographic, historical and, to a considerable extent, hermeneutic accounts of particular urban places. My concluding argument is that both these ways of seeing must be employed in any adequate attempt at understanding the urban.

Sources

In the course on which this book is based we make considerable use of unconventional sources. These fall into two categories. The first comprises 'representations' in the form of novels, travel writing and film / TV. The second consists of the 'virtual footprints' of places on the World Wide Web. Throughout the book I will suggest examples of films and fiction which illustrate the themes I have raised. The books will be referenced in the normal way. To locate the films or videos, use the latest edition of Halliwell's guide.

Let me begin with a general suggestion about getting to know places. Guide books, and in particular the excellent Lonely Planet and Rough Guide series, are well worth reading because they are designed to 'explain' both the history, the process of becoming, and the form, what is now, of cities and towns. They are excellent sources of illustrative material and I use them all the time in order to get a sense of a place. See, for example, either or both of the Lonely Planet or Rough Guide guides to Poland on the City of Lodz, an extraordinarily interesting and significant example of a place which experienced both capitalist and Stalinist industrial development.

Likewise, look on the Web for the virtual footprint of cities. Use search engines and enter the place's name as the search term. Again,

Lodz is a good locus with a large and interesting virtual footprint. In the Americas, Medellin is worth a virtual visit and Mumbai (Bombay) is a fascinating South Asian locale.

We can also use novels and films. It is very hard for us now in Western and really even in Central and Eastern Europe to appreciate the nature of the lives of peasants before the industrial world, and almost as hard to appreciate the lives of rural proletarians. For the latter, the work of Thomas Hardy remains one of the best guides, and the film of *Far from the Madding Crowd* does show what that kind of life was like. The numbers of people engaged were very different but the nature and rhythms of work then were very similar to when I worked as a harvest hand at North Trewick Farm in Northumberland in the 1960s, nearly one hundred and fifty years after the period in which that story was set.

For pre-industrial peasant life, Flaherty's film *Man of Aran* remains superb. *The Field* is a brilliant account of land relations in post-famine Ireland. Brody's anthropological classic *Inishkillane* (1986) describes rural County Clare in the 1960s. The Scottish trilogy *A Scots Quair* (1990) by Lewis Grassic Gibbon is especially valuable because it follows its characters from farm to city in the early twentieth century and puts war as central in their lives. In the contemporary world the film *Going North* illustrates exactly the experience of Latino immigrants, indeed Indios of pre-Columbian stock, in their transition into the urban labour markets of Los Angeles.

When we turn to the urban world of the early nineteenth century, we have novels of which Mrs Gaskell's *Mary Barton* (1993) and Dickens's *Hard Times* (1995) are two of the best. A wonderful book about the early twentieth century industrial city is Upton Sinclair's *The Jungle* (1985) which describes that combination of stockyard and factory, the Chicago of 1910. Jack London's *The People of the Abyss* (1998) describes early twentieth-century London in similar terms.

A lot of contemporary material on China illustrates the character of the emerging urban world very well indeed. Paul Theroux's travel book *Riding the Iron Rooster* (1989) is particularly useful, not least for his remark that anybody who grew up in an American or European factory town of the 1940s or 50s knows exactly what contemporary China is like. Shanghai is an amazing place to visit on the Web. The recent UK TV series *Shanghai Vice* was a brilliant portrayal of the contemporary Shanghai scene.

1

The city at the beginning of a new millennium

The task of this chapter is to establish the nature of the urban world at the beginning of the twenty-first century. Cities are diverse: they are localities, and specific context, both economic and cultural, always matters when we are dealing with things which have a local character. However, cities are embedded within a global system and changes in that system matter for the character of specific places.

We will begin by considering both the significance of industrialisation for the generalisation of urban ways of living, and the transition from industrial world to postindustrial world. As always, we must consider both what is to be understood ('the urban') and the ways in which we actually do understand ('urban theory'). We must bear in mind that the transition from industrial to postindustrial involves 'combined and uneven development'. Much of the world is still urbanising on an industrial basis. The next section will consider the scale of that continuing industrial urbanisation, particularly in the enormous countries of East and South Asia. Then we will consider 'all the posts'. The terms postindustrial, postFordist, and postmodern – all neologisms which incorporate as prefix the Latin word for after – are much employed in discussion of urban issues. We will review them as description of contemporary circumstances, as explanation for it, and, in the form of the relativism of postmodernism, as method of understanding. This chapter is one in which themes are brought onto the field of play. One which matters a great deal is culture. We will consider ideas about culture and identity which will be developed in both Chapter 3 in our discussion of community and in Chapter 6 when we return to the theme of culture, widely considered.

The industrial and postindustrial city

> Our urban system is based on the theory of taking the peasant and turning him into an industrial worker. (Roger Starr, New York's Housing and Development Administration Chief 1976, quoted in Fitch, 1993: viii)

Starr was absolutely right. The mass urbanisation of the world is based on taking peasants and turning the hims into industrial workers and the hers into industrial workers and / or reproducers of the industrial workers' labour power. Starr went on to say: 'Now there are no industrial jobs. Why not keep him a peasant?' The implications of the transformation of industrial into postindustrial cities in the metropolitan core of capitalism will be crucial to our considerations. However, industrial urbanisation continues across the world. Using 1989 data, Angotti identified 62 metropolises (urban areas with populations greater than one million) in China alone (1993: 145–6). The overwhelming majority of these are industrial cities.

The industrial urbanisation of China has resulted in the creation, in the delta of the Pearl River, of the world's largest industrial metropolis incorporating Hong Kong and Gwandung together with the wholly new industrial city of Shenzhen. This conurbation has a population of 30 million people. Most of them are peasants who have been made into industrial workers. In the New Industrial Zones there is only industrial production and the reproduction of the labour power of those now working. Young workers live in dormitories and when they are not sleeping, they are working. Pregnant women go home to their villages as late in pregnancy as they can. Elites live well and the workers have much higher incomes than they would in their villages, but work is all.

China is not unique. India, Indonesia and Brazil have enormous numbers of industrial workers in cities which are growing apace. True, there is a postindustrial shift even in these new zones of industrial urbanisation. Mumbai (Bombay) and Hong Kong have lost many industrial jobs as they have been transformed into specialist financial centres for the industrial complexes of which they are a part. However, the industrial production of commodities remains at the core of urban life.

How can we understand this world of cities? The argument that the industrial production of commodities is the basis of life in cities points towards a combination of political economy and economic geography as the basis for interpretation and / or explanation. However, there is another domain which also matters. Although the combination of realism and complexity theory which informs this book implies necessarily a rejection of the extreme cultural relativism of the postmodern turn in cultural studies, that does not mean that culture is unimportant. Culture matters. It matters as a component of the political economy of postindustrial cities, given the significance of cultural industries in those cities – the significance of the production of signs rather than material commodities. It also matters as a domain of life which is different from, but always related to, the material and natural bases of our social existence. We will explore both these dimensions in Chapter 6.

Although this book argues for realist understanding, we should note the character of the relativist alternative. As Jacobs notes in 'Urban Studies', the relativist mode of understanding is founded on the principle that 'the boundary between social reality and representations of that reality has collapsed' (1994: 830). In an important collection, Tagg asserts:

> The discursivity of the city is indelibly multiple and heterogeneous and the discursive regimes across which the city has been constituted do not coincide. This city, therefore, is not one: it is not identical with itself. (1996: 180)

Tagg is explicitly rejecting 'master narratives' of explanation in favour of a multiplicity of individual interpretations in which economic base has no explanatory privilege. That is not the view taken in this text. In understanding our urban world, we have to begin from a recognition of a fundamental material reality. Cities are the places in which things are made by people; and the labour power, the capacities of those people to make things, is renewed and replaced by other labour power expended to that end. Indeed, the materiality of human social existence involves not only the products of labour but our relationship with the natural world.

The use of the word 'thing' to describe products does not mean that everything which is made has a material form. With the crucial exception of raw food, the overwhelming majority of material commodities which we use to live by are made in cities, but so are the 'signs' of Lash and Urry's in their book *Economies of Signs and Space* (1994). The call centre is even more of a panopticon, Jeremy

Bentham's idealised prison of surveillance, than the factory; and Taylorist principles of production management are even more rigidly employed in such contexts than in the manufacture of material commodities. Even most aesthetic signs are produced by labour working in an industrial way. Moreover, this is not a new process. Commercial art dates from the second half of the nineteenth century and its techniques of mass production were perfected, as with so much else that is modern, in the years between 1900 and the First World War. Tools of production have changed but the overall pattern of organisation remains what is was then. When Lash and Urry assert that:

> The 1980s have surely sealed Marx's coffin for good and confined him and his monstrous books to the dustbin of history. Even if we are not at the end of history, we are surely at the end of his history based as it was on the unfolding contradictions of *industrial* [original emphasis] capitalism. That society and those contradictions have unequivocally gone for ever. (1994: 1)

they should consider whether this would square with the experiences of call-centre workers in Middlesbrough and elsewhere.

Assertion of postindustrialism is certainly western centric since the most important social phenomenon of the second half of the twentieth century is the general extension of industrial and urban production and ways of life on a global scale. Even on the old home ground, it is wrong because it confuses form with content. A commodity is a commodity is a commodity and that commodity can be an answered call, or health care, or the emotional labour of a bartender or PR person, just as much as it can be a sack of wheat, or a loaf of bread, or a sack of coal, or the electricity coming down the wire, or raw cotton, or a shirt. These things are made by people who sell their labour power for wages, and the places in which they (other than the sack of wheat or the raw cotton, or, sometimes but not always, the coal) are made are cities.

The deindustrialisation of industrial cities matters in ways which are both economic and cultural and which have profound significance for sources of power in a capitalist system, but the key thing to understand about cities is that they are places in which production and reproduction are brought together outwith the domestic sphere. For the subsistence peasant, the home is the locale both of production of food and other essentials, and of reproduction of self and family. You grow it, you eat it, you make it, you use it, a lot you sell to pay the landlord – the Orcadian crofter's three grains of oats: 'ane to saw and ane to gnaw and ane to pay the rent withaw'. In the city, production is separated from the home in the iconic structure of industrial life, the factory. I do like the Russian word *Zabod* which translates as 'Works', a term used as well in the north east of England and Scotland – the Great Works; that is something to conjure with: 'The Great Works was spread out over miles of snow-covered work yards, all the way from the workers' quarter to the sea' (1975: 54). This is Serge's description of the industrial zone of Petrograd on Vassilsky Island, Bely's unknown island of that city, from which the revolutions of 1917 had started and in which, in 1920, revolution was being transformed into a regime based on totalitarian bureaucracy.

A world becoming urban and postindustrial

The statistical publications of the United Nations describe the scale of industrial urbanisation and the simultaneous trend towards post-industrialism. In 1996, India, China, Pakistan, Bangladesh and Indonesia all had less than a third of their people living in cities. This set of enormous Asian countries together with some of their neighbours are the largest reservoir of rural life in the contemporary world; although in all of them, urbanisation is proceeding apace and they are so big that their urban areas form a large part of the urban world. Sub-Saharan Africa (other than South Africa) remains predominantly rural although again there is both very rapid urbanisation and a set of enormous cities. Europe, North, Central and South America, Australasia, North Africa and Western Asia are all predominantly urban (United Nations, 1996).

India and China are so huge that even with only a quarter of their people in cities, they still have enormous urban industrial populations. In 1993, China had nearly 93 million manufacturing workers which can be compared with Japan's 15 million, Brazil and Indonesia's 8 million each, Russia's 19 million, the UK's 8 million, Germany's 10 million, Korea's 5 million, Poland's 4 million, Mexico's 16 million and the US's 21 million (United Nations, 1995; 1997). It is important to note that in all cases other than Indonesia and Mexico these totals were smaller than five years previously – deindustrialisation is almost a general process, although its proportionate scale is far higher in some places, particularly the UK, than in others and there are places which are still zones of growth. The urban world is still industrial, but it is changing all the same. Let us try to get a grip on the character of those changes.

'Being after' I: postindustrial

The actual mechanisms, direct processes and social consequences of deindustrialisation will be the subject of the next chapter. Here, we will consider the broad character of the social transformations which have been given a variety of labels incorporating the word 'post'. Our world at the end of the twentieth century, and particularly its Western and Northern parts, is variously described as 'postindustrial', 'postFordist', 'postmodern'. The Latinate prefix 'post' means after. The implication of these adjectives is that there has been a qualitative change involving the ending of one sort of system and its replacement by something which is the product of historical evolution from what was before, but which is also of a different kind. Let us consider the content and implications of these terms.

'Postindustrialism' refers to a change in the character of employment. The term 'industrial' usually describes the traditional forms of the production of both material goods and services by wage labour working in the factory system as mode of organisation of the factors of production. Plainly, manufacturing is industrial, but it is conventional to include mining, construction, energy and water, and marine, rail and road transport. In terms of production relations, the form of labour's remuneration and the way in which work is controlled, a great deal else could be added to this set, but the list indicated has value because it does contain the core sectors of industrial capitalism. Note that although the workforces of these sectors are predominantly blue-collar and manual, they are also large numbers of white-collar office workers, technical staff and managers. Note also that although industrial employment, particularly in mining and transport, has always been predominantly male, there are massive numbers of female industrial workers in textiles, clothing, light engineering, and the manufacturing of food and drink.

Although we will examine deindustrialisation intensively in Chapter 2, we need some idea of its scale here before we proceed. Let us take the most extreme example of deindustrialisation in the world's oldest industrial country, England. Here it is useful to consider the world city of London and the provincial cities separately because the differences between them are important for our considerations in Chapter 3. Both the provincial cities and London lost about half of all their industrial jobs in between 1971 and 1991. London had a catastrophic collapse of manufacturing, losing 700 000 jobs which was 70 per cent of the original total. Other industrial numbers held up due to a strong construction sector and growth in communications despite the loss of thousands of port-related jobs. In the provincial cities the number both of manufacturing and other industrial jobs halved so the industrial total fell from 3.5 million to 1.7 million. The growth sectors were financial services and health and educational employment, particularly in the provincial cities. In both the provincial cities and London, overall employment declined by 16 per cent and full-time male employment declined by more than 30 per cent. Full-time female employment declined in the provincial cities by 10 per cent but stayed roughly the same in London. The only dramatic increase was in part-time female employment which went up by 50 per cent in the provincial cities and somewhat less dramatically in London.

These changes are not just a matter of numbers of people employed. Although a good part of the reduction in manufacturing employment resulted from productivity gains, much also came from plant closure. Not only factories, but also docks, railway yards and coal mines closed and were demolished. The consequence was not only redundant and redeployed people but also redundant and redeployed land. There are crucial political, economic and cultural consequences of the massive destruction of industrial employment in cities and we will explore them in more detail in Chapter 2. Let us for the moment turn to the other terms in the 'post' litany.

'Being after' II: postFordist

We can begin with postFordism. Amin specifies the nature of this best:

> The 'post-Fordist' debate concerns the nature and direction of ... epoch making change. It is debate about the putative transition from one

dominant phase of capitalist development in the post-war period to another thirty to fifty year cycle of development based upon very different economic, societal and political norms. It seeks to identify the driving forces in each historical phase and, through this process, to elaborate how these forces constitute a paradigm or system capable of securing relative economic stability over the long term. Different positions within the debate each accept that history can be periodized into distinct phases, guided by a coherent frame of dominant principles, but giving way to a period of uncertainty and transition during which the elements of a new paradigm may develop and mature. (1992: 3)

In order to understand post-Fordism we need to define Fordism. Jessop (1991: 136–7) begins his account by reference exactly to the production line pioneered by Henry Ford and identifies four levels at which the term can be analysed. These are:

1. In terms of *labour process* where Fordism is a system of mass production based on the assembly line and semi-skilled assembly labour. This can be distinguished from manufacture in which production depends on the work of skilled labour with the skilled worker retaining considerable control over work management, and machino-facture in which the worker is tied to the process of the machine but for the production of piece rather than complex goods. Of course both manufacture and machino-facture remained important in the Fordist and even into the postFordist era.

2. In terms of *macroeconomic organisation* (the regime of accumulation) Fordism saw a virtuous circle of growth in which mass production and economies of scale generated economic growth, which in turn sustained higher real wages and hence higher demand, which ensured the consumption of goods produced.

3. In terms of *economic organisation* where Fordism is characterised by large corporations in which ownership is separated from control and organised capital – organised in terms of a clear corporate structure with specific managerial levels, and organised labour, organised in trade unions, negotiating wages which reflect both rises in productivity and general price inflation. In consequence, real wages rise and there is developed a system of credit support for continued consumption.

4. In terms of the *development of a system of state activity* which provided a large element of welfare goods directly, sustained generous levels of wage substitution benefits, and regarded the maintenance of full employment as a central objective – the Keynes / Beveridge Welfare State. It is important to note that this was not merely a national programme. The system of international institutions established at Keynes's initiative at Bretton Woods were intended to manage international economic relations to the same end.

I have modified Jessop's account because he brings into his description of Fordism 'the consumption of standardized mass commodities in nuclear family households', which has been part of industrial capitalism since its foundation; although this pattern did become absolutely prevalent during Fordism. It would also be usual to consider the aspects described under headings (3) and (4) above as together constituting the Fordist regime of accumulation, although Jessop reserves this description for (3) alone.

Originally, discussions of postFordism centred on changes in the relations between labour and capital at the point of production. Micro-electronic technology was identified as the basis for a de-skilling of manufacture and machino-facture because machines could be programmed to work in a variable way. This meant that the detailed division of labour through the mass production assembly line could be extended to batch production. However, this production centred account soon became overlain by a consideration of changing patterns of consumption in which standardised goods were supplemented by a much greater variety of differentiated products made in systems based on 'flexible specialisation'. Microelectronic flows of information from consumer to producer meant that consumption patterns could be used to determine production runs.

For regulations theory (see Lipietz, 1988), postFordism is a transformed social order in which new relations exist between labour and capital, full employment is achieved only if real wages are massively reduced, and welfare expenditures are under constant ideological assault, although other than in the United States, they have actually generally maintained their Fordist levels as proportions of GDP.

'Being after' III : postindustrial capitalism

Nelson, writing from a US standpoint quite separately from the Fordism / postFordism debate and drawing on the ideas of Schumpeter, has identified the present era as 'postindustrial capitalism'. This means rather more than the loss of industrial employment discussed earlier in this chapter, although that loss is important. For Nelson managerial control over production, marketing and politics is crucial to the reformation of the social order. He describes the consequences thus:

> post-industrial capitalism does not involve any shift in the fundamental processes of capitalism, as reflected in the competitive search for economic advantage or political dominance ... What this new and blended form of capitalism does, however, is produce a transformation, a qualitative and discontinuous shift in class structure. That is, the contrast of past and present is indicated not merely by the blended form capitalism assumes but also by its influences on inequality. In a previous time, economic development fed social development by diminishing inequality; today economic development escalates inequality. (1995: 14)

Nelson's approach is more coherent than the general postFordist account but many of the essential features are the same. If we follow Nelson's lead we are directed towards agency, towards actors who have made this happen. In Chapters 7 and 8 we will look at the nature of those actors and actions in relation to urban governance and planning.

'Being after' IV: postmodernism

The last of the 'post' words is postmodern. This term is both a description of the social world and an account of, and even prescription for, forms of knowledge. To 'understand the urban' we have to keep coming back to the debates about how we understand. We need to consider the terms realist, modern and postmodern. These have different content in science and in criticism, and that different content is the source of enormous confusion. It is easiest to distinguish between the ideas of modern and postmodern in science and philosophy. Here the key thinker is probably Lyotard. A very useful and coherent account of Lyotard's position is provided by Cilliers (1998):

Scientific knowledge, [Lyotard] claims, habitually legitimates itself by appealing to a coherent metadiscourse that provides a general unifying function. Should such a metadiscourse be found, it will be possible to incorporate all forms of knowledge into one grand narrative.... Postmodernism is consequently defined as 'incredulity towards meta-narratives' ...Instead of looking for a simple discourse that can unify all forms of knowledge, we have to cope with a multiplicity of discourses, many different language games – all of which are determined locally, not legitimated externally. Different institutions and different contexts produce different narratives which are not reducible to each other. (1998: 113–14)

In Cilliers's interpretation different social groups work with their own specific local narratives which 'are instrumental in allowing them to achieve their goals and to make sense of what they are doing' (1998: 114). These local narratives cannot be combined into an overarching grand theory of everything. Above all else, there is no possibility for a unique and *universal* privileged account. However, Cilliers, whose book is exactly about *postmodernism* and *complexity* argues strongly for the possibility of local knowledge. We cannot have laws which hold everywhere and always but we can construct knowledge specific to particular contexts in time and space.

On this basis, Cilliers asserts that Lyotard's account must not be interpreted as a licence for absolute individualistic relativism. It is true that it has been seized on in that way by those working in a critical tradition in 'cultural studies' mentioned in the introduction to this chapter. Absolute relativism appeals to such 'critics' because it provides a license for the individual aesthetic sensibility. However, in general, postmodern urbanism emphasises group rather than personal knowledges. Nonetheless, even those who argue for multiple collective accounts and recognise class as a proper, if not privileged, basis for one such account, still tend to assert the infinity of possible knowledges rather than their localism. From the localist position it is fair enough to dismiss a singular, objective or unchanging 'reality' (Graham, 1992: 398).

However, Graham goes on:

In other words, the 'truth' of particular knowledges is not adjudicated in a universal forum but is particular to certain social settings and validation practices... In the context of an overdeterminist epistemology, it becomes possible to theorize an infinite multiplicity of knowledges and, at the same time, to acknowledge an infinity of potential validation practices, all justified according to criteria that are themselves a matter of contention and debate. (Graham, 1992: 398)

This is Tagg again and the 'city which is not one'. Short *et al.* have a pertinent comment here:

> Cities, like all environments, are texts in which are inscribed values, beliefs, and the exercise and struggle for power... But if the city is a text, it is written as well as read, (re)constructed as well as (re)interpreted, and (re)produced as well as consumed. (1993: 208)

In other words we are in the business of understanding causal processes, as well as, and more importantly than, merely interpreting the consequences of those causal processes.

Here we need to return to the scientific use of the term 'realism'. We must distinguish between realism and positivism. Realists understand causes in terms of complex generative mechanisms and recognise the role of the social processes of observation in the generation of the empirical which is the object of science. This is absolutely antithetical to positivism's central canons. Banai explains the implications of this approach:

> Although critical realism accepts a place for hermeneutics, it differs from hermeneutic philosophies in insisting that there is also causation in society. It posits a hermeneutic which is 'historically' situated and a social science which allows for interpretative, critical, systematic, and practical inquiry of the concepts and activities of how we constitute our social world. (1995: 466–7)

The use of the term realism in literary criticism is somewhat different. It is associated not only with an account of what is, rather than the use of literary form as an object in its own right, but also with a linearity and singularity of narrative. Harvey puts this well:

> How was it possible, using the narrative structure of realism, to write anything other than a parochial, and hence to some degree 'unrealistic' novel in the face of all this spatial simultaneity? Realist narrative structures assumed, after all, that a story could be told as if it was unfolding coherently, event after event, in time. Such structures were inconsistent

with a reality in which two events in quite different spaces occurring at the same time could so interact as to change how the world worked. (1989: 265)

Harvey considers that this problem was resolved by the early twentieth century development of the 'modern' novel. I think the best examples of the modern and realist, in the scientific sense of complex and contingent, novels are those which use the strategy of multiple narrative strands pioneered by Dos Passos in *Manhattan Transfer* (1925, 1987) but also emerging in Bely's *Petersburg* (1916, 1983) and used by Serge in *Conquered City* (1932, 1975) and other works. The blurb for *Manhattan Transfer* describes it thus:

> Using experimental montage and collage techniques borrowed from the cinema, and the jumbled case histories of a picaresque range of characters from dockside crapshooters to high-society flappers, Dos Passos constructs a brilliant picture of New York City as a great futuristic machine filled with motion, drama and human tragedy.

I think we have to call this modernist realism and note that it is specifically urban.

The idea of the postmodern as a condition of life in general and of culture in particular has more to it than simply a position in epistemology. Of course the epistemological uncertainties are seen as central by postmodernists. However, there is a much wider sense of cultural crisis, although this is scarcely postFordist in timing. There are those who argue that what we live in is not different from modernity but simply the late stage of that epoch. Jameson (1984) sees postmodernism as nothing more than the cultural logic of late capitalism – a position which has much to commend it. It is plain that most of the elements seen as characteristic of the heterogeneity of the postmodern have existed throughout the modern, particularly in the colonial spaces of the modern era (King, 1996). Indeed Lash and Urry consider that:

> postmodernism is not so much a critique or radical refusal of modernism but its radical *exaggeration* [original emphasis]. It is more modern than modernism. Postmodernism hyperbolically accentuates the processes of increased turnover time, speed of circulation and the disposability of subjects and objects. (1994: 3)

Lash and Urry seem never to be quite sure if the situation they are describing does represent a new epoch or not. They do, pertinently, identify important tendencies, for example 'the extent to which culture has penetrated the economy itself, that is, the extent to which symbolic processes, including an important aesthetic component, have permeated both consumption *and* production' (1994: 61). However, we must ask, so what else is new? The significance of popular culture as commodity is as old as urban capitalism. The breaking down of boundaries between high and popular culture, with the former becoming commodified on a mass scale, has been going on for a long time. In fiction, the gap between the literary and the popular exists only for academic critics and those influenced by them. Film was academicised and rendered high by the application of critical principles to a popular form. In the visual arts, the 'revolutionary' impressionists have been providing chocolate box covers for two generations. What should surprise us about this? Commercial art and industrial design were established through state sponsored educational systems in the 1860s and have always been important, not only for the production of consumer goods but for capital goods as well through the influence of constructionism on industrial design. Jacobs identifies the pertinent issue:

> It is arguable whether this sudden shift in what might generally be defined as the cultural dimension of the city is responding to a material shift in cities, or if its simply the city being seen anew. (1994: 225)

It is true that the city is 'being seen anew' by those who write about it. There is a clear cultural turn in the nature of accounts of the urban and urban change. This has to some extent replaced the use of political economy as the major frame of reference, although Zukin contends that: 'The most productive analyses of cities in recent years are based on interpretations and interpenetrations of culture and power' (1996: 43), and it is plain from the context here that power means economic power manifested through the different circuits of capital. In this book we will follow this sensible approach.

Harvey (1989) attempted a massive confrontation of political economy with cultural theory. There is much of interest in Harvey's approach but we should note that the political economy which informs his work is one in which social actors, and in particular social classes, scarcely figure at all. However, Harvey is absolutely right when, quoting Colquhoun (1985), he contends that:

> Whereas modernism looked upon the spaces of the city, for example, as 'an epiphenomenon of social functions', postmodernism 'tends to disengage urban space from its dependence on functions and to see it as an autonomous formal system' incorporating 'rhetorical and artistic strategies, which are independent of any simple historical determinism'. (1989: 304)

Postmodernism as meta-theory regards space as autonomous and more important than time in the construction of the social world. I wonder if this is little more than a kind of continuing mental gloss on the use of the word 'local' as a way of establishing difference. In contrast, complexity theory certainly does allow for the simultaneous use and ultimate reconciliation of space and time in the construction of explanations of the social world as dynamic process, and faces down absolutely Shields's argument when he says: 'Representations are treacherous metaphors, *summarizing* [original emphasis] the complexity of the city in an elegant model' (1996: 229). Complexity founded models are not summaries but descriptions, a very different thing, and we do more with them than reflect. Plans are never merely representations. They are declarations of intended action.

Here we should note the significance for Harvey of the development of an electronic global economy based on markets in 'unreal' derivatives and other financial instruments, as a crucial factor in making our social lives at the end of the twentieth-century postmodern. There is no doubt whatsoever that the virtual financial markets, which come to ground in specific places have enormous significance for contemporary urban form and urban processes. We will come back to this theme in Chapters 2 and 3.

Even if we reject 'postmodernism' as theory, the idea of 'the postmodern' as a distinctive epoch has value. We might describe this epoch as postindustrial but that terminology does not so clearly incorporate the cultural dimension of change. I find little to argue with in Dear's description of postmodern urbanism:

> The tenets of modernist thought have been undermined, discredited: in their place a multiplicity of new ways of knowing have been substituted...
> Analogously, in postmodern cities, the logics of previous urbanisms have evaporated; absent a single new imperative, multiple forms of irrationality

clamour to fill the vacuum... The localization (sometimes literally the concretization) of these multiple effects is creating the emergent time-space fabric of what may be called postmodern society... Traditional concepts of urban form imagine the city organized around a central core; in postmodern urbanism, the urban peripheries are organizing the centre... There is no longer a conventional center in philosophy or in urbanism: what you see depends upon where you are seeing it from. In science, as in all human affairs, knowledge is inseparable from the people and places employed in producing it. (2000: ix)

This is not wrong but it is incomplete. The crucial missing phrase is: what you see depends upon what you are seeing – complex systems are local, contextual, varied in their causal properties and potentialities. Of course knowledge is socially contextual but to say that is to do no more than make an epistemological point. As a critique of nomothetic universalism this is not enough. We need to think about the local character of the real – to think ontologically. If we think in this way perspectives are not the source of unique accounts but the grounding points for our theodolites in triangulating the nature of the locally real – a task of surveying if ever there was one.

Culture in the 'post' world

There is an absence of culture in the debates about the transition to a postindustrial/Fordist/modern world. This may seem a surprising thing to say: after all, the discussion of postmodernism was in large part a discussion of 'culture' but it was a discussion of 'culture' only in one of the meanings of that important word. Cultural theory is a queer critter for anyone coming to it from a background in Sociology or Anthropology because it does not have within it any kind of notion of culture as that is classically defined in those disciplines.

The major exception is the work of Raymond Williams who was fully aware of the at least double meaning of the term. The cultural turn in thinking about the urban has paid a lot of attention to culture as documentary, as: '... the body of intellectual and imaginative work in which in... a detailed way, human thought and experiences are variously recorded' (Williams, 1965: 57). We might well add 'expressed' since the idea of culture as a sector of production is central to Williams's whole account. There has also been a good deal of debate about universal aesthetic principles, the foundation of 'high culture', understood both as general standards – the attack on this is the basic of the postcolonial and / or feminist programmes of critical reconstruction – and as frame of reference, postmodernism's 'grand narrative'. In challenging this approach Taylor *et al.* (1996) turn explicitly to Williams's idea of the foundations of the collective 'structure of feeling' in order to manage their research materials which were founded on qualitative research in two deindustrialising northern English cities, Sheffield and Manchester.

This seems to me to be the right turn to make. If there is one great absence in the discussion of the 'posts' it is a discussion of consciousness. The political economy stories do, always, however much they mean it to be in the last instance, subscribe to the proposition that Base determines Superstructure. They pay remarkably little attention to the equally crucial Marxist canon: Social Being Determines Consciousness. This is because the theoretical ideas organised around the 'post' propositions, are remarkably unhistorical. This is an extraordinary thing to say when the whole content of their arguments is that there has been a qualitative change through time – an essentially historical statement (although of course the epistemological version of postmodernism would not see things in this way – that would be far too much of a grand narrative). However, this assertion has almost no empirical foundation, either quantitative or qualitative, which addresses people's own feelings (and particularly collectively expressed feelings), about the significance of these social changes for them and their lives.

Let us think about what culture is from a sociological / anthropological viewpoint. Williams put it like this when he described:

the 'social' definition of culture, in which culture is a description of a particular way of life, which expresses certain meanings and values not only in art and learning but also in institutions and ordinary behaviour. The analysis of culture, from such a definition, is the clarification of the meanings and values implicit and explicit in a particular way of life, a particular culture. (1965: 57)

Contemporary social anthropologists can help us proceed. Jenkins (1996) takes us through what they are saying. He discusses the work of Cohen noting that for Cohen communal membership is an emergent: 'The similarity of communal membership is thus imagined; inasmuch as it is a potent symbolic presence in people's lives, however it is not imaginary' (1996: 105). Cohen himself remarks:

culture – the community as experienced by its members – does not consist in social structure or in 'the doing' of social behaviour. It inheres, rather, in 'the thinking' about it. It is in this sense that we can speak of the community as a symbolic, rather than a structural, construct. (1985: 98)

Jenkins is right (1996: 109) when he contends that this dichotomising of thinking and doing is an issue. People think while doing. Much of the time, if we accept any sort of notion of habitus, then they do without thinking, although contra Bourdieu they can always think if made to, and, what E. P. Thompson (1981) called Experience I, the harsh reality of social change, has a way of making them do exactly that. Nonetheless, the idea of community as mental construct works.

The significance of this for a consideration of the 'posts' is that we need to think hard about the ways in which changes in the structural organisation of economic life in cities in the late twentieth century have generated a crisis in culture. We have an extensive literature about the turn to cultural as opposed to material production, Lash and Urry's 'economies of signs'. We have much less on the implications for personal and collective identities, the crucial 'imagined but not imaginary' constructions of the social world which articulate the principles of both inclusion and exclusion. This will be an important theme of the next chapter – postindustrial capitalism is a cultural system as much as an economic system, but the cultural forms of industrial capitalism survive into it and may well represent the most important challenge to it.

Concluding remarks and further resources

We have covered a lot of ground in this chapter because we had to get set at three levels:

● at the level of *history* – in terms of the changes in our world as it becomes urbanised and the changing character of the urbanised components of that world as they become postindustrial.

- at the level of *theory* – in terms of the character of scientific accounts of the changes in our world and of the urban systems within it.

- at the level of *meta-theory* – in terms of the nature of the claims to knowledge which social scientists make when they formulate theoretical accounts of the nature of the social world and of the ways in which it changes.

We have considered both the scale of urbanisation and the changing character of urban places as they become postindustrial. The key information was statistical: quantities measured, simply measured by counting in categories, and examination in changes in those quantities over time. We used secondary data collected by states for their own administrative purposes (the origin of the world statistics) to see how the world was changing. Then we considered theoretical accounts of the nature of those changes, the postFordist account, Nelson's account of the nature of postindustrial capitalism, and the story of postmodernism. All these accounts have, however much this assertion may displease postmodernists, a foundation in political economy, in social science's description of the way human beings organise the production of commodities and the reproduction of labour power.

We also considered accounts which focus on culture and identity. Of course these things are related – base does determine superstructure in terms of setting limits but social being determines consciousness and consciousness is the basis of social agency which turns back to remake base itself. In other words the possibilities we have for culture and identity depend on the material bases of our lives but the way we think about ourselves is fundamental to the actions we take which in turn transform the material bases of our lives.

All the way through these discussions we kept coming back to issues of meta-theory, to arguments about how we can understand the urban world. The debate is essentially between 'postmodern relativism' and 'complex realism'. Postmodern relativism focuses on the epistemological problem of how any understanding can claim to be better than another understanding. In addressing the very real issue of how 'universal' claims for knowledge serve as a source of power and a basis for domination, postmodern relativism often argues for the supremacy of the individual sensibility. There are collective versions of postmodern relativism which get beyond this

kind of solipsism by arguing for post-colonial and/or feminist under-
standings, for perspectives which are different from and just as valid
as that of science.

Note that the word 'science' rather than 'scientism' was used in the
last sentence. Postmodern relativism denies that any account of anything has any status greater than that of any other account. It not
only dismisses universalist nomothetic scientism – the project of
establishing laws which hold always and everywhere – it denies the
possibility of establishing even a local account – the project of 'complex realism'. Whereas postmodern relativism is fundamentally an
epistemological project, complex realism has ontological foundations. It is organised around the notion that the world is composed
of nested complex systems with emergent properties and in which
causes are complex, contingent, and due to mechanisms which can be
considered to 'lie behind' the world in which we live, which we
observe, and which we change by our actions. Complex realism is
an anti-universalist programme. We can only know these systems
locally – there are no universal laws. The general character of complex systems and similarities among complex systems of the same
kind, can help us through a process of comparative reasoning and
inference, although this can never be more than a set of guidelines.
We must always take account of context. However, we can know – at
the level of the local there is a true story which we can try to find.

Complex realism accepts absolutely that knowledge is a social
product. The social context in which we construct our knowledge –
quantitative in the form of statistical measurements just as much as
qualitative in the form of language-based accounts – matters a great
deal. That said we make our knowledge out of something, not out of
nothing. Our knowledge may be local and in very important respects
contextual and socially constructed, but we can know, and on the
basis of that knowledge we can act.

The themes addressed in this chapter can be illustrated in three
ways. The first is by looking at measurements of trends over time.
The best single source of such measurements are statistical publications of the United Nations which enable us to look at the world as a
whole, or at least that very large part of the world in which states
are well enough organised to conduct regular systematic censuses.
There is no substitute for going to the tables. Look at them and see
how the world is urbanising. Look at them more closely and see how
the industrial world is becoming postindustrial.

A very useful exercise is to select a city in a country about which you know very little and have never visited. Examine the urbanisation trends in that country using the United Nations publications. For the city you will have to look more deeply. Here, there are two ways to go. One is to access the statistical data of the individual nation state. For some countries, particularly the USA, this is relatively easy because there are good sources on the Web. For others you will need to fish harder – searching bibliographical sources for articles which give information in a language you can read. Almost any social science article about any city anywhere in the world gives some trend information about that city.

The other source is the Web itself. Look at the Web footprint of your chosen city and scour it for information about changes in that city over the life of the city. Almost all big cities have a Web history page – very useful these are too, not least because they are usually quite short summaries. Almost all big cities have some economic development agency which gives lots of information about the economic structure of that city and about potential for inward investment to that city. The Web pages of these agencies are good sources of information about economic structure and the way in which it is changing. Finally, there is an enormous amount of cultural information in Web footprints – information about cultural events and agencies, but even more interesting information about the way people lead their lives. When I looked up the Web footprint of São Paulo, the world's second biggest city, one thing which I found and had never expected was large numbers of personal pages in which middle-class educated women were advertising for North American or European husbands. These were not sex adverts of which of course the Web is full. They were genuine adverts from women wanting to marry and have a family. The implications of this for a cultural understanding of North / South relations is considerable.

In terms of literature and films I have some suggestions here. The brilliant *Central Station*, a journey in reverse in which a woman takes a small boy back from Rio de Janeiro to the Brazilian North East, is full of wonderful images of the rural / urban transition. Lisa See's detective novel set in modern China, *The Interior* (1999) shows clearly the modes of urbanisation and industrialisation in that enormously important country and the meaning of this for people's everyday lives. The novels of Marge Piercey whose biographical entry usually begins 'Marge Piercey was born in Detroit and grew up there' have a background of urban and industrial change which is very useful indeed. A native of the city of Ford can write very well about the transition to post-Fordism – see *Small Changes* (1998) and the brilliant *The High Cost of Living* (1978) or indeed almost anything she has written, including a lot of her poetry.

2

The genesis and the implications of the postindustrial city

In this chapter we are going to consider a general process which is significant for all urban spaces. Deindustrialisation does not imply that there has been a reduction in the amount of industrial goods produced. Rather it describes the enormous decline in both absolute and relative numbers of people employed in the making of industrial goods. It is unlikely that we will ever reach the situation with industry which advanced societies have reached with agriculture where a tiny handful of people feed the rest of us, but that change happened and something of the same kind seems to be happening with industry, particularly but not exclusively in the older industrial countries.

Cities were machines for making peasants into industrial proletarians who made physical commodities, and into the reproducers of the labour power of those industrial proletarians. Now they are becoming something else. In the older industrial countries, cities are becoming places in which signs and services rather than things are made. This chapter is about that change and about the processes which have caused it to happen.

Four good questions which social scientists should always ask when looking at the dynamic development of any spatial aspect of the social world are: What? How? Why? and Who benefits? That is to say that they should consider:

- What is the nature of the place considered both as geographical location and as social system? This question must always be dynamic; it must not be a snapshot of now but a moving picture which describes how the place got to now from then past and how it might go from now to then future.

- How did this place become what it is? This is a question about causes. It is inherently systemic – how did the dynamics of the social system generate this place as it is now and might become?
- Why did this place become what it is? 'Why' questions require answers in terms of reasons whereas 'how' questions require answers in terms of causes. In other words, we are looking here at actions and their consequences. We are dealing with conscious human beings and the reasons why they act in particular ways, with such action being understood as both individual and collective.
- Who benefits? In the social world, changes are almost never neutral in distributive consequences even if there is seldom a zero sum game in terms of absolute resources. Everybody may become better off in absolute terms. However, relative distributions are a zero sum game. If the poor become better off relative to the rich in monetary terms then the rich are worse off relative to the poor. Money is the obvious case, not only as a measure of benefit but as motive. We might also consider other things including status and coherence of cultural identity in relation to the distribution of benefit. All these matter.

In this chapter we are going to consider the transformation of cities from industrial to postindustrial in terms of the first three of these questions. Question four is the subject matter of Chapter 5. The transition to postindustrialism is the biggest change of the last thirty years of the twentieth century and we need to appreciate it in all its aspects.

We will begin with a consideration of the causes of deindustrialisation. Then we will consider the role of active social agency with reference to Lovering's (1997) discussion of what he calls 'The Simple Story' offered by those who actually manage the restructuring of cities. A third level between the macro level of the whole economy and the micro level of the management of particular places is the meso level of the transnational enterprise. Massey has reviewed the organisation of firms in a globalised postindustrial system and we will consider her ideas here. Much of the literature on deindustrialisation is, appropriately, about manufacturing, but we must never forget the significance of construction, of the making of the built environment, for the economy as a whole. We will consider this in detail in Chapter 7 but it is appropriate to begin a discussion of it here. The built environment matters for the system because it is the basis of a 'secondary circuit' of accumulation in a capitalist system. However, even more relevant for us here where we are considering deindustrialisation is the role that the actual physical restructuring of urban space plays in deindustrialising particular places. This process of restructuring is intimately linked at all levels with what Castells calls the informational global economy. It is connected at the abstract level of world system because of the determinant influence finance capital now exercises over all economic activities. At the meso level, global companies operate through information nets which now might be considered to constitute the real structure of the enterprise. At the local level, processes of urban governance restructure the form of cities to facilitate the operations of 'networked capitalism'. We will return to this theme in Chapter 4 when we consider the idea of 'world city'. Here we will link the idea specifically to this chapter's central theme of deindustrialisation as a social process.

The causes of deindustrialisation

Rowthorn (1986) suggested that three main sets of causes could be identified in discussions of deindustrialisation in Britain, the first industrial and now most severely deindustrialised society. These were the 'Maturity Thesis', the 'Trade Specialization Thesis' and the 'Failure Thesis'. In a review of deindustrialisation as a general global phenomenon, Rowthorn and Ramaswamy recognises a fourth set of causal accounts which:

> suggest that deindustrialization is a result of the globalization of markets and has been fostered by the rapid growth of North-South Trade (trade between the advanced economies and the developing world). These critics argue that the fast growth of labor-intensive manufacturing industries in the developing world is displacing the jobs of workers in the advanced economies. (1997: 1)

Let us take Rowthorn's list as amended above in order. The maturity thesis requires consideration of both processes of production and patterns of consumption. In terms of production the thesis is simple. Improvements in both technology and production management have led to massive increases in manufacturing productivity. A comparison with construction costs where there has been far less growth in productivity illustrates this. Cars, for example, now cost about a quarter of what they did relative to houses fifty years ago. Productivity gains in manufacturing have been enormous and many have occurred exactly since the 1960s, the peak period for industrial employment in Western economies.

In contrast, there has been little productivity gain in services other than in the important, especially for women, area of domestic technology. However, in general, purchased services remain labour intensive and the development of technology in service sectors, particularly in biomedicine, can lead to greater labour intensity rather than less, for example, in intensive care nursing. There is always a combined and uneven aspect to these things in services. In health care, bio-analyses which used to require the skilled labour of a trained scientist can now be conducted routinely by a semi-skilled technician using electronic equipment. At the same time the task of the nurse has become much more complex, both in heavy science in relation to processes like intensive care, and in personal inter-relationships with mental health nurses moving from being custodians to counsellors. Reinforcing the production shifts are trends in consumption. As people become better off in absolute terms they can spend more of their income on services as opposed to, first, basics such as food and shelter, and second, manufactured goods.

An important consequences of these changes is a new pattern of urban land uses with formerly industrial locations being transformed into places in which services are delivered, whether that service is the conspicuous consumption of positional goods in an exclusive restaurant, or investment in personal future-income flow through attendance at an institution of higher education. In the postindustrial city many of us live by taking in each other's washing.

Rowthorn and Ramaswamy in a publication produced for the International Monetary Fund (IMF) assert the strong version of the maturity thesis:

deindustrialization is primarily a feature of successful economic development and . . . North South trade has very little to do with it. Measured in real terms, the share of domestic expenditure on manufactured goods has been comparatively stable over the last two decades. Consequently, deindustrialization is principally the result of higher productivity in manufacturing than in services. The pattern of trade specialization among the advanced economies explains why some countries deindustrialize faster than others. (1997: 1–2)

The trade specialisation thesis derives from that key dogma of economics, the doctrine of comparative advantage. This, typically for economics, is a story of the achievement of an equilibrium in market mechanisms which creates a spatial ordering which optimises output from the system as a whole – the spatial expression of Smith's invisible hand. All economists recognise that this may not be a description of any real economic system, however globalised, because of the intervention of 'secular factors'. This expression usually refers to what the IMF and other organised priesthoods of the free market, such as *The Economist* which has been pushing this line for more than a hundred and fifty years, regard as the irrational intervention of misguided ideologues through political processes.

One of the many advantages of the complexity founded account of social reality is that it renders fatuous searches for equilibric situations. Reality is non-linear and complex, not linear and equilibric. This doesn't mean that these kinds of economic approaches do not matter but instead that we can turn their claims for universal rationality back on themselves. They constitute an ideology based on erroneous ontological premises. Indeed Martin and Rowthorn's remark in the 1980s seems a far better general description than the simplistic story being peddled by Rowthorn and Ramaswamy in the 1990s:

> deindustrialization manifestly has not occurred in a social or spatial vacuum. It is not a simple or mono causal economic mechanism with undifferentiated social and geographical consequences, but rather a diverse set of complex processes affecting different localities in different ways... (1986: vii)

The failure thesis was defined by Rowthorn for the UK, primarily in terms of the weak relative performance of manufacturing industry against its international competitors from the 1960s to the 1980s. There is a good deal to be said for this, but the failures were not merely failures of management and workers, separately and in interaction, they also included failures in macro- and meso-economic management. The very rapid UK deindustrialisation of the early 1980s derived in considerable part from the very high value given to the pound by UK central government's macro-economic policy. For example, in the early 1980s, the Northern Ireland synthetic textiles industry, a key sector for the modernisation of that province's economy and an important base for non-sectarian trade unionism, was wiped out precisely because its product was not price competitive against US and German output, despite high quality and levels of productivity which were above the international norm. That is a general story for UK textiles and for much of the UK clothing industry.

Conservative macro-economic policy in the UK in the 1980s favoured the financial services sector of the city against manufacturing industry. There was an explicit justification of this in terms of a thesis of modernisation towards a service-based economy and a usually implicit but sometimes explicit programme of destroying the bastions of trade union organisation, however economistic and reformist that organisation was (see Imrie, 1997, for a good account of this). In the UK the secular interventions were real and uni-directional.

The meso-economic/meso-spatial level of the region is significant here. Regional integration of manufacturing production and social reproduction, and in particular the development of infra-structure and the provision of highly trained labour makes for successful modernisation of manufacturing production and the development of regional economic systems with a considerable manufacturing content – witness the long-term success of West Germany.

However, accounts of failure, like accounts of trade specialisation, are accounts of differentiation within the world system, not accounts of general tendencies within that system as a whole. The maturation thesis is a world system story, but in its simple economistic form it is merely part of that story. We also have to consider the role of active agency and recognise that such agency can be local as well as global.

The simple story: global determines everything

Lovering provides us with an excellent guide here with his interesting conception of a

> Simple Story that has become almost as much a part of popular political culture as it has become of academic and political orthodoxy. According to

this story, the problems of the great industrial cities (plus large parts of London) are rooted in Britain's century long decline from being 'the workshop of the world'. Industries have disappeared into oblivion under the impact of technological change ... or moved to cheaper workforces elsewhere ... Newly industrializing countries, with cheaper labour and new factories, will continue to take over the production of consumer goods, moving up-market from low-to high-tech products. The global mobility of capital, including the growth of multi-national corporations, has increased this likelihood, making it easier to transfer work to cheaper labour areas abroad. Britain's cities have ceased to be centres of production. The more fortunate amongst them have become instead centres of consumption and administration. Out with factories, in with offices, shopping malls and clubland. (1997: 68)

What we have here is a story of trans-national capitalist interests using space as a way of maximising profits by producing in the cheapest zones available to them. The extreme version of this story is that recited in the UK but it has also been told in the USA across the rustbelt and is now being shouted very hard in continental Europe. Even in this simple form there is a good deal to be said for the story, although as Lovering goes on to indicate we must never make the mistake of neglecting the crucial significance of local agency in this process. However, let us for the moment concentrate on the larger geographic scale. Here the work of Doreen Massey (1984) is of particular interest. Massey's account operates at the meso level, at the level of real places within the macro-global system. Despite her considerable hostility to the actual role of conscious agency, her story is one of action in the real world. In particular, she developed an account of the way in which large corporations not merely seek the best locations for production, but have actually developed a procedure of internal spatial differentiation of their own functions so that these are separated and located in different places on a global scale. Mass production will be in some places, design engineering in another and head office management in yet another, often in a 'global city' as part of a network of command and control. Massey's ideas played an important part in informing conceptions of 'locality' which we will examine in Chapter 3.

Although Massey allowed for 'the local' a role in restructuring, particularly of the skill base and industrial culture of local labour forces, she only grudgingly admitted a role for agency:

the nature of the interaction, of the impact of local specification on the operation of wider processes, may vary in kind. It may be thought that it occurs through self-conscious local activity. In the UK of the early 1980s, it was this which was the political focus of attention and enquiry. As the local political activists aimed to demonstrate and as the locality projects showed in their research, there was a huge variety – of varying effectiveness – of local activity, resistance and practice ... in these cases the focus of 'local impact' was the local government, but it could be other agencies, social movements, or constellations of these. Moreover the mutual conditioning of local and wider processes need not be a product of conscious local agency. Local impact may equally well, indeed more frequently, come about through the structural interaction of social processes without any deliberate local social agency. (1991: 271–2)

In fact one of the great weaknesses of locality studies was precisely their failure to take account of local histories of social action. We should perhaps concentrate on the significance of local social actions which have created restructuring, rather than those which drawing on older traditions of industrial organisation have operated to resist it, since the first sort have usually won.

Lovering's criticism of 'The Simple Story' for its assertion both of the inexorable logic of capitalism as a global system and of the irresistible power of transnational capital, is founded exactly on a recognition of the necessarily local element in the restructuring process. For him 'The Simple Story' echoes the nineteenth-century assertion of a global modernity which was universal in opposition to local particular cultures. We should note the ironic reality that in the transition to postindustrialism the oppositional local cultures are founded on the experiences of the industrial working class, which in socialist accounts of modernity were the embodiment of the universalist principle itself. In high modernity the proletariat was universal and capital was national. In later modernity capital is transnational and workers are local.

'The Simple Story' is an account of the global logics of capitalism, expressed both systemically and through power, and Lovering has identified its inherently ideological character in the most pertinent way: 'Prominent users of "globalisation" often elevate to the status of a social scientific fact what is really only a partisan view from the boardroom of a corporation with global reach' (1997: 75). As such it is a capital-logic account. This term was coined by Cleaver

(1979) to describe 'Marxist' accounts of social processes which asserted the overweening power of capital, usually through a systemic account of its internal logic, and thereby disempowered the working class in its resistance to capital. In other words a Marxist story is played for capitalist purposes. In fact the simple story is not only 'Marxism for capitalism' in systemic terms, it endorses, often explicitly, the profound pessimism of Gorz (1982) who bid farewell to the working class because it had been beaten in a war of movement.[1]

There is another story about the different trajectories of urban spaces towards postindustrialism. It is one derived from an interweaving of the 'locality' perspective as means of understanding the nature of places with the general postFordist account of the transition to postindustrialism. We will encounter the policy approaches informed by this account in Chapter 8 when we consider the nature of urban governance. Basically it is a story of place centred agency, often agency at the level of regional rather than urban space, in which places are developed through corporatist mechanisms as spaces of innovation and growth. This approach is the justification for the enormous growth in regional and local economic development as an activity of government in old industrial countries. This growth is not just a matter of resource commitment: more importantly it has involved placing 'economic development' at the centre of local governance with a consequent privileging of business interests in the processes of government. The English Regional Development Agencies established in the late 1990s typify this approach. Central to the whole strategic vision is the notion of enhancing the competitiveness of one space against others within the global system.

Graham (1992) presents an important critique of this approach and shows how regulation theory has provided a discourse of development for capital. We do not have to accept her arguments for an eclectic postmodernist deprivileging of any specific knowledge claim in order to agree with this. Her point that this is an approach serving capitalist interests stands. Lovering (1997) argues for the significance of local action in restructuring and for the importance of other factors apart from comparative 'competitiveness' in the constitution of social life in the postindustrial city. He is absolutely right but we can develop that theme further if we first consider two other approaches to the issues with which we are engaged.

The built environment: urban space as commodity

So far we have not considered the way in which space itself can be commodified. Classical political economy before Marx, and particularly in the work of Ricardo, was very concerned with the way in which space became commodified through the private ownership of land and the consequent requirement that rent be paid for the use of land. Originally this was a theory applied to capitalist agriculture, but the economic theory of rent and the market reality of rents also matter in urban contexts. Many of the major fortunes of industrial capitalism were founded not on industrial production but on land development, a process which was particularly beneficial to the estates of the British landed aristocracy and was also the source of great wealth in the USA and Australia. The story of Los Angeles is a story of land development as the basis of everything else which happened in that global metropolis.

Land was valuable when it could be converted from agricultural to urban uses. This process of conversion involved development: the application of capital to land. Of course agricultural land usually has capital applied to it, sometimes very considerable amounts of capital as in the draining of the East Anglian fens which was important in the development of capitalism in England. However, the production of the built environment is much more capital intensive than even that level of agricultural development. Moreover the buildings which are created fix the character of urban spaces over a long time period and have potential for enormous changes in value during that time period.

Any commodity which incorporates a land element is a different sort of commodity. We have to think about the production and circulation of this kind of commodity when we consider the nature of urban spaces and the trajectory of their development. The most important recent discussion of this has been attempted by Harvey (1985) who identified three distinctive circuits of capital accumulation, namely: the primary which involves the industrial production of commodities, the secondary which involves the production and realisation – sale into the market in exchange for money – of the built environment, and the tertiary which is concerned with the reproduction of labour power.

Harvey endorses Marxism's conception of capitalism as a crisis-prone system. When there are crises in the primary circuit of capital accumulation in consequence of the inherent tendency for capitalism to overproduce, an important mechanism for the resolution of such crises is the channelling of investment into the production and / or realisation of the built environment. Realisation is the process by which capital investment yields an actual return when the products of that investment are sold. The realisation of the built environment is a continuing process precisely because it is so long lasting and so fixed in space. It is often realised through a flow of rents and even when sold outright, as with most speculative housing, is constantly revalued and realised again on resale. In consequence, in contrast with the overwhelming majority of material commodities, elements of the built environment appreciate over time rather than depreciate. In other words, capital is accumulated not merely through the initial process of construction, which is actually part of the primary circuit of accumulation, but through speculation in land, as part of the development process, and in buildings, when constructed.

Although the turn to the secondary circuit of capital accumulation soaks up surplus capital, the secondary circuit itself is a source of crises. There are two aspects to this. The first is that the built environment being relatively permanent can become obsolescent and an obstacle to future development. However, we must note that it is only relatively permanent. The built environment can be remade and is remade. Go to Web pages illustrating Berlin to see this happening in Alexanderplatz, the biggest building site in the world.

The other aspect of the secondary circuit which matters is that it is an inherently speculative process. In economists' terms the built environment is very inelastic in terms of supply. Urban land is in limited supply; limitations are imposed first by the way in which urban values are a function of specific locations, although of course transport developments, changes in fashion, and other factors change location values over time. Land availability is also affected by state development control in planning systems. The result is that when money is poured into the built environment it can lead to enormous valuations being attached to elements of that environment which bear no relationship to the potential income streams which the assets might generate. An example is provided by Japan in the 1980s where investment in the built environment was so intense that real estate in the City of Tokyo was worth more than all assets in all forms, industrial, commercial, residential and agricultural, real property, equities, securities and money, in the very large developed nation state of Canada.

Speculative booms always burst, although typically the cycle is repeated from a higher basic overall valuation than in the previous cycle. Nonetheless, the bursting of a land speculation boom can provoke a general crisis in capitalist accumulation because of the impact it has on the asset value of financial institutions which are heavily committed to property values both through direct investments and through loans to property developers.

The idea of the secondary circuit of capital matters in relation to the general process of deindustrialisation because potential development gains from changing the uses of industrial land are an important motive in actual local processes of deindustrialisation. This provides us with a convenient link to the next set of processes which we need to discuss in relation to the genesis of the postindustrial city – those local processes combine the planning activities of the local state with the development activities of urban capital.

Ranting globally, acting locally, spreading the simple story

'Think globally – act locally' has long been a slogan of the Greens. Lovering points out that in fact it is also a good description of the practice of those involved in the restructuring through development of specific localities although the direction of cause is quite the reverse of the Green intention. The Greens want autonomous local action as a way of changing the global situation. The restructurers see the global as determining everything at the local level. 'The Simple Story' is regularly invoked:

> by property speculators and developers who argue that the only economic solution for cities is to bow to world market pressures and seek to attract international firms to new office complexes...or by politicians, business people and cultural commentators, who seek to demonstrate that little can be done to improve the lot of the urban poor. (Lovering, 1997: 70)

This is a very important point because it shows us how 'systemic pressures' are translated through ideologically informed social action into actual development practice. The inevitability of global forces are asserted as a way of overcoming opposition to development processes which are 'deindustrialising'.

In the United States and the UK the redevelopment of port and industrial land has been crucial for deindustrialisation. The Baltimore Inner Harbor scheme is generally considered to have pioneered this process. In the UK the principle agencies were the Urban Development Corporations established in a first wave in 1980. The best known of these was the London Docklands Development Corporation (LDDC) which was given planning and development powers over enormous tracts of land in East London. The port facilities in these areas were redundant but the elected Greater London Council intended to use the land released by port closure for a mixture of social housing and light industry on a new town pattern. Instead 'Docklands' were developed as a mixture of offices – an eastwards extension of the City of London – and expensive private housing. One important industrial plant was located in the area – the Wapping printing worlds of Rupert Murdoch's News International organisation. This plant was used to break the hold of the printing unions on UK national newspaper production, and the relocation of production just a couple of miles from Fleet Street was important in this. LDDC's operations were financially a failure and the one of the world's largest development companies, the Toronto-based Olympia and York, went bust in consequence of its engagement with the key site of Canary Wharf in Docklands.

In provincial UDC areas, development is generally a mix of office parks, housing, and retail malls with associated leisure facilities. Many of the office parks house 'call centres' the IT and telecomms based new form of corporate connection with consumers. Call centres replicate many of the social relations of the factory, although the product – the answered call containing information and / or a sale – is a sign rather than a material commodity. Call centres are very important postindustrial employment locales. In the UK there are more than 200 000 workers employed in them. This work is categorised as 'service employment' but in reality it takes the form of the factory production of signs.

It is plain that there is considerable spatial flexibility in the location of call centres and related office activities. At one point the north of England based Child Benefit Agency, which delivers universal cash social benefits to the mothers of dependent children throughout the

UK, was threatened through 'market testing' with the relocation of its work to the Philippines where routine administrative computing could be done by English-speaking workers at much lower cost. This was a data-processing exercise and it is harder to envisage speech-based transactions being quite so easily moved. However, the move from speech-based telecommunications transactions to those based on Web sites means that there is potential for this. I buy books from Amazon without any speech acts at all. Amazon could locate anywhere on the globe with a decent basic parcel post service.

But, and this is a big but, much of the employment in these new postindustrial spaces created by the transformation of land uses in formerly industrial cities is not in these global activities at all. Much of it is in retail or in leisure activities centring around the consumption of alcohol and dancing. These are locally focused and serve local consumer markets. Shopping malls, apart from those specialising in 'factory shops', deliver global products to the locality. The dance, drink and dine-out scene is explicitly local and depends on local consumers. The culture of these spaces always has a local or at the very least regional dimension. Given that a favourite postindustrial use of industrial sites is for sports stadia, then these sites become spaces which promote specific regional identities in a direct and particular way. In Manchester more people are employed in leisure activities operating after the hour of 8 p.m. than are employed in manufacturing industry.

Fitch, and the developers on whom he drew for his information, associate this kind of leisure development with world cities. For Fitch 'Post-industrial New York is a mutation masquerading as a modernization' (1993: 235). Fitch reminds us that the cities of the pre-industrial world were the spatial locations of elites and that the non-elite people who lived in them, the great majority of course, were those who provided services for elites and were paid out of the surpluses the elites extracted from those they dominated in the rural world.

There is a lot of mileage in this account, and Fitch's discussion of the under-development of New York is a brilliant piece of contemporary history and absolutely one in the eye for, as he puts it, those: 'academic Marxists for whom the capitalist is only the personification of abstract capital and who believe, austerely, that any discussion of individuals in economic analysis represents a fatal concession to populism and empiricism' (1993: xvii). However, it is remarkable that the kind of deindustrialisation he describes has been active policy, not only in truly global cities like New York, but in clapped-out industrial dumps like Sunderland in the north east of England. There is an enormous amount of service development in such places and those buying it are by no means only 'Masters of the Universe' working in the core of global finance capitalism.

The US City of Cleveland, Ohio: 'the quintessential blue-collar, working-class American city' (Warf and Holly, 1997: 208) is an excellent example of the way industrial places have become transformed into postindustrial places. Although overall employment levels in the Cleveland metropolitan region have not fallen dramatically, this is due to an increase in public employment. Manufacturing employment which peaked in the late sixties at 307 000 had fallen to 185 000 by 1993. Service employment totalled 592 000 but service wages averaged only 56 per cent of manufacturing wages. In commenting on these figures, Warf and Holly conclude that: 'Cleveland, like much of the nation, has seen the substitution of relatively well-paying blue-collar jobs by lower-paying pink-collar [personal service] and white-collar jobs' (1997: 217). We will note the consequences of these changes in Chapter 5 when we examine social polarisation in the postindustrial city.

These changes are perfectly explicable in terms of the 'modernisation' account of economic activity offered by Rowthorn. For many people, especially in Europe although to a lesser degree in North America, real incomes are higher. The cost of food and most manufactured commodities is much less. Many people have more to spend on leisure and spend it they do. This does matter, a lot, for the day-to-day experience of people in the postindustrial city. Indeed there is a good argument to the effect that in a postindustrial service centred world, cities are less globally dependent than they were when they were locales of specialised manufacturing. The production of health care and leisure is necessarily local. We will return to this theme later in the chapter.

Before leaving this issue of the local element in the process of deindustrialisation, it is important to note that it is a general phenomenon on a world scale. Plainly the core industrial cities of the American heartland (see Kleinberg, 1995) are deindustrialising or deindustrialised. However, the process is occurring in the South – the location of manufacturing within the New International Division of Labour. For example, in a discussion of redevelopment

processes in Mumbai (Bombay), Dimonte notes of textile employment that:

> what was probably the single largest unionized labour force in one city in
> one industry anywhere in the world, with around 250,000 workers, has
> now been reduced to a third of its former size. (1998: 283)

The sites of the textile mills are being redeveloped for commercial
and high-value residential uses in the same way as former docklands
have been redeveloped in London. The same thing seems to be
happening in Shanghai (see Olds 1997; Wu, 1999), although there it
is mediated through the power structures of the Party and state
apparatuses, whereas in Mumbai a key factor was the massive defeat
of the textile union in the great strike of 1984. The significance of
the New International Division of Labour is considerable, but deindustrialisation is a global process. Around Mumbai this has involved
the relocation of industrial employment from the originally unionised
plants on high-value land on Bombay Island to other cities such as
Poona in the city's hinterland. India is big enough to conduct a new
spatial division of labour within its own territory, something which
also happened in the USA in the 1950s and 60s with the relocation of
garment plants from unionised New York to 'free labour' sunbelt
states. Now the US plants are going to the Caribbean and Latin
America and areas in formerly rural India are receiving plants not
only from Mumbai but from Scotland. Coats and Paton, originally
located in Paisley – hence Paisley patterns, which were Indian designs
in the first place – now employ far more people in Indian plants than
in their UK operations.

Active underdevelopment in the network society

Castells's trilogy *The Information Age: Economy, Society and Culture*
(1998) has as its central theme the notion of a new economic structure
which he calls the informational / global economy. This remains
capitalist – indeed, it is predicated as a global system on the extension
of market capitalism to the former statist societies of the Soviet block
and to China. For Castells: 'Productivity and competitiveness are the
commanding processes of the informational/global economy. Productivity essentially stems from innovation, competitiveness from

flexibility' (1998: 341). This has much in common with the matura-tion thesis but there is rather more to it. This 'more to it' does not just derive from Castells's embedding his economic story within a wider narrative of social and cultural change, although that is important and he raises issues which we will address in subsequent chapters. The maturation thesis is a thesis of production and consumption but it does not really describe the social organisation of either process. The postFordist/regulation theory account is one which does address the social organisation of production but does not get beyond a story of distribution systems and marketing in relation to the organisation of consumption. Postmodernist accounts with their central notion of lifestyle give a cultural context to consumption.

Castells takes this further by making a distinction between the roles of generic and self-programming labour in informational capit-alism. To a considerable extent this argument reproduces the account of central and peripheral labour offered by theories of segmented labour markets since the 1970s. However, Castells's distinction is couched in terms of the adaptability of educated labour as compared with the inflexibility of merely task-specific trained labour. The relative power positions of these two groups are very different since the informational system does not need much generic labour and there are large reserves of it.

Actually these are old ideas. Indeed the crucial Marxist conception of the distinction between the expropriation of absolute surplus value from basic workers and relative surplus value from more highly-productive skilled workers describes the political economy of the situation rather well. However, Castells does have a point about the actual real organisational situation of these groups in the contem-porary context. Individualised remuneration packages for the infor mational workers, including their access to stock option schemes and their engagement through savings with capital markets, mean that despite the fact that they are plainly exploited in work, they do not have a basis for class solidarity with generic labour.

It must be emphasised that Castells does not see generic labour as surplus either in economic form or in terms of being in a condition of permanent unemployment. As he correctly puts it:

Comparative data show that by and large, in all urban societies, most people and / or their families work for pay, even in poor neighbourhoods and in poor countries. The question is: what kind of work for what kind of pay under what conditions? What is happening is that the mass of generic labour circulates in a variety of jobs, increasingly occasional jobs, with a great deal of discontinuity. (1998: 344)

This system is not just a product of new technologies and forms of work organisation. On the contrary, Castells assigns much of the causal power to innovations in financial markets through the instantaneous globalisation of trading on an IT base. The kind of futurology Castells engages in is always chancy and his assertion that the Pacific rim nations were emerging as a powerful competitive economy (1998: 337) now seems very dated. However, for the moment his argument, that there are differentially high profits to be obtained through engagement in financial markets, and that in consequence all forms of capital have become to a considerable degree dependent on their investments in it to the extent that the global financial markets stand as the basis of capitalism as a whole (1998: 343), does have considerable force.

The potential implications of this for inducing crisis are very considerable. Already US stock prices reflect four hundred years of earnings in important sectors, which is an absurd and over inflated level by any standard. Indeed many 'dot com' companies would have an absolutely negative value if earnings were the basis of their valuation, because they have never made any profit at all, only losses. This is acceptable in the investment phase but when are the profits going to come? The financial markets seem to have become part of a secondary circuit disconnected from real earnings or even from land assets. Castells was far too sanguine (1998: 343) about the forecasting capacities of market leaders and their ability 'to colonize the future'. The Barings fiasco and the collapse of Long Term Capital Management, a company founded by the inventors of the basic mathematical device for long-term forecasting, demonstrate that this is not the case.

Castells is always an interesting writer, but one who seizes on the extremes and generalises them. He does recognise that a response to much of his description would be to say 'so what's new', particularly if the contemporary flexible economy's similarities to the economy of the Edwardian era is recognised. He tends to generalise a description of an (admittedly) crucially significant set of sectors to all economic sectors. For example, in the production of the built environment, the exercise of craft skills remains crucial. The story is a good one, but there is another way of casting it by reference to the autonomist Marxist conception of linked development and underdevelopment.

> [D]evelopment and underdevelopment are understood here neither as the outcome of historical processes (as bourgeois economists recount) nor as the processes themselves (as many Marxists use the term). They are rather two different *strategies* [original emphasis] by which capital seeks to control the working class... they are always co-existent because hierarchy is the key to capital's control and development is always accompanied by relative or absolute underdevelopment for others in order to maintain that hierarchy... By development I mean a strategy in which working class income is raised in exchange for more work... The alternative strategy, in which income is reduced in order to impose the availability for work, I call a strategy for underdevelopment. (Cleaver, 1977: 94)

Let us consider deindustrialisation as a strategy which makes possible the combination of underdevelopment and development as described by Cleaver. This seems a very good way of thinking about the genesis of the division between Castells's informationally programmable and generic labour. We must distinguish between the content of the words 'process' and 'strategy'. If we consider deindustrialisation to be a process, then we turn to systemic explanations which emphasise the inherent characteristics of dynamic economic structures.[2] The maturation thesis is such a story. Of course the maturation thesis is true. The point is that it is not the whole truth. The maturation thesis describes the inherent tendency of capitalist economies to change through what Schumpeter called the process of creative destruction. The issue is not the liability to change, but the consequences that will flow from the changes. There are alternative futures. It is the agency which determines the character of those futures.

Discussions of the role of agency have been just as global as the systemic accounts. The stories of the New International Division of Labour and of transnational corporate organisational restructuring are stories of global actors. This is even more the case for the story of the role of the new network of instantaneous global financial markets. The truth is that much of the action is local action. Local action is crucial in the selection, and the voluntarism implied by that word is absolutely deliberate, of different urban futures.

Concluding remarks and further resources

At first glance, the story of deindustrialisation is a story about the global system of capitalism and one which identifies three crucial processes in that global system. The first of these is the general tendency towards ever increased productivity in the manufacturing of commodities which means fewer people can make more. The second is the freedom of movement of industrial capital which means that industrial jobs can be put wherever they can be done most cheaply. The third is the freedom of movement of financial capital and the emergence of a global system of speculation based on purely financial instruments, which means that production as opposed to circulation has become, at least in the short term, less important for the capitalist system.

However, it would be a mistake to think that deindustrialisation is simply a global process with consequences for urban places. In cities everywhere the processes which make up the secondary circuit of capital accumulation operate as an important part of the capitalist system. Land speculation drives deindustrialisation forwards on the basis that sites are worth more in other uses – Mumbai, Shanghai, Sunderland, Newcastle (New South Wales), New York – these very different places all exhibit this phenomenon. This is a globally general process but it is one which operates in particular places and is absolutely fixed in space in terms of its immediate and medium term consequences.

Land speculation is not an abstract process which 'just happens' in the global capitalist system and somehow materialises out of thin air in particular places. It requires action by people. Of particular significance here is something which will be a central theme of both Chapters 7 and 8 – the role of planners and developers working through city governments in order to shape and change our urban futures. The global system becomes real in particular places through the actions of particular people. That is very important because it means that there is a potential for things to be done differently and for cities to be made in a way which is not wholly subordinate to the overweening logic of global capitalism. In this context, the fact that so much of the economic activity of postindustrial cities takes the form of the local production of locally consumed services, a necessary consequence of the modernisation process, means that cities may actually have much more global independence than 'The Simple Story' suggests.

Deindustrialisation is mostly visible through its consequences, particularly in terms of social polarisation, and we will examine these in subsequent chapters. However, there are some illustrations of the process. The first lies in the numbers. Students should select an industrial city region and look at the composition of its labour force around 1970 and today, or as close to today as they can get. There are printed and Web sources of data – typically in the form of Census volumes, usually (in the UK and the USA in particular) based on censuses held every ten years. It is also worthwhile looking at land use maps for those two dates and comparing aerial photographs if available. Here access to Geographical Information Systems (GIS) is helpful. Again I recommend the memories of parents and grand-parents as a source of information about changes in their lifetimes.

Processes of urban development can be examined in a number of films because the dramatic character of cityscapes is appealing to cinematographers. Amber Films in the north east of England have made a special study of changes in my region and their work is described on their Web site. The redevelopment of London's industrial docks into postindustrial Docklands is the background to a range of films including *The Long Good Friday*. The role of financial speculation in deindustrialisation is the basic theme of *Wall Street*. An outstanding novel of women's experience of industrial life in 1950s Australia is Dorothy Hewett's *Bobbin Up* (1959). The author's reflective preface to the 1989 edition is a thoughtful and fascinating account of changes over thirty years.

The Web is full of images of urban change and hence of deindustrialisation. Again Shanghai and Mumbai are good places to visit in the virtual world but see also real estate images of places like Newcastle (both the original and its Australian namesake), Pittsburgh, Cleveland (again both the UK original and the US namesake), Detroit, Katowice and Lille.

3

Locality and community: the significance of place

This chapter deals with the way people experience space in their daily lives. It begins by examining two key social scientific concepts used for organising our understanding of such experience. These are 'community' – a term which in this usage originates in the intersection of social anthropology and sociology; and 'locality' – in this sense a term originating in social and economic geography and the 'locality studies' of the 1980s which examined processes of 'restructuring' as places underwent the transformation from industrial to postindustrial status.

Each term will be considered in turn and in relation to each other. The contemporary significance of the two concepts will be examined by means of a case study of Upper Silesia in Poland – central Europe's largest industrial district and almost an ideal type of the rust belt regions found in all 'industrial societies' in both the western advanced industrial world and in the former second world of former communist societies. Upper Silesia is particularly interesting because of the extreme rapidity of its social transformation. A clear implication of the accounts of social change on a global scale which were discussed in Chapters 1 and 2 is that this kind of very rapid transformation is likely to be a general experience, even in 'newly industrialising countries', in the early years of this new millennium.

In this book, we will always keep coming back to 'ontology' – to accounts of the nature of the urban world, and to the ways in which complexity and realism taken together can help us in understanding the nature of this world. This chapter will be no exception. Throughout the discussion, we will keep picking at the dual meaning of the word 'interaction', a meaning to do with the way causes work together and a meaning which deals with the way people relate to each other in everyday life. The penultimate section of this chapter will examine this again with particular emphasis on the emergence of urban cultures and on the implications of restructuring for the continued survival of such cultures. The chapter will conclude with a further discussion of the themes of 'culture' and 'identity', topics to which we will return in Chapter 6. It is important to continue this discussion in relation to our consideration of community and locality because the spatial interactions which arise from day-to-day life in particular places, *and* the common experience of radical changes, as the recasting of global systems of production and consumption lead to the restructuring of those places, are together of crucial importance for the formation of culture and identity. This matters because culture and identity are two of the most important sources of social action – we have to remember that 'cultured and identitied' people are at least as important social actors as 'economic' man.

Community: network and meaning in places

Community is the older term so we will consider it first. Most of the studies described in Frankenberg's 1966 book *Communities in Britain* were social anthropological investigations of rural places. There was, however, a chapter on the work of the Institute of Community Studies in Bethnal Green, the base of perhaps the most famous social study of the 1950s, *Family and Kinship in East London* (Willmott and Young, 1957), and a chapter dealing with 'Urban Housing Estates'. In that chapter Frankenberg posed a significant question:

> In the Irish, English and Welsh countryside, we found people who lived together and prayed, played and worked together. In the housing estates to be discussed, people live together or at least side by side. To what extent do they work together, play together or pray together? (1966: 197)

In other words, in the estates where planning and design policy had attempted to create a replication of the social relations of the 'English village' was there something like the 'community' of the rural world? Frankenberg was well aware that the rural communities reviewed in his book were by no means the idealised stable places which constitute the basis of Töennies's concept of *Gemeinschaft*. In his English deep rural example, the Cumbrian parish of Gosforth, even in 1951 a third of household heads were not local in that they had been born beyond a ten mile radius of the parish.

In fact, in the world of modernity nowhere is disconnected or stable in the sense that places might have been in the pre-modern world. Nowhere represents *Gemeinschaft* in a pure sense. Leyny in Sligo before the famine was the kind of place which that term implied, but even it was based on a relatively new economic and social system, intensive potato cultivation, which was less than two hundred years old. The construction of a whole social system in the bogs of Connaught around the cultivation of a vegetable from the Andes illustrates that the globalisation of the world was well under way. Certainly by the time Brody carried out his modern classic study of *Inishkillane* (1986) in a similar townland in County Clare, emigration and tourism meant that deep rural Ireland was intimately connected to the modern world.

We have to ask ourselves whether there can ever be community within modernity, if community is taken in technical language to be the translation of *Gemeinschaft*. In particular we have to ask whether community can ever be possible in an urban world, a question which certainly is implicit in Töennies's own specification of *Gesellschaft*. Simmel's classic discussion of 'The Metropolis and Mental Life' (1950) defines the daily experience of the urban as absolutely opposite to the holistic relations which seem to characterise community.

And yet community is a term which is very widely used in social science, in the media, in politics, and in the general discussions of everyday life. What are we dealing with when we talk about community? Day and Murdoch put it like this:

> people's location within particular places tended to be an important part of their lived experience . . . and a major resource drawn on for many purposes . . . so far as individual actors and their social experiences are concerned, the boundaries between analytically distinct components of life, such as economic relations, cultural understandings, and political goals, may be extremely ill defined. (1993: 184)

In a study which combined the approach of biography and community study, Williamson defined community thus:

> the notion of community embraces not just the idea of locality or social networks of particular kinds: it refers to the rich mosaic of subjective

meanings which people attach to the place itself and to the social relations of which they are a part. It is in terms of these meanings that the community can be recognized and the people who live there can recognize themselves. The pattern of these meanings is what constitutes the culture of the community. (1982: 6)

Cohen's conception is very close to this:

the reality of community lies in its members' perception of the vitality of culture. People construct community symbolically making it a resource and a repository of meaning, and a referent of their identity. (1985: 118)

What we have here, as Day and Murdoch (1993: 84) show, is a combination of themes. There is an idea of the significance of place and of the interactions which are set within place, an assertion of place as a basis for a holistic lived experience, and a notion of the distinctiveness of 'ways of life' in different places. Morgan considers that community as a social scientific concept is concerned with 'the extent to which locality functions as a site for the construction of cultural meaning in contemporary society.' (1993: 523) However, as he pithily puts it: 'Community is what Marx would call a chaotic abstraction, that is one which combines various elements and lacks conceptual leanness and clarity, (1993: 532).

Certainly the older generation of 'community studies' and the concept of community as used within them were trenchantly criticised in the 1960s. Gans (1962) and Pahl (1968) both noted that the concept failed to distinguish between geographical space and distinctive way of life. It seemed to assert that spatial proximity created social interaction and on the basis of that interaction, a distinctive collective social reality. Stacey, one of the participants in the important community study of Banbury in Oxfordshire, concluded that in the modern world, spatial proximity did not necessarily promote any kind of collective identity and argued that 'it is doubtful whether the concept "community" refers to a useful abstraction' (1969: 134).

There are two aspects to this questioning of community as a concept which can be logically employed in contemporary urban society. The first is simply a matter of scale. The rural communities investigated by social anthropologists had small populations. Holistic interpersonal relations were possible because everyone could be known. Towns are not small. Remember that by the end of the nineteenth century industrial Gateshead had a population as large as that of the whole of County Sligo. Any approach to community studies in County Sligo, a good location for such investigations, would take the townland as the unit which represented community. The spatial area of the townland would be much the same as that in Gateshead. The population would be a tiny fraction of the population of Gateshead. In the urban context most people are mostly strangers, known if known at all by the fractional part of them we meet in specific roles. The same comparison can be made anywhere in the world. Imagine the difference of experience for someone from a Chiapas pueblo in Mexico who goes to Mexico City or Los Angeles, as so many do, or for someone from a Chinese village going to Shanghai. Indeed instead of population ratios being fifty to one, they are now five thousand to one in contrasting the rural and the urban places.

The other factor is openness and change. Community has always implied spatial stability and a high degree of spatial closure. In the ideal of community, not only do people lead their present lives within the confines of the spatially delimited social system, they always have done so and always will. In other words they do not have external contacts to any significant degree and they have stayed and will stay where they are. The globalised world is the complete antithesis of this.

This openness to the global is addressed in an interesting collection *Living the Global City* (Eade, ed., 1997) which combines theoretical discussion with a range of studies in the global city of London. The use of the phrase 'global city' is crucial. Global cities are the spatial locations of the command processes of globalisation, exactly the processes which operate against the maintenance of the stability of social relations over time and the limitation of the spatial range of social relations, the twin pillars of community as the concept is traditionally constructed. In the collection, Robertson's (1995) formulation of 'glocalisation' is mobilised as a basis for understanding the contemporary form of social relations in London, one of three cities in the world which is unequivocally agreed to be 'global'.

Most of the empirical studies in *Living the Global City* deal with the level of 'neighbourhood', of residential area within localities, rather than the larger scale of whole place which was the focus of 1950s and 1960s community studies. However, even at this small scale the social worlds of people can only be understood in terms of both the local and the global, and indeed of every possible scale in between. As Albrow puts it:

> The locality is criss-crossed by networks of social relations whose scope and extent range from neighbouring houses over a few weeks, to religious and kin relations spanning generations and continents. (1997: 53)

There is nothing new about this. That part of my family which came out of Ireland in the famine sent siblings to both the north east of England and North America. My family has photographs from the 1880s of a visit made by my great-grandfather's sister who was a hotel housekeeper in Atlantic City, New Jersey, to her brother, a miner in South Shields, England, both having been born forty years before in Ireland. Other relatives were in Queensland and South Australia. The Irish are a particularly globalised people but the limiting case demonstrates the theme.

And yet these studies do not by any means dismiss the significance of local social spaces as a basis for social action. O'Byrne puts this very clearly when he argues that:

> localities can be seen as constructions of a tentative social order in a world of flows. Indeed it is my contention that identity – such as that of being working class – is constituted only with reference to: (a) the objective structure of material conditions, physical localities, and flows of people; (b) the normative structure of values and traditions; and (c) the interaction of people and cultures in a given physical locality, which produces a constant negotiation and renegotiation of the 'local'. (1997: 74)

The word flow is very significant here. Albrow draws on Appadurai's notion of 'scape' (1990) as a way of representing the character of social structures in a world of movement and flows, but extends the idea beyond Appadurai's original formation by arguing that under the conditions of modernity, and even more of the exaggerated modernity of postmodernity, there are no stable and invariant communities but instead 'socio-scapes' which are equally part of a shifting global system. It might actually be helpful to employ the realist conception of 'relatively permanent' social mechanisms here, an idea which we will return to in our subsequent discussion of locality.

Albrow coined the term 'socio-sphere' as a way of grasping the multi-scale connectedness of individual lives with the global system. People's spatial location, for those for whom such location is crucial which means most but not all of us, is where this inter-connectedness actually comes to earth, in much the same way as the complex virtual economy of networked global finance is grounded in particular world cities.

Albrow's emphasis on selves, a necessary product of his research strategy which involved individual interviews, leaves open the question of how congeries of socio-spheres might constitute something more than networks. In other words we still have to consider the possibility of spatially grounded emergent communality, of the inter-actions in place of people as being the basis for an emergent collective identity. Before doing that, let us clarify Robertson's (1995) important and useful concept of adaptation of the business / marketing term 'glocalisation':

> My deliberations... on the local-global problematic hinge upon the view that contemporary conceptions of locality are largely produced in some-thing like global terms, but this certainly does not mean that are all forms of locality are thus substantively homogenized... An important thing to recognize in this connection is that there is an increasing globe-wide discourse of locality, community, home and the like. One of the ways of considering the idea of *global culture* is in terms of its being constituted by the increasing interconnectedness of many local cultures both large and small... although I certainly do not myself think that global culture is entirely constituted by such interconnectedness. In any case we should be careful *not to equate the communicative and interactional connecting of such cultures* – including very asymmetrical forms of such communication and interaction, as well as 'third cultures' of mediation – *with the notion of homogenization of all cultures*. (1995: 31, original emphases)

Robertson is arguing that contemporary conceptions of the local are themselves in no small part a global product, even in their local expression, but that at the same time there remains a distinctive sphere of the local. Although he allows a domain of local autonomy, Robertson does see causal relationships as being from the global to the local. We might consider that they do, and indeed must, run in both directions. The global is open to influence and indeed even potential transformation from the local.

Locality: space and structure

> the locality study as a *method* has arisen from the attempt to address the complexity of spatially intersecting causal processes...We derive our sense of the local from a realist perspective, by paying attention to the *spatial ranges* of the many causal elements that impinge on any chosen area...All of these overlie each other and can enter into substantive relationships where they overlap, involving sometimes the same and sometimes different collections of individuals and other subjects. Social reality from this perspective, is made up of the totality of these significant inter-relationships over space...(Bagguley *et al.*, 1990: 8, 10, original emphases)

The essence of the idea of locality is the emergence of a specific local system through the spatially delimited interaction of economic and social systems with each other and with the physical geography of a particular place. Although the accounts do not use the language of complexity theory, this emergence is understood as historical and evolutionary. It happens through time and that which happened before has a time irreversible significance for what is now, just as the contemporary in interaction with history has an irreversible significance for the future. This is more than just a matter of spatial differences and consequent contingency – a word which is in effect a synonym for local:

> Over and above this contingency effect, causal effects may be locally derived. This is our second level. Furthermore a combination of these may create what can be called a 'locality' effect. The sum of locality derived causes is greater than the parts. In both these cases, our second and third levels of socio-spatial interaction, local variations are active in the sense of causally producing outcomes rather than just contingently affecting them. (Duncan, 1986: 28)

We can understand locality as the product of interaction in both the senses in which that word can be used in the social sciences. It is the product of interaction among causal forces which involve both natural and social structures. It is also the product of the human interactions of everyday life in which we construct our social world on the matrix of the natural world and of the equally real, and in the case of the built environment, equally material, social world which is the product of previous human action in history.

Bagguley *et al.* (1990) use the word 'interaction' to mean interaction among causal forces, interaction in the sense of classical causal modelling in which the relations among variables produce outcomes other than those which would be anticipated by the simple summation of their effects. We must also recognise the absolute centrality of interaction among agents rather than forces in line with Emirbayer's (1997) demand for a relational sociology. We need a Copenhagen interpretation here. Just as in quantum physics, photons can be interpreted as both waves and particles, so we have to think about social causation in terms of both structurally expressed forces and individual and collective motivated agents. There are real natural and social structures and there are people.

An important part of the 1980s discussion of locality was founded around the notion of the significance of 'restructuring'. As originally developed by Massey (1984) this was a more sophisticated approach to the traditional geographic problems, usually designated by the title 'location theory', when she employed a Marxist understanding of the relationship between a global capitalist system and particular places. Central to Massey's approach was the 'geological metaphor' which used an analogy with the physical geographical process of sedimentation in order to understand the social and economic geography of particular places. Places had a history, and just as palaeontology finds a history written in successive layers of sedimented deposits, so the history of places consisted of different sequences of the relationships of those places with global capitalism. Although explicit reference was not always made to Wallerstein's idea of a world system, something like it was implicit in discussions in the restructuring tradition.

Massey's account was implicitly evolutionary – in other words, history had a determinant effect (in the sense of the word 'determinant' implying the setting of limits rather than exact specification) on what came next. There was interaction among the different phases of the relationship with the global division of labour. In human history there is always such interaction, not least through the reflexive influence of the way people understand their past on their present and future.

Massey was reluctant actually to label her account as historical, perhaps because she was influenced by Althusserian structuralism which explicitly dismissed the validity of the historicist current in Marxist thinking and thereby denied the significance of conscious human action as a source of social change. If we do employ the rich and fruitful potential of historical materialism instead of arid structuralism, then we can begin to think about restructuring in a useful way. In particular, whilst continuing to regard developments in economic systems as of fundamental importance for places, we can also pay attention to the character of lived experience. We can address what Raymond Williams (1980) identified as the two key propositions of Marxism, rather than only the first of this pair:

> Base Determines Superstructure
> Social Being Determines Consciousness

In this connection it is useful to employ a distinction made by E. P. Thompson between 'Experience I' – lived experience, and 'Experience II' – perceived experience:

> Many contemporary epistemologists and sociologists, when they hear the word 'experience', immediately reach for experience II. That is, they move directly to what Marx called social consciousness. They then go on to show that experience II is a very imperfect and falsifying medium, corrupted by ideological intrusions, and so on... Historians within the Marxist tradition – as well as many without – have for so long been using the term 'experience' in different way that in *The Poverty of Theory* I did not adequately explain it... What we see – and study – in our work are repeated events within 'social being' – such events being indeed often consequent upon material causes which go on behind the back of consciousness or intention – which inevitably do and must give rise to lived experience, experience I, which do not instantly break through as 'reflections' into experience II, but whose pressure upon the whole field of consciousness cannot be infinitely diverted, postponed, falsified or suppressed by ideology... Experience I walks in the door without knocking... Experience I is in eternal friction with imposed consciousness, and, as it breaks through, we, who fight in all the intricate vocabularies and disciplines of experience II, are given moments of openness and opportunity before the mould of ideology is imposed once more. (1981: 406)

Thompson is saying that base, the material foundation of our lives in terms of work done in relation to nature and the way that work is organised as a system of production, does determine superstructure. If we use the Althusserian get-out that such determination happens only in the last instance, we have to recognise that the last instance has a nasty habit of arriving. In other words our lives are based on material production and the forms of that production always matter. At the same time, we make our lives in different places and in different times and in different ways. Come stark material reality, then things happen in a way which is a product of that reality. But, a very big but, we are also conscious agents and act socially in relation to the concerns of our consciousness. It is necessary to be rather careful here. Culturalist accounts can be just as deterministic as economist accounts – we can end up with people dancing to the tune of culture without much free will on their part in much the same way as crude economic rationalism gives us a programme of behaviour for economic men.

Before turning to the example of Upper Silesia we need to sort out the different spatial levels of region and locality. The distinction between regions and localities is not as clear in social geography and related studies as one might expect. There seems to be general agreement about the 'small' scale of community, even when this is understood in terms of the rural social relations which stem from systems of agricultural production. Likewise, region is understood largely in terms of the administrative level which seems to correspond to the spatial level at which co-ordination of production and social reproduction through governance is most easily achieved.

However, localities have been rather oddly defined in operational terms rather than on a clear relating of their supposed structural foundations to space. In the UK Economic and Social Research Council funded locality studies of the 1980s, localities were typically defined as local labour markets operationalised as journey to work areas as these are constructed on the basis of census information about travel patterns. The boundaries of UK journey to work areas typically change between censuses as economic restructuring changes the relation between residential and employment patterns. Given that most regions in the contemporary urban world are actually city regions – spaces organised around one or more metropolises with the great majority of the region's population living in the urban areas – this definitional issue is not crucial, but we should be aware of it.

Economic restructuring towards postindustrialism is certainly an example of the coming of stark material reality. At the beginning of the third Christian millennium in the world of informational / post-industrial capitalism, our discussion of places is not a discussion of places in a stasis, but must inevitably be a discussion of places undergoing a process of radical change. In other words the locality debate is not just about a process of categorising, of distinguishing among places: it is always about how places are changing. This means that despite its structural form, the idea of locality has a dynamism which is not inherent in the idea of community. On the contrary, community is an idea which implies the absence of transformational change.

Katowice / Upper Silesia: locality and community in a context of restructuring

Let me illustrate this with an example based on one of the most industrial places in the world which has a rather close relationship with what was until very recently one of the strongest peasant cultures in the world. Upper Silesia in Poland is now, as it was from the middle of the nineteenth century until 1945, a zone of carboniferous capitalism. The industrial development of the urbanised region, which contains just 2 per cent of Poland's area but 10 per cent of Poland's population, was founded on the geological reality that it is a coal basin.

Not only was there enormous capital investment in deep coal mines, but other coal using and coal related industries developed around the mining system. This included iron and steel making, chemical manufacture, and heavy engineering. The industrial development attracted enormous amounts of immigrant labour, and large urban systems were created around existing urban settlements or even more spectacularly on green field sites. Katowice city did not exist before the 1850s. By the time of the First World War, Upper Silesia was one of the most important industrial capitalist regions in the world. This was Central Europe's Pittsburgh, Black Country, Ruhr – in fact the mirror image of the Ruhr at the other end of the Prussian empire. The industrial regions of Russia in the Donbas or Urals have a very similar character.

With the establishment of the Stalinist regime in Poland after 1945, Upper Silesia remained the powerhouse of Polish industrialisation and did not experience the pressures for industrial diversification which were so significant in industrial regions embedded within the Fordist culture of mass consumer capitalism, particularly those in North America, Australia and the United Kingdom. Here the

European regions, the Ruhr, the Basque country, Le Nord/Pas de Calais, were in an intermediate position with some diversification pressures but not subject until recently to untrammelled free market processes.

The actual spatial level we are dealing with when we discuss Upper Silesia is that of region rather than locality, but we can regard the regional level as the product of spatial interactions with the spatial system of discrete localities. In any event, the main urban centre of the region comprises such a large part of both its area and its population that it actually takes the form of a city region. In this connection Cooke's specification of the nature of region is helpful. He defines it as: 'a socio-spatial scale at which it is possible to place in focus the specificity of class formations... regional boundaries are largely co-terminous with class practices' (1985: 213). However, this account is not simply one of consciousness. Rather for Cooke, there are five elements which have to be taken into account in our understanding of place at the level of region: productive base in terms of economic structure; the character of labour processes; the forms of the owner-ship of capital; the nature of social relations in civil society; and the specific character of institutional forms including forms of govern-ance. For Cooke, what matters is 'the rich interaction of economy, community, culture and history' (1985: 239). We can see these expressed very clearly in the city region of Katowice/Upper Silesia.

The Katowice industrial district is now fully subject to the pres-sures of transformation which were described in Chapters 1 and 2. Gorzelak makes the important point that changes are not really the product of the shift from communism to market economy, rather:

> the restructuring processes that dominate in the post-socialist transforma-tion very strongly resemble the phenomena which shaped economic life in more advanced Western countries since the 1960s and specially during the 1970s... With a great deal of simplification one may say that the post-socialist transformation is a shift from fordist to post-fordist type of organization of economic, social and political life. This shift was not possible in a closed system, separated by economic and political barriers from global markets and therefore not exposed to economic and political international competition. (1996: 32–3)

Sociological studies of Katowice and Upper Silesia (see Wodz, ed., 1995; Blasiak *et al.*, 1994) all treat community as a reality. This is so commonplace that we take it for granted. We have a notion of 'mining community' which stands almost as strongly in the popular cultures of industrial societies as the notion of 'rural community'. And yet the mining 'communities' were actually the product of enormous social dislocation in which people moved from rural lives into an urban or semi-urban industrial system. This process was still going on in Poland until the 1970s.

The 'communities' of the mining areas were, as Williamson puts it, 'constructed communities' that: 'have to be seen as part of a moment of historical change when the special circumstances of capital invest-ment in mining require the creation not just of labour camps, but of communities' (1982: 6). The capitalist logic which created commun-ities rather than mining camps was that the costs of the reproduc-tion of labour power were much less if this was done through the domestic labour of women in families. However, the small mining communities of pit villages did resemble in scale the rural commu-nity. It is for exactly this reason that they have been a classic locus for social anthropological informed community studies, notably Dennis *et al.*'s *Coal is Our Life* (1969).

Pit villages are at best semi-urban, but what of the big industrial cities? Katowice is a big industrial conurbation with a substantial amount of mining still going within it. What we have to recognise is that these sorts of places too were created as communities in the nineteenth century. Throughout the English speaking world the opening credits of *Coronation Street* show the gridiron pattern of terraced streets characteristic of northern English industrial towns. Katowice was constructed, and this is the term actually employed, on the Scottish system with blocks of workers' flats built in the nine-teenth century explicitly modelled on Owen's pioneering develop-ments at New Lanark in the late eighteenth century.

The male inhabitants of these new industrial districts worked in mining, engineering and related industrial activities. The important point is that they too lived in a 'created community' in which labour power was reproduced by the intensely hard work of women and in which the institutions, particularly religious institutions, of the pre-industrial world were injected into these 'workers' dormitories' with an explicit intention of maintaining the fabric of civil society.

In the case of the Katowice industrial district this process did not stop at the end of the nineteenth century. Throughout the period of 'real socialism', young adults brought up on peasant farms throughout Poland flocked to work in Katowice, just like the Irish to Birmingham in England. This is the process in China today. The essentially contingent separation of spatial residence between these new arrivals and the existing proletariat – basically, incomers were put in new housing schemes whilst many Silesians remained in the nineteenth-century barrack flats of the 'familiok' old mining settlements – made for a divided community in some senses (both groups were Polish and Catholic) but for strong neighbourhoods in which family and religious institutions provided a communal frame within a society nominally organised on very different principles.

In Katowice the institutional framework of community was by no means simply a matter of imposition from above in terms of the assertion of a general collective interest under Communism. It was exactly in these workers' communities in Upper Silesia and nearby areas, particularly in the vast post-war industrial suburb of Cracow, Nova Huta (literally the New Forge) built around the enormous Stalinist steelworks, that the social relations of Solidarity were put together from a combination of Catholicism and peoples' daily experiences. The organisation of Catholic parishes on a spatial basis is very interesting. In urban Poland there was another social form which was that of the neighbourhood and which existed outwith the frameworks of the state.

In Upper Silesia in the 1950s and 1960s, a key resource of people in everyday life, and even in politics, was a communalist solidarity founded around a class-based industrial and urban set of collective identities. The local and regional levels of governance were under the control of a Communist Party which, nominally at least, drew its legitimacy from the supposed interests of this class identity. During the Gierek era in Poland, there were quite real ways in which this connection was expressed in terms of policies for industrial and urban development. The solidaristic sense was expressed in 'communal terms' – something which, as Jenkins pertinently puts it, is 'imagined but not imaginary' (1996: 175). Communism and community had more in common than the first two syllables of the words. Obviously one derives from the other. The proletarian Catholics of the Polish industrial suburbs, the most formidable popular force against communism in the post-war world, operated on a deeply communal basis.

Restructuring involves the disruption of all of this on the basis of a reconstitution of the relationship of the labour systems of a place to the changing global economic system. Here I must make it clear that by labour system, I do not by any means simply mean remunerated work 'at the point of production'. The labour system includes the unpaid labour of women in social reproduction. There is a kind of almost wilfully ignorant feminist account of deindustrialisation, exemplified by Campbell's *Goliath* (1993), in which men are seen to a considerable extent as having got what they deserved with the destruction of 'macho' cultures. Not only does this almost invariably ignore the significance of remunerated industrial employment for women in the Fordist period which can be equated with Stalinist industrialisation on Fordist principles in Poland, it also fails to take into account the role of women in the politics of reproduction as part of the foundation of labourism as a political culture.

In this sense restructuring is a process of fragmentation. It does not fragment localities. The actual economically defined locality may be re-ordered in spatial terms: at the simple level by new patterns of daily commuting to work, in more complex terms by the creation of whole new spatial forms – the 'edge cities' – and Katowice now has edge city shopping areas. However, the places remain, remade by processes of governance and economic change. What is fragmented is the set of collective social identities which form the basis of spatial collectivity. We will return to this theme in Chapter 6, particularly in terms of a discussion of consumerism as a source of identity as opposed to identities founded in work.

This process is essentially complete in the older industrial regions of the UK and USA; its consequences in the mining communities of East Durham are brilliantly described in Hudson's *Coming Back Brockens* (1994). We are familiar with the urban expression of these changes largely from literature and films rather than from comprehensive sociological studies. In Katowice these changes are both immanent and imminent. In other words there are tendencies and potentials in the social and cultural structure of the place and its inter-relationship with the global system which make such changes possible, and they are actually just about to happen. The original mining workforce of more than 300 000 miners and ancillary workers is being reduced to less than half of that total. This process is already under way with the non-recruitment of pupils from specialist technical secondary schools into the industry for which they have been prepared. Moreover, very large numbers of women employed in the 'enterprise social services' of mining have been made redundant as this aspect of the industry has been effectively eliminated. This is the reality of restructuring towards postindustrial capitalism. Wodz and her co-workers have documented the way people think and feel about these processes. It is very evident that they feel threatened. Things which were central to their identity – in particular the significance of hard manual work and strong family relations – are challenged far more by the transition to postindustrialism than by communism. Communism applauded hardwork and could live with the family as a source of social order and stability. There is a considerable decline in respect for the Catholic church, so long the symbol of both communal and national identity, as priests become external authority figures rather than part of the resisting community itself. Developing and evident material inequalities, much more evident than the cynical and hypocritical inequalities under real socialism and the relative advantages of the nomenklatura which were a major source of political discontent then, seem to challenge principles which are central to the basis of what a community should be. The restructuring of the city region represents a major assault on people's individual and communal identities.

The significance of emergence: locality and identity considered as complex forms

In the literature on localities, there is constant use made of the word 'interaction'. In the social sciences this word has two meanings and we need to think carefully about both of them in our consideration of community and locality. In general, in the locality literature the word is used in a way which is analogous with the idea of interaction among causal forces in the physical sciences, for example, although it does not use the word interaction itself, Bagguley *et al.*'s describes the complex set of social causes thus: 'All of these overlie each other and can enter into substantive relationships where they overlap' (1990: 8).

There is reference in this passage to actors but the emphasis is on the causal powers of social structures and there is a clear sense of the emergent character of the local as the consequence of the interaction of these causal powers. Remember that in this sense, interaction does not mean that the combined effect of causes is the sum of them taken separately. The use of the term implies non-additivity. When things work together, that which is produced cannot be predicted from the effects taken alone. This is the meaning of the word 'emergence' in this context.

Compare this with Giddens's use of the idea of 'locale': 'Locales refer to the use of space to provide the *settings* of interaction, the settings of interaction being essential to specifying its contextuality' (1984: 118). Given that for Giddens a room can be a locale, it is plain that by this term he means the spatial location of interaction among social actors, rather than causal forces. This is an approach which resonates with the idea of 'community' not as the emergent product of structural causal forces, but rather as something which emerges out of the ways in which people relate to each other in the conduct of life.

Here are both of the dichotomies which Mouzelis (1995) considers are fundamental in sociology: the dichotomous contrast between structure and action, and the dichotomous contrast between the micro level of individuals and their relations on one hand, and the emergent social structures on the other.

Concluding remarks and further resources

We will return to the inter-relationship between urban cultures as the emergent products of people's urban lives, and the restructuring logics of global postindustrial capitalism. Here let me begin to conclude by reference to Ekström's discussion of the 'Causal explanations of social action':

> From the generative standpoint, causal explanations are directed not towards the production of empirical correlations between variables or towards the making of predictions on the basis of empirical laws, but towards the uncovering of causal properties and the processes whereby social actions arise out of the complex interaction of internally related mental dispositions, meanings, intentions, social contexts and structures. (1992: 107)

Most people's social interactions are mostly local although we do have much wider socio-scapes, the range of which has been extended by the new technologies of communication. I can email colleagues in South Africa or the USA as easily as I can email colleagues five feet away in the next office to mine. Moreover in networked global capitalism, there are some very significant people whose social inter-actions are not local – the global superclass of movers and shakers; but, email notwithstanding, most of us most of the time make our lives in places.

O'Byrne summarises things in a way which will do very well as a conclusion to theoretical discussion in this chapter:

> localities can be seen as constructions of a tentative social order in a world of flows. Indeed it is my contention that identity – such as being working class – is constructed only with reference to : (a) the objective structure of material conditions, physical localities, and flows of people; (b) the norm-ative structure of values and traditions; and (c) the interaction of people and culture in a given physical locality, which produces a constant nego-tiation and renegotiation of the 'local'. (1997: 74)

People live in places which are changing. Indeed people themselves change both in terms of character through time, and in relation to place of residence as they move on an increasingly global scale. They have significant social connections at a range of spatial levels. In this world of flows everything is inherently plastic. The character of places changes as much as the character of people. We may well think that there are different stiffnesses of plastic. Although the whole economic and social base of a place may change, for relatively long periods, places do have a relatively stable character: structures do endure for a time. Indeed culture may be a very stiff thing indeed, outliving the material forms within which it was generated. We will come back to all this in Chapter 6.

There is no substitute for reading the community studies them-selves. Some now appear very dated from a contemporary stand-point; Willmott and Young's *Family and Kinship in East London* seems so patronising, it actually makes me angry. In contrast, the rural studies (best represented by a late example in Brody's *Inishkil-lane*) and the mining studies (of which Dennis *et al.*'s *Coal is Our Life* is the most significant) are outstanding. The one I really do not like here, *Family and Kinship in East London*, does pay attention to the world of women and there is a perfectly justifiable criticism of the industrial studies, of *Coal is Our Life* in particular, to the effect that they are male centred. The critique of the restructuring thesis on feminist grounds developed in Bagguley *et al.* (1990) is unconvincing because it seeks to separate gender out as a dimension from the actual complex interactive lived experience of class and gender (and ethnicity too where that signifies), but there is a real tendency in economistic analysis to miss gender as a crucial component of the complex formation of experience.

There are US-based community studies although, as with the UK examples, the form was much more popular in the 1950s and 60s than it is today. Indeed books like Lynd's *Middletown* (1959) were major best-sellers. Gans has maintained a life-time commitment to first-class locally based and theoretically informed sociological research and his *The Urban Villagers* (1962) and *The Levitt Towners* (1968) are classics. There are interesting studies of rural community in China, notably Myrdal's *Report from a Chinese Village* (1963) but far fewer studies of urban community in the South. However, there is excellent literature on restructuring in Mumbai – see Harris (1995), O'Hare *et al.* (1998) and Kamdar (1997).

There are some very interesting literary and filmic representations of community, locality and change. I particularly like Amber Film's *Dream On* set on Tyneside because it manages to be funny, intelligent and surreal, whilst at the same time conveying the nature of post-industrial lives in a very clear way. *Flashdance* does give at least the visual images of change in Pittsburgh. Wodja's films convey exactly the reality of Polish life under Stalinist industrialism and resistance to it – see *Man of Iron* and *Man of Marble*. In a sense, all urban soap operas are about community, and are usually set on a neighbourhood basis. After all, the most famous of all Australian soaps is not called *Neighbours* for nothing.

4

Grounding the global: cities in a world system

Under the onslaught of globalization, North American cities are changing dramatically. This process – anything but new – today exhibits a new character and intensity that places cities within dramatically transforming economic and social networks. Hyperactive flows of investment, seamlessly penetrating the city, transform aging downtowns into glittering consumption landscapes. Business decisions thousands of miles away close plants and factories, thereby sending cities into tailspins. Cities compete desperately and ferociously to attract jobs and investment in a fight for survival. And the dizzying arrival of new commodities and fashions reverberates through the urban everyday to resculpt cultural fabrics. In this city, a heightened commodification and search for global purpose, alter urban culture, politics, and civic life in fundamental ways. (Wilson, 1997: 8)

Delete 'North American' from the above passage and it remains an absolutely valid statement. It is happening everywhere. Globalisation is not a new process. Wallerstein (1974) dates the world system from the development of the European seaborne empires at the end of the fifteenth century. The colonial world just before 1914 was more globally open with a greater volume of measured production traded internationally than is the case today. However, then the world was not a world of cities, and the structure of places, despite the enormous significance of colonial relations, was not so absolutely a product of global ordering.

Our contemporary world has almost no refuges from the global system and the majority of people experience their relationship with that system because they live in an urban world. Before 1914 most people in the world were connected globally through cities but not in them. In China, a land where a wheelbarrow was wealth, Shanghai distilled that wealth outward to the world through a particular form of colonialism that was policed in the International Settlement, where the Europeans and Americans lived outside Chinese law, by a force recruited in large part from Connaught in Ireland! Shanghai was and is a great world city, but until very recently the great majority of Chinese were peasants.

In historical terms we have to recognise the significance of the geopolitics of the late twentieth century for the re-establishment of an open global system. China was largely closed off from the global system from 1948 until the 1980s by the impact of a peasant-based revolutionary transformation of that enormous nation's social order. It is precisely the abandonment of 'the "socialist" alternative' which makes our world so unequivocally global again.

However, these political changes have not occurred in isolation. They have been associated with a transformation of markets and the control of enterprises based on the development of new technologies of communications. Castells calls this system 'informational capitalism' and describes it as the economic base of a 'networked society':

> Networks constitute the new social morphology of our societies, and the diffusion of networking logic substantially modifies the operation and outcomes in processes of production, experience, power and culture. (1996: 469)

The world network of communications is not new, even in an electronic form. However, the scale and implications of those communications are now qualitatively different both through their generalisation in everyday life and as the basis of a virtual economy of money which has become largely disconnected from real commodities but which offers the opportunity for super profits and sustains a particular form of urban lifestyle in those cities where it comes to ground in real space.

This chapter is about 'world cities'. Usually this expression is used to designate particular places as the crucial nodal points of command and control of both the real and the virtual global economies (see Sassen, 1994). The idea can then be employed in the construction of an 'urban hierarchy' in which places are ranked according to their role in the global system, and the amount of real space which they connect to that global system. In this scenario the prime function of urban governance is to seek the most advantageous possible place for a particular city in this hierarchy (see Brotchie *et al.*, eds, 1995). We will begin by thinking about money. Underlying the construction of the ideal of a global urban hierarchy is a belief in the fundamental significance of the global financial system – the world of money traded electronically twenty-four hours a day across the electronic networks of our wired world. The first section of this chapter will examine this system which Castells calls 'networked capitalism'. We will then consider the idea of 'world city' and review attempts to define that term and to rank urban spaces by locating them in a hierarchy in which their status is determined by the character of their relationship with the world system. Next we will begin to examine urban social division. If the global financial networks are seen as the driving force of the global urban system, then social polarisation is the major social characteristic of cities in that system. Chapter 5 will examine this in detail but it is necessary to begin a discussion of it here. Finally, we will refer back to the themes of Chapter 3 by examining the relationship between the global and the local in world cities in a postindustrial global system.

Funny money: the world after big bang

The original version of the global city account emphasised the role of particular places as locations for corporate headquarters and saw the spatial separation of the control of production from actual production, an important theme of Chapter 3, as the origin of the increased significance of particular places. This, and the associated development of producer services separate from actual production, do matter but perhaps the best way into the global city debate is not through a consideration of real production but instead through a treatment of the global virtual economy.

Traded financial products have been part of city functions since the creation of the world system more than four hundred years ago. However, the traded financial products were things which existed only at one remove from real commodities. Eric Newby in *The Last Grain Race* (1956) explains how the big sailing barques (my grandfather was first mate on one of these before the First World War) which brought wheat from the Murray-Darling basin in Australia to Europe up until the 1930s, carried cargoes which were bought and sold ten times over in the course of the voyage. They were actually both transport and warehouse. Wheat futures were part of a market, but at least the wheat futures had eventually to be translated into the real wheat which was made into real flour which was made into real bread. Many of the things of the new global economy have no such reality.

We are dealing here with derivatives – enormous bets placed on mathematical functions of the movements of the real markets. The illegal numbers game in the USA is a simple derivatives process which is random within limits. People bet on the last four numbers in stock market turnover. To all intents and purposes this simple activity of criminal capitalism has been generalised as a crucial component of the world system.

It is estimated that the daily total of world banking and financial transfers is somewhere between three and seven trillion (US – old UK billion, that is, a million million) dollars per day. The inexact nature of the estimate shows the extent to which these transfers exist outside any effective regulatory system. Knox (1996: 124) asserts that only 10 per cent of these transfers have anything to do with the traditional world economy of trade in goods and services. The rest are to do with virtual money.

Although the profit margins on derivatives trades can be tiny, the actual size of such trades means that the volume of profits is enormous. Derivatives trading is possible because of instantaneous electronic communication, massive electronic-based computational power for calculations, and electronic recording of trades to enable a market to cash up at the end of the transaction period. Castells makes a distinction between the world economy of the world system since the sixteenth century and what he identifies as a contemporary global economy (1996: 92), in terms exactly of the contemporary capacity of markets to work as a unit in real time on a planetary scale. This sort of system has been described as 'neo-mercantilist' in that gains flow from trade rather than direct processes of production.

Castells sees the development, post financial deregulation, of these markets as shaping the whole character of the global world. He puts this very strongly:

> because of the differential between the amount of profits obtained by the
> production of goods and services, and the amount that can be obtained

from financial investments, individual capitals of all kinds are, in fact, dependent on the fate of their investments in the global financial markets, since capital can never remain idle. Thus, *global financial markets, and their networks of management, are the actual collective capitalist, the mother of all accumulations.* (1998: 343, original emphasis)

In effect the financial markets are the control system of global capitalism. This is not, as Castells recognises perfectly well, by any means the outcome of natural processes. Rather it is a consequence of the interaction of technological possibilities with the political actions of governments in the US and the UK in the 1980s which expressed the logic of liberal market ideologies of deregulation. The UK's big bang in the City of London combined new electronic trading with deregulation of capital flows.

Things were already moving in this direction through the criminal evasive and legal avoidance use of banking facilities located in small sovereign or semi-sovereign statelets with loose regulatory practices – the offshore bases of tax avoidance and money laundering. Deregulation linked the world economy intimately to these salubrious locations. The linkages are so powerful that when Long Term Capital Management, domiciled in the Cayman Islands, went bust, thereby demonstrating that Castells had perhaps been oversold the hype of market analysis when he remarked that: 'the programming and forecasting abilities of financial management models makes it possible to colonize the future' (1998: 343), the US Federal Reserve was obliged to inject a volume of funds into the rescue of its trades which would have gone a substantial way towards meeting the Millennial Jubilee objective of paying off the debts of poor Third World nations.

We will not understand the idea of world cities unless we grasp a central point. The thesis is that the transformation (still of course ongoing and demonstrating all the usual characteristics of combined and uneven development) of our world, from one in which most urban people were industrial proletarians to one in which many of us lead postindustrial lives, cannot be understood without appreciating that money has taken over from goods as the basis of economic life. Money always mattered but now it matters most. It is the reality of economic life rather than a symbol for economic life. That is the matrix within which is embedded the idea of world city.

World cities or cities in a world system?

The term 'world city' is usually associated with Friedmann's 'world city hypothesis' of 1986 although it had been used as a book title by Hall in 1966. Friedmann's hypothesis has seven elements. Knox (1996: 124) identified these as a 'series of statements' to the effect that:

1. Processes of urban development are now determined by the extent to which particular urban spaces are integrated into the world network and the role that the particular spaces play in the world network.

2. There is a hierarchy of cities: topped by the command, control and market centres of the global system with others arranged below this at levels which are a function of their role in connecting subordinated places to the global system.

3. The spatial and social ordering of world cities – the places highest in this hierarchy – is a function of their global control functions.

4. World cities are key locales for the accumulation and concentration of capital.

5. World cities are attractors for immigration.

6. The major contradictions of industrial (we might rather say postindustrial) capitalism are expressed in world cities in terms of socio-spatial polarisation.

7. The growth of world cities can impose social costs which exceed the fiscal capacities of government, especially municipal government.

Friedmann's original formulation has been described by Schachar as having:

> the built-in ambiguity of being a heuristic framework for asking questions about urban restructuring and phases of change in urban development processes, and/or . . . a. new definitional description of a new type of particular cities which are different from other urban agglomerations by specific characteristics. (1994: 381)

In other words the idea has been the basis of a description of some places – the world cities. At the same time it is an assertion of the significance of global processes for all places – cities in a world system.

Quantitative indicators are generally used in defining world city status. Two of the commonest are numbers of major corporate headquarters and the proportion of workforces engaged in producer services. Producer services are high-level, often professional, activities which used to be part of the organisational framework of large productive corporations, or were small-scale professional adjuncts to the work of such corporations but are now carried on by separate bodies outside those corporations' own structures. Legal and accountancy services were always somewhat separate from production, but now management (through consultancy), engineering design, recruitment and a range of other functions can be outsourced. These services frequently interface with financial services and may link productive enterprises to financial services.

Beaverstock *et al.* (1999) have prepared a 'roster of world cities' in terms of level of advanced producer services, namely, accountancy, advertising, banking / finance and law. They combine their data into a scoring system in which London, Paris, New York and Tokyo score twelve, with Chicago, Frankfurt, Hong Kong, Los Angeles, Milan and Singapore scoring ten. These are Alpha world cities. Beta world cities scoring more than six but less than ten include San Francisco, Sydney, Madrid, São Paulo and Mexico City (two mega cities) and Moscow. Gammas scoring less than seven but more than three include Amsterdam, Melbourne, Boston, Warsaw, Atlanta, Kuala Lumpur and Shanghai.

It is perhaps surprising that a world which Massey (see discussion in Chapter 2) can describe in terms of the spatial separation of the functions of large corporations, should be displaying such concentrations of market, command, and high level producer services in particular places. However, we have to draw a careful distinction between these strategic levels and the actual levels at which routine work is done. For example Swindon, a former railway town in the south west of England, has become a key location of back-office routine data-processing and call-centre operations for a large number of financial institutions (see Boddy *et al.*, 1997). Office space and labour costs are lower than in London and these functions do not require the inter-personal networking that seems to be a central aspect of the command-level functions of such enterprises.

We have an apparently contradictory set of processes in the global economy. On the one hand we see a global dispersion of manufacturing and a within language zone dispersion of much of routine office functions, with a lot of US insurance claims being processed in Limerick in Ireland; on the other we see a concentration of command functions in particular places. Amin and Thrift (1992) explain this in terms of the role of urban centres as the locales for the three processes of 'representation', here understood as the process of establishing the nature of the global system itself; social interaction   the social mixing of elites which is the basis of informal communication, networking and the establishment of personal trust; and innovation in that in these places and through these processes new products can be brought together with marketing and financial systems. Essentially this is a story of personal networking at the top. The global becomes local in particular places so that elites can meet face to face.

Sassen (1994) identifies global cities as the postindustrial production sites for financial and producer services as well as being the location of the key financial markets. We might add media production to this list, and the significance of the production of aesthetic as well as informational signs is something we will return to in Chapters 6 and 7. This approach, of course, privileges the unequivocally global cities, London, New York and Tokyo   the locations of the three major financial markets which maintain the twenty-four hour real-time, virtual global financial network.

The 'hierarchy' approach to cities, which locates them in a descending order and relates places to the global networks of control and command, has wider implications. Castells (1996. 403–4) recognises that not all cities, not even mega-cities, are command nodes of the global economy. However, the typical specification of 'urban hierarchy' describes the way in which particular cities link territories to that global economy – connecting to it 'huge segments of human population'. King (1990) has criticised the general global city hypothesis as having no real historical perspective. In particular he wants us to chart the process of transition from the merely world system, which was intrinsically colonial, to its global successor. This is an important point particularly when, as King suggests we must, we consider the implications of world cities for all parts of the urban system.

Let me illustrate by an example. In the global city's hierarchical framework, we can see London as the organising node towards which all UK urban systems are connected. However, below London are regional nodes. In the north west of England this is the function of Manchester which has succeeded in becoming the location of producer services for the economy of the north west of England, a role which has displaced its traditional manufacturing function and which has sidelined Liverpool, previously a major location of financial operations connected with transatlantic marine transport. Manchester scores two on Beaverstock *et al.*'s (1999) scale. Liverpool does not score at all. The argument is for a global penetration of all urban systems and the subordination of them to global processes.

In this scenario we have a reconstruction of colonialism with a spatial dislocation of the colonial power. The Maoist dislike of Shanghai, the classic locus of Marxist revolutionary activity in China, was based on Shanghai's function as a link with Western colonialism. Shanghai certainly contained the largest urban proletariat in China but its prime role was as the base of 'comprador' capitalism, the system through which China was exploited by the colonial system using indigenous collaborators. The non-Chinese comprador system even had its own territories, the French Concession and the International Settlement, which were wholly outside Chinese rule. Comprador capitalists got pretty short shrift after the Communist take-over, in marked contrast to national capitalists engaged in indigenous production.

Mao Zedung understood that Shanghai was entryport and conduit. In the global world all 'connecting cities' serve these functions for the territories they connect. Colonial power no longer resides in imperial systems except perhaps in the United States although even that imperial nation is drawing in its military horns other than in relation to the external sources of its oil. What this means is that every urban space is somehow subordinate, dominated by something external to it but which has no privileged spatial locale. In other words everywhere is colonised.

What we are dealing with here are not the colonial cities of a supposed Terra Nullis in Australia, but rather the kind of cities which were injected into existing highly organised social orders by colonialisms imposed on large productive populations. The spatial form of world cities with their high degree of internal differentiation has much in common with the colonial form of such comprador cities in the past and is very different from the spatial form which industrial cities had when they contained powerful organised working classes pursuing their own political objectives in the sphere of social reproduction. In former colonial zones this similarity is very evident. Dick and Rimmer (1998) demonstrate that contemporary South-East Asian cities are becoming more like Western cities and that it is inappropriate to see them as having a radically distinctive form. The similarities, it can be argued, are in fact the product of a mutual convergence rather than simply a matter of the westernisation of former colonial and / or indigenously distinctive spaces.

The general story of world cities is, as Sassen puts it, one in which: 'The master images . . . of economic globalization emphasize precisely these aspects: hypermobility, global communications, the neutralization of place and distance' (1998: 193). And yet, as she points out, the hypermobile global economy must be grounded and much of what it does has to be embedded in places. We have a continuing story of global elites and of cities remade for them to play and work in; but the global cities are also cities, not of permanently excluded underclasses (which contention is with limited exceptions a myth of postindustrialism see Byrne, 1999a) but of the working poor, many of whom are employed in the subordinate generic labour positions of financial and producer services, and many more of whom are the service workers in the facilities which cater for the consumption of the new global elites.

Whilst it has to be admitted that Short *et al.* have a point when they argue that in the discussion of world cities: 'Hypotheses are repeated rather than tested' (1996: 698), there is now a substantial amount of empirical research organised around the 'world cities' theme. This includes Sassen's own work on global producer services (1994), and interesting sector studies such as that by Boyle *et al.* (1996) who examine the role of Executive Search Firms as enabling mechanisms of the global high-level labour market, by Beaverstock (1994) who pursues a similar theme in relation to the global employment patterns of employees of major banks, and by Schacher (1994) who examines how the multi-polar urban complex of the Randstad (Amsterdam, Rotterdam and the Hague), one of the world nodes of the original world system and one of Hall's world cities of the 1960s, is undergoing a process of urban reordering which is directed at relocating it in global terms.

We should distinguish here between 'place centred studies' including the useful monograph series on specific world cities edited by Johnson and Knox, and accounts of the whole global system of cities. Smith and Timberlake (1995) argue for the use of formal quantified network analysis in exploring the actual dynamic character of that system. Their approach examines the system taken as a whole, understood in terms of the network of relationships which constitute it. The account is explicitly dynamic. In other words the relationships are understood as changing over time. Smith and Timberlake see the network of cities as existing alongside and intersected with the network of nation states, the traditional focus of attention of political geography and related disciplines.

World cities as unequal cities

In this literature there are some constant themes. We find urban social polarisation, with a continuing (not really demonstrated by comparative study) assertion that world cities are particularly socially polarised; culture as subject of inquiry, which inquiry often adheres to the relativism of cultural studies' general epistemological position and rejects any general account of 'the urban'; and spatial mobility of global elites, tourists and migrants. Much of the discussion of mobility has centred on the elite of cosmopolitans. These people can be understood as the global element in the higher service class. Indeed global connectedness and mobility might well be regarded as a key demarcator of higher-service class membership.

The cosmopolitans are not only a class. In Weberian terms they are also a status group with their identity being constructed in large part by particular patterns and rituals of consumption. This is by no means simply a product of differentially high incomes. Sassen has noted that:

> The income of the new workers was not sufficient to explain the transformation. Less tangible factors also matter: an examination of this transformation reveals a dynamic whereby an economic potential – the consumption capacity represented by high disposable income – is realized through the emergence of a new vision of the good life. (1996b: 27)

We might see even this account, with its clear recognition of the cultural dimension in world city practices, as being still somewhat

unidirectional and economically deterministic. Zukin (1996) identifies and distinguishes between two general accounts of the built
environment. One, typified by Sassen's account and by those elements of Castells's work which have been discussed thus far, is an
account grounded in political economy and in the processes of capital
accumulation. In principle, as Zukin recognises, this should also be
an account of classes in action, but that dimension is much less
elaborated than the discussion of the processes of capital circulation.
The other centres on a symbolic economy in which 'endless negotia-
tion of cultural meaning in built forms . . . contributes to the construction of social identities' (1996: 43). Zukin is a cultural realist. For her
the city can be known in terms of its interacting complexity, a
position for which she is roundly criticised by Tagg (1996). These
epistemological battles have been mentioned before and we will come
back to them in our discussion of culture in Chapter 6. Here we need
to note both that culture is a demarcator for world cities and that the
production of culture, both mass and highly differentiated, may
actually be an important part of the real political economy of the
symbolic economy.

As Zukin described in her pioneering *Loft Living* (1988), art as
commodity can become the basis of art as lifestyle which in turn is
commodified. It is certainly true that the processes of commodification of differentiated lifestyle and the upward valuing of differentiat-
ing aesthetic signs as commodities is dependent on the availability of
money made in other locales. At the end of the twentieth century the
key cash cow is plainly financial markets with associated producer
services. However, the mass production of aesthetic signs, the mass
media as industry, is not a second order activity in this sense. We
have to distinguish between the status culture which flows from
money and the mass culture which is a means of making money.
The idea of positional good is helpful here. People pay more than my
weekly food and drink bill, which is not small, for a single meal at an
upmarket London restaurant. They are not getting ten times what I
get when I eat out. The point is to spend ten times as much money –
the positional good is the expense itself. In contrast, mass culture –
say Pizza Hut – is about making money from ordinary consumers.

The account of capital accumulation in world cities and of the
kind of labour which is engaged in this accumulation suggest that
cities will be polarised and that the principle of division will be
income. Whatever the principle of polarisation, whether this is simply

income or the differences are drawn, as for example by Castells, in terms of command over diverse and flexible informational skills, the actual labour forces of postindustrial capitalism's commanding heights, money processing and producer services, are themselves polarised. On the one hand are very highly remunerated 'knowledge' operatives, on the other are the hands of generic labour who clean and guard the spaces of global capitalism in real cities. Actually this story of polarisation can be overdrawn. The middle white-collar grades of informational capitalism, the predominantly female wage slaves of the secretarial grades, remain moderately well paid in world cities. It is also true that all world cities, and cities of any ranking in the world hierarchy of cities, are also cities of health and knowledge with very large labour forces employed in hospitals and universities, many of whom are middle-income public sector professionals and semi-professionals like the present author. What in Britain are becoming known as the '999' professions – nursing, paramedics, junior doctors, the police and the fire service – are an important component of all urban populations. Moreover, cities, especially but not exclusively in the developed world, are rapidly becoming cities of students. In some cities, for example Mexico City, student numbers approach half a million.

The existence of these groups 'in the middle' in terms of income means that Hamnett (1996) is making an important point when he considers that we should question the notion of the absolute polar-isation of world cities, although this is perhaps not so much a func-tion of different welfare and urban regimes, as Hamnett suggests, as of the actual dynamics of global cities in general.

We must also not forget that deindustrialisation and the develop-ment of postindustrial capitalism have not eliminated industrial pro-duction. What has changed are the conditions under which that production is carried out. New York's garment industry is an extreme case. The original mass unionised industry was virtually eliminated by the export of employment to US sunbelt states with 'free labour' (that is, anti trade union) labour legislation. New York again has a garment industry based around the employment of immigrants who are often illegal unlike the legal, and therefore unionisable, immigrants who founded the International Ladies Gar-ment Workers Union which dominated Fordist New York's garment production. In Los Angeles a relatively new garment industry exists in very close proximity to a very new 'downtown', something which

Los Angeles lacked until it became a node of financial connection between the Far Eastern and US economies. This industry is one in which the real estate is often owned by the Anglos who founded modern Los Angeles, the small entrepreneurs are legal Korean immigrants, and the employees are undocumented Latinos working for what are by US standards low wages, but which may when remitted back to central America be the basis of middle-class standards of life in the country of origin.

In the contemporary literature on world cities, it is function and not size which demarcates significance and level in a world hierarchy. There are mega cities, usually identified as urban agglomerations with populations of more than ten million people, and there are world cities. New York and Tokyo are both. London if defined by GLC boundaries is a world city but not a mega city, although the London conurbation is plainly a mega city. However, there are mega cities which are as big as the three unequivocal world cities but which have much lower positions in the hierarchy. For example, no sub-Saharan African city outside South Africa would rank as anything other than a bottom-level entryport for its national economy, although places like Lagos, Ibadan and Nairobi are huge urban centres.

The origins of the mega-city lie in the interaction of local, regional and national spaces with the world economy. In other words they are always to a very considerable degree the product of migration from rural to urban areas, a migration driven by pushes in the form of the transformation of peasant into capitalist farming and / or the demographic pressures of large peasant families, and by pulls in terms of the wage and lifestyle attractions of urban centres.

Two such mega cities are Mexico City, the world's second largest urban space in 1990 with a population of more than 20 million, and São Paulo in Brazil, third in the size league with a population of 19 million. Both are beta world cities in Beaverstock *et al.*'s (1999) ranking. São Paulo is a good illustrative case. This place, originally founded as a slaving station by Brazilians raiding the Guarani settlements organised as a Utopian Christian commonwealth by the Jesuits in what is now Paraguay (see the film *The Mission*), has in the twentieth century become Brazil's largest city through industrialisation and the attraction of rural migrants from the environmentally-challenged ranching and sugar economies of Brazil's northeastern states. São Paulo rather than the political capital of Brasilia or the former political capital of Rio de Janeiro (itself a mega city with a population of more than 11 million in 1990) is the connecting node between Brazil and the world economy. However, with a population which would put it in the top half of member states of the United Nations by population size, it is plainly a gigantic and to a considerable extent self-sustaining system.

Angotti (1993) makes an important point about contemporary metropolises. They are so large as internal markets and represent such enormous commitments of capital to the built environment that they are remarkably robust as human systems. In general, urban areas of this size persist almost regardless of economic trends, whereas smaller industrial cities can be challenged by changes in the international division of labour. Whatever the reality of that distinction of scale, Angotti's point does indicate that we cannot regard urban life as simply some consequence of the interaction of global economic forces and local particularities in 'glocalisation'. Urbanisation, considered as a consequence of sheer scale and as a universal process, which happens in particular places but happens in all those places, is a distinctive world shaper in its own right. We will return to this theme in the Conclusion of this book.

It is true that we can almost always detect the footprint of globalising forces which demonstrate the relationship between the global systemic hierarchy and particular cities. We should remember the example of Mumbai (Bombay) cited in Chapter 2 in which the sites of the textile mills which were the industrial base of the city are now being redeveloped for world city office and residential purposes (see Dimonte, 1998: 283).

The background to this was a major defeat in the early 1980s for the textile workers' unions. This permitted both a relocation of textile production by Indian capital to other locales both within India and elsewhere in Asia where labour costs were lower, and a redevelopment of the land occupied by textile mills. This redevelopment, in which criminal capitalism is deeply involved, reflects Mumbai's role in relating India to the global economic system. Deregulation of a previously highly bureaucratised economy has opened India up to the global system as a whole. This is more a matter of Indian capitalists' capacity to export capital and participate in world trade, rather than of a massive penetration of non-Indian capital into India. India's mercantile and industrial capitalists are now players on the world scene, and Mumbai is their location of choice. The result is that mill sites are now very valuable for redevelopment as residential zones for the new Indian rich and upper middle classes whose affluence derives primarily from their role in international markets and producer services; although we must never forget Bollywood's role in the production of aesthetic commodities of mass culture. Corruption and violence are two of the means by which sites nominally reserved for high-employment volume industrial development are being 'deindustrialised'.

The global and the local under postindustrial capitalism

We have to think about the implications of globalisation for all components of urban systems. The version of the world city story, which sees all cities as part of a global hierarchy of places, generally includes a notion of relative connectedness of populations. Clarke and Gaile identify:

> new stratification problems based on links to the global economy. An emergent class of cosmopolitans has weak community ties since their interests and resources transcend communities. In contrast, most citizens remain locals, defined by particular places and limited opportunities; although many are weakly linked to a global web through their involvement in global practices, their well being is dependent on decisions of world class citizens. (1997: 32)

Beauregard might well identify the above passage as an example of privileging the global in our consideration of these issues. He puts it like this:

> 'thinking globally' is privileged over 'thinking locally'. Dominance is conceded to actors and forces operating internationally, and local actors resist, adapt, or acquiesce, but do not *fundamentally* alter global intrusions. The thrust of this diverse literature is to nest national and subnational scales of activity within an overarching global framework. (1995: 232, original emphasis)

Beauregard is quite right to the extent that he is identifying the general globalisation story and the world city component of it, in part an ideological device of dominance. Essentially we are dealing here with the specifically urban version of Lovering's Simple Story (1997) which we discussed in Chapter 2. This is a theme we will take up in Chapter 8 when we consider issues of urban governance, now very much acting as the pander of places to the global system.

Concluding remarks and further resources

There is a curious dualism of the presence of both ends and absence of the middle in discussions of globalisation. In this chapter we have reviewed a literature concerned with the implications of the restructuring of capital accumulation on a global scale, although it does recognise a distinctive cultural dimension with culture understood as being to do with the production and consumption of aesthetic commodities. There is a literature on urban politics and power in global world, which we will consider in more detail in Chapter 8. We have political economy and we have cultural studies. What is lacking is any detailed consideration of the way in which people actually live their lives – of cultures as ways of life – the territory of sociology, social anthropology, and social history. Of course that statement is a grotesque exaggeration. There is interest in social polarisation, quite a lot of discussion of the ways of life of elites, and the usual surveillance of the lives of the poor. There is also an extensive and valuable social anthropology of immigrant groups. What is, however, noticeable by its absence is the ethnography of the ordinary. Eade's *Living the Global City* (1997), discussed in Chapter 3, is an honourable exception but it is by no means as complete a study as Gans's account of Levittown (1968).

There is an interesting literature describing everyday existence in the mega and other large cities of the South. Wikan (1995) gives us an important account of the modes of everyday survival for poor people in Cairo, poor people who have become less poor over her more than twenty years contact with them. She suggests that the collaborative social actions of the poor are vital to the maintenance of the integrity of the urban system, a point made explicitly by Parnwell and Turner in their account of 'sustaining the unsustainable in Indonesia':

> It is not mega-urbanization per se that is self-sustaining so much as the system being held together by the cement (or Sellotape) of coping, surviv-

alism and tolerance. . . . The mechanisms of coping and survival are pivotal and necessary components of the urban system, because of the nature and shortcomings of the process of urban development (or maldevelopment) – given added impetus in recent years on account of the 'retreat of the state'. . . – set against the continued failure of the market to support and improve the quality of life of more than a segment of the region's urban population. (1998: 150–1)

An exception to the relative dearth of empirical studies of these sorts of social relations in the North (the developed world) is Morris's examination of family lives in Hartlepool (1995) through a quantitative account of household contacts and network relations rather than an ethnography of lived experience. The Institute of Sociology at the Silesian University in Katowice has conducted a series of important studies of lived experience in that region of Poland, which in terms of income just counts as part of the North (see Wodz, 1995). What these studies show is a remarkable similarity of coping strategies and networks in Poland and northern England, and a considerable similarity with the coping strategies of the urban poor of the South, with networks of family and neighbours mattering a great deal. We have to remember that these mundane and daily social interactions are just as much constitutive of the modern urban as the global processes which dominate academic concern and political world views.

The relative absence of investigation of the nature of everyday life matters a great deal in relation to discussions of politics and collective modes of action, which we will consider in Chapter 8. There are excellent 'city studies' with different emphases, for example, Cybriwsky's account of *Tokyo* (1998) and Lane's account of *Liverpool: Gateway of Empire* (1987). In these historically grounded books we can see places as the locales of life and social action. Actors, other than business and political elites, do not otherwise figure very much in contemporary discussions of the urban in the global system.

There are a number of novels and films which deal with lives in world cities in different ways. Jay McInerny's *Bright Lights: Big City* (1994) deals with the life of financial and cultural elites in New York in the 1980s. The film *Wall Street* showed the life of the peons of global financial capitalism. Melanie Griffiths in *Working Girl* was convincing as the working (not under) class woman from Staten Island who was trying to claw up from secretary to broker.

Web sites are particularly informative on this topic because any city worth thinking about in terms of global hierarchy has a virtual presence. Invariably (a bold word to use but correct in this context), a large component of that presence is the publicity material of urban development agencies which are all about world city positioning and producer services. Dublin is a good case to examine here but see also, yet again, Shanghai. Look at adverts for the spaces in which producer services locate, so often the old industrial docklands of the port cities of the colonial era.

5

The divided city: the ecology of postindustrial places

The cities of the modern world are divided cities. Incomes are unequal and statuses are differentiated and ranked. People live in neighbourhoods which reflect and reinforce these inequalities of income and status. In premodern cities rich and poor often lived in close proximity, sometimes at different levels of the same dwelling. The emergence of residential segregation in cities was one of the bases of the political origins of modernity. The sans-culottes, the trouser (and skirt) wearing urban poor of Paris, especially the artisans of the notoriously radical working-class suburb of the Faubourg Saint-Antoine, made the French Revolution and created a new political order as the foundation of the modern world just as Bely's people of the islands – the proletarian districts of Petrograd – made the Russian Revolution of 1917 and shaped the history of the twentieth century.

With the generalisation of the urban way of life, the significance of spatial segregation in cities becomes crucial. One of the first commentators to remark on this was that sharp-eyed participant observer in the practices of industrial capitalism, Friedrich Engels, who noted of nineteenth-century Manchester that a capitalist like himself could come from his rural Cheshire home into the city centre and never see the dwellings of the workers who made his fortune for him.

In this chapter we will examine both perspectives on the origins of social differentiation within cities and the contemporary character of such differentiation. There are patterns which characterise advanced industrial societies – the late twentieth century extreme polarisation of the urban core into zones of wealth and poverty; the shift of the 'middle masses' to the suburbs from the 1920s onwards; the late twentieth-century development of 'edge cities'. There is the general European phenomenon of what in the UK and Ireland is called the 'overspill' estate, but which in France goes by the generic term of 'banlieue'. There are the distinctive patterns of shanty towns, favelas and communas in the South. We will begin with a consideration of 'human ecology' as this has developed since the work of the Chicago School between the wars. We will then examine divided cities both in the postindustrial world of 'advanced capitalism' and in the cities of the South. Then we will turn to a consideration of the form of the suburb – the twentieth century's distinctive urban innovation, and extend this discussion to examine the character of the 'exurb', of the 'edge city', the first built environment in which the centre may matter less than the periphery.

In everyday life, one of the key aspects of urban division hinges around the way in which people obtain their dwellings. This is not simply a matter of renting versus owning. In Switzerland, one of the world's richest countries, most households rent, and the economic advantages of a particular tenure depend on complex interactions among tax systems and housing finance processes. However, in much of Europe, social housing, housing provided by the state, is the tenure of residence of the residualised poor. We need to consider the implications of this and of the very different patterns of tenurial division which exist in other sorts of society. This is important because in the 1980s sociologists proposed that tenure, with its associated implications of possession or lack of real assets, might be replacing occupationally derived class as the key principle of social hierarchy in advanced societies. This was a very British obsession but we should consider it. Finally we will consider the ways in which ethnicity, age and gender constitute principles around which urban socio-spatial systems are organised. In the USA, ethnicity has traditionally been considered the key principle of differentiation, but this is most unusual in the advanced industrial world. The significance of age cohort is relatively new, but has interesting implications for patterns of consumption through urban space. Gender is largely a matter of the exclusion of single mothers and their children, but the inequalities predicated on that are enormous. The penultimate section of the chapter will consider the processes which have engendered social polarisation, referring back to our discussion of global processes in Chapters 1 and 2 and forward to our discussion of urban governance in Chapter 8.

Urban ecologies: Chicago and beyond

The origins of social scientific urban ecology lie in Chicago in the 1920s. Here it is not difficult to become confused by nomenclature. The Chicago School, those working at the University of Chicago in this period, pioneered two radically different approaches to empirical social science. Chicago sociologists initiated systematic 'social scientific' qualitative observational work in urban industrial locations, whereas Park and Burgess (1925) developed a Darwinian positivist account of the actual socio-spatial organisation of the city in terms of land use functions and residential segregation.

Park and Burgess argued for a process of ecological competition in an urban environment. The analogy was with the competition among species to occupy niches in natural environments. The competitive groups were differentiated by ethnicity and class. All groups were not equal. Park (1952) noted that natural environments are often characterised by the presence of a dominant species which seems to impose order on the whole system. In the urban context, dominance was understood not in terms of a social group as such but rather by reference to the component of urban space which commanded the highest land values – in Chicago School language: the central business district. The pattern of land uses was then that of a series of rings, of annular zones, surrounding the central business district. Development took the form of invasion as uses pushed out with urban growth and became successor uses displacing the uses previously in that space. Successors might be a new ethnic group or lower social class displacing an established group as that group moved further out into suburbia.

Kleinberg summarises the perspective thus:

> in classic urban ecology the structure of the city is viewed as the product of the operation of the market in land interacting with the demographic characteristics of its various social and economic groups. The life and growth of the city are ultimately governed by supposedly unconscious *biotic processes of competition*, out of which there evolves in an unplanned spontaneous way, a spatial mosaic of culturally and economically segregated natural areas representing the placement of each group into its appropriate ecological place. (1995: 12, original emphasis)

Kleinberg pertinently identifies a fundamental contradiction in classical urban ecology. On the one hand there is a biotic account of the urban socio-spatial system as the product of unconscious competitive processes. On the other, the Chicago School were concerned with the sociological project of understanding social order as an overarching whole. The problem of getting from the competitive components to a holistic account of society was never satisfactorily resolved.

Classical ecology has been substantially criticised from two directions. Castells in *The Urban Question* (1977) attacked it as irredeemably positivist and to be dismissed on methodological grounds. Most Marxist-influenced social scientists abandoned the insights of Engels and tended to ignore intra-urban social differentiation for nearly two decades. This had the unfortunate consequence of permitting accounts of the nature of the relationship between the global and the local in which localities were understood as undifferentiated wholes.

Simultaneously in social geography a 'neo-classical ecological theory' was developed on the positivist foundation of the classical approach. Whereas classical ecology retained a sociological interest in normative structures which were seen as factors operating alongside processes of economic competition, neo-classical accounts are Schumpeterian, emphasising the role of technological development, both through innovations in urban transport systems and in relation to the role of technology in capitalist production as a whole.

Duncan (1964) argued for the existence of a systemic ecological complex formed by the simultaneous interaction of population, environment and technology, with, as Kleinberg (1995: 17) points out, social organisation understood as a fourth element but as the dependent variable with the other three being independent factors. Kleinberg observes that this creates a fundamental problem for social action about urban issues in that it regards the domain of conscious and reflective social action as a dependent consequence of factors beyond active control (1995: 17). This kind of systemic conception gels with the chaos/complexity understanding of urban systems, although the chaos/complexity framework allows us to be more optimistic about the possibilities of consciously directing the evolution of urban futures and certainly does not consign conscious action to dependent status.

Explicit discussions of urban social ecology are inherently modernist in form and still depend in important respects on the Chicago School model. Dear (2000) has proposed an alternative approach which he argues is postmodernist in two respects. First, it is explicitly postmodernist at the meta-theoretical level, arguing for a relativist perspectivism, an approach which we discussed in Chapter 1.

Dear's second statement about the postmodern city is that it no longer takes the annular form dependent on the central business district. Although he explicitly rejects Los Angeles as a general urban model for the postmodern city in the way that Chicago was a model for the modern city, his observation that whereas in Chicago we had the city organising around a central core, in Los Angeles we have 'the periphery organizing the center' (2000: ix) is extremely important. Here we have a different ecology in what we might better call postindustrial rather than postmodern cities. This is the theme of 'Edge City' and we will consider it in detail after we have examined both contemporary urban inequality and the nature of the suburb.

Divided cities

In order to describe socio-spatial systems in a systematic way, we need to measure. Of course impressionistic description does matter. We are happiest when the results of our measurements correspond with our impressions, and both correspond to people's everyday knowledge of the differentiated character of their own particular locality. Callaghan (1998) shows this spatial knowledge to be a key element in the general repertoire which people use in understanding of their own position in the social order. The measurements we use are generally the product of population censuses which record characteristics of individuals and households and locate those individuals and households in space.

The regular censuses conducted in advanced industrial societies generate 'small area' data sets which describe the organisation of urban space: see for example the discussion of the UK version in Dale and Marsh (1993). There are various statistical methods which can be applied to these data sets. Here we will consider the two commonest approaches, the use of 'factor analysis' approaches and the construction of numerical typologies.

Factor analysis was invented for biometric and psychological work. We are not going to deal here with the mathematical details of the technique but rather with its underlying logic of explanation. This can be most easily explained by considering the way factor analysis is used in the analysis of psychometric measurements. Scores

on psychological tests are at best indirect measurements of underlying mental attributes. The scores are not direct measurements of
causes, but of the effects of causes which cannot be directly and
specifically measured. Factor analysis and related techniques use
sophisticated mathematical methods to identify the underlying causal
factors whose indirect effects are (supposedly) observed in the form
of psychometric scores.

Factor analysis fits very well with the kind of explanations offered
by positivist social ecology in both its classical and new forms. Social
ecology considers that the form of the city is the product of an
underlying general mechanism of causation which can be established
through the analyses of measurements. These measurements take the
form of the construction of social indices using census and / or similar
spatially organised data. Factor analyses are then carried out and
factors are labelled on the basis of examinations of the social indices
with which they are highly correlated. These factors are then identified as the causal forces which generate the shape of the city as a
socio-spatial system.

From a realist / complexity perspective, factor analyses are not an
appropriate way for us to manage our accounts of socio-spatial
systems and the ways in which those systems change over time.
This is because they are part of the general linear model. In other
words the underlying causal account implicit in them is one of incre-
mental changes rather than one of whole systems transformations.

The construction of numerical taxonomies, heavy-duty quantitative stamp collecting, can deal with non-linear change. These taxo-
nomic techniques were developed by biological ecologists in order to
differentiate among habitats on the basis of very large sets of measurements of those habitats. Since Linnaeus, biology has been a
discipline based on classification, on sorting things into categories.
Biological categorisation seems in many ways to be a development of
an innate human capacity – certainly scientific and lay classifications
of species generally correspond rather closely across places and
human cultures. In any event, we can sort things into types using
multi-variate social indicators as the basis of the sorting.

The unfashionability of urban ecology, even as description, means
that there are not as many examples of cluster-based accounts of
socio-spatial systems in the academic social science literature as one
might expect, although the approach is widely used in marketing, for
insurance rating purposes, and in epidemiology. An exception is the

work of Morenoff and Tienda (1997) who explored changes over time in the classic locus of social ecology, Chicago. They found considerable social polarisation over the period of deindustrialisation. Transitional working-class neighbourhoods, which comprised 45 per cent of all census tracts in 1970 formed only 14 per cent of such tracts in 1990 (1997: 67). Hispanic immigration has modified the social ecology of Chicago with concentration of Hispanics leading to the transition of many stable middle-class neighbourhoods to the transitional working-class category. In Chicago, 'underclass' neighbourhoods were overwhelmingly (90 per cent on average) black. The process of transition was not uniformly downwards. Many transitional neighbourhoods became stable middle class, but in Chicago this usually meant stable middle-class black. Those which became 'gentrifying yuppie' became more white. This middle-class segregation of Afro-Americans, almost uniquely among ethnic groups in the developed world, is extremely important.

My own examinations of two locales in the north east of England, Northern Tyneside (Byrne, 1989) and Teesside (Byrne, 1995a), show a similar shift from the social inequalities of the Fordist era, which were real but stepped and continuous, to a much more polarised urban system in the postindustrial city. Here we can see a real advantage of the quantitative typology approach. Essentially it deals in relations. In other words the classification depends on the differences among the entities being classified. The resulting typology is a description not just of the categories taken separately but of the whole set of them considered as a socio-spatial system. Unlike factor analysis, this is not a reductionist approach. The existence of time ordered data sets means that we can use the approach to see if things have changed and in what way they have changed. Morenoff and Tienda's work is an example of exactly this.

The cities of the South have somewhat different urban patterns but to the extent that they are subject to globalising forces, there is a convergence of their urban forms towards the postindustrial norm. We must be careful to distinguish between cities in post-communist systems and those in countries without that history of detailed control. Shanghai (see Wu, 1999) has much in common with post-Soviet cities in Central and Eastern Europe in that on top of pre-communist patterns of urban differentiation – extreme in this semi-colonial city where the Western and westernised elites lived in the International Settlement and French Concession outside Chinese law, and the

Chinese proletariat lived in something very like London's East End – there was imposed a homogenous development of new housing areas. The cadres or nomenklatura did have their special districts but such cities were more uniform than their Western or Southern counterparts. They certainly lacked the self-built squatter housing of the unregulated South, although in Hungary people did build for themselves, subject to some regulation, in the suburbs.

Mumbai provides a good South Asian illustration of the more typical Southern city. O'Hare *et al.* summarise the situation thus:

> The reality is that over one-half of Mumbai's population live in conditions of abject poverty, squalor and deprivation... The poor live in overcrowded slums and hutments, on pavements, along railway tracks, beside pipelines, under bridges, on ill drained marshlands and in other vacant spaces available to them. Although not strictly categorized as 'slums', many others live in relatively old and dilapidated single room tenement chawls... The slums and hutments are located in highly polluted and unhealthy environments as a result of proximity to industrial emissions and effluents, and/or from poorer sewage, drainage and irregular garbage clearance. (1998: 270)

The extent of urban inequality in Mumbai is illustrated by Das and Gonsalves's estimate (1987) that the rich have 90 per cent of Mumbai's urban space and the poor have the remaining 10 per cent. Mumbai represents an urban form found where there is massive rural inmigration into urban centres without much in the way of regulation of urban construction, coupled with extremes of inequality in wealth and income. Its pattern is not different in principle, although there are contextual differences of form, from that of most Brazilian cities. However, there are significant differences of degree in the cities of the South. Medellin in Columbia has its communas but conditions in them are massively better than in Mumbai or Rio's equivalent areas because of significant municipal investment in infrastructure (Steinen, 1999). It would be wrong to see the South as undifferentiated.

The suburbs

Let us turn now to the very substantial changes in the socio-spatial arrangement of urban space in the cities of the developed world which happened, in the USA and UK at least, during the development and high period of the Fordist era. The most important of these was 'suburbanisation' but we should also think about the beginnings of gentrification and the impact of urban renewal on the spatial location of working-class people in the UK, and ethnic minorities, especially Afro-Americans, in the USA.

The word 'suburb' originally referred to a built-up area outside the walls of the city, but from the nineteenth century onwards, in large cities it began to take on a new meaning. Suburbs became possible once people could live at some distance from the place where they worked, and began as early as the late eighteenth century. The development of suburban railways and tram systems led to massive suburban development during the second half of the nineteenth century with increasing car ownership accelerating the trend during the twentieth century.

In the UK much of the post-1918 suburban development was of social housing, housing built for rent by local authorities. The original estates built under legislations of 1919 (Homes fit for Heroes) and 1924 were deliberately built to high quality for the skilled working and lower middle class, using garden city layouts and housing designs. This approach was repeated between 1945 and 1956, the great period of council-house building. However, other estates were built in the 1930s and after 1956 specifically to house residents whose original dwellings had been 'slum cleared', and these were generally of lower standard and took on some of the social reputation of the slums they replaced (see Merrett, 1979).

In the United States suburbanisation boomed in the inter-war years. That iconic representation of Roosevelt New Deal local communitarianism, Frank Capra's *It's a Wonderful Life*, hinges around the activities of an honest (those were the days), able and hard-working manager of a local 'Savings and Loan' Company, the US equivalent of a building society, who created a decent suburb in his home town of Bedford Falls. In the post-war period, with very generous funding available for mortgage advances to returning veterans of the World and Korean Wars, suburbs were created on an enormous scale.

Perhaps the most suburbanised of all societies is Australia typified by the Western suburbs of Sydney (see Forsyth, 1999). Here there was massive inmigration from Europe in the post-Second World War period, but these migrants were vastly more prosperous than the poor peasant migrants of the South, explicitly excluded from Australia by the White Australia policy even if they had had the resources to travel there. Between 1948 and the 1990s, Sydney's population more than doubled to nearly four million and the bulk of this was suburban development in Western Sydney. Other Australian cities had similar growth. *Neighbours* – the TV soap opera set in Melbourne – illustrates the character of the places which resulted.

The suburbs are very important indeed. They are the product of a complex combination of factors and have different significances at different points in their development. Crucial to their very possibility was the substantial increase in the real incomes of skilled and white-collar employed workers which began in the core capitalist countries in the second half of the nineteenth century. These higher wages were the product of working-class organisation and of the technological response of capitalism to that organisation which led to a shift from absolute surplus value expropriation – the extraction of profits by paying workers less – to relative surplus value expropriation – the increasing of profits by making workers much more productive. Under the latter process real wages rose.

The design of the suburbs owed much to the radical anti-urban and anti-industrial aesthetic programme of William Morris. The ideal suburb, Letchworth, was developed on a Utopian basis as a garden city by Ebenezer Howard and it was the adoption of forms influenced by this approach, if not necessarily by Howard's philanthropism, which spread suburbs throughout the English speaking world; although in Europe only Brussels took this 'English' form, with high-density apartment housing remaining the norm as it did in New York, although not in most other North American cities.

The suburbs flourished because people wanted to live in them. The new houses were cleaner, healthier, much easier for women to manage (constantly available hot water is perhaps the greatest single innovation for the housewife of all modern technologies) and they had a good social reputation. The politics of suburban development is complex. Certainly the suburbs were seen as the basis of order: rent strikes in the UK during and immediately after the First World War expressed social discontent and were seen as prefiguring Bolshevik revolution. Suburban development of owner occupation was understood as a 'bulwark against Bolshevism'. Lower middle-class and upper working-class people were incorporated into the existing social system by suburban residence. At the same time the improvement in real living standards was a significant social gain for them.

However, the suburbs were not available to all. The urban poor under industrial capitalism never really gained access to them, even at the end of the Fordist era. In the 1960s, massive overspill housing estates were built on the edge of UK cities. These estates were typically of good quality in terms of construction but as slum clearance replacement they were always more marginal than 'general needs' housing. There was also redevelopment using non-traditional style on inner city sites: Dunleavy's 'mass housing – large flatted estates of uniform housing quite distinct in form from the kinds of housing provided by market mechanisms' (1981: 1). The suburbs and the poor working-class areas were separate. In France the massive development of the Parisian banlieues, the 'Red Belt' of industry and workers' housing, had a very similar form. Indeed this was the pattern for much of Europe and in particular for societies undergoing Soviet style industrialisation. Most of Saint Petersburg is made up of block after block of flats built in this period and this is the norm in post-Soviet cities in general.

In the UK, differentiation was largely a function of class, although all post Second World War immigrant groups (other than Asian doctors) originally did not live in suburban areas. In the US, race also signified although in the massive post-war suburbanisation of Los Angeles, segregated black suburbs were developed. This can be seen clearly in *Devil in a Blue Dress*, the filmed version of Walter Mosely's book starring Denzil Washington as a southern black ex-serviceman who settled in California as a factory worker but becomes a private detective. The protagonist makes great play of his home ownership. However, despite the existence of some black suburbs, US cities throughout this period were virtually absolutely segregated for blacks on racial lines. Indeed in *The Two Jakes* the Jewish developer of a West Los Angeles suburb justifies his exclusion of Latinos from purchase by pointing out that he could not, as a Jew, live in the scheme himself.

It is important to recognise the spatial scale of suburbanisation. The Tyneside conurbation provides an interesting illustration. The population of the conurbation in 1911 and in 1991 was of almost exactly the same size at just about one million people. However, the one million people of 1991 occupied nine times as much built-up area. This spatial spreading makes social differentiation much easier and much more severe. Lever describes the same process in Glasgow:

> This outward expansion of the conurbation has permitted much great social polarization within the built-up area. Those with secure incomes have been able to buy themselves pleasant environments, good local services, a political locale within small towns and local authorities where there has been considerable scope for individuals to exercise significant political power and choice, low taxes and enhanced employment opportunities. The poorer households, however, have been trapped either in the inner city of Glasgow or in the inner areas of the older industrial towns, or, when relocated through the processes of urban renewal, assigned to equally unpopular high rise flats or peripheral housing estates which are poorly serviced, highly taxed and in areas with few employment opportunities. (1991: 987–8)

The UK is a highly centralised country where most local services are funded from national taxation according to formulae which are supposed to reflect need, in which low-income households are cushioned against destitution by 'safety net' cash benefits, and in which other than white ethnic minorities both form only a small proportion of the population (6 per cent overall with a maximum of 28 per cent in London) and are not spatially segregated in constrained ghettos. If social differentiation occurs here, then it is even more the case in the United States where 'white flight' to the suburbs has left central cities as fiscally impoverished minority ghettos.

The extreme case of this is Detroit in which the original city of Fordism has become deindustrialised, predominantly black, with a poor local tax base and a virtually derelict Central Business District. At the same time the white suburbs (see their portrayal in the film *Gross Point Blank*) remain affluent and ordered. This grim picture has been substantially modified in the United States by the increasing Latinisation of almost all the US's core city areas which has important implications for the US's urban structure in postindustrial capitalism. However, the spatial reordering of suburbanisation remains extra-ordinarily important in understanding the urban.

There are some classic studies of suburban life of which Gans's *The Levittowners* (1968) for the US and Bell's *Middle Class Families* (1969) for the UK are probably the best known. These studies were conducted more than thirty years ago. Yet again we encounter the problem of the missing contemporary ethnographies of everyday life for the middle groups in the postindustrial social order.

Tenure: a British obsession?

In the UK there is an interesting literature of the 1960s through until the 1980s which takes housing tenure as a key principle of social differentiation. This began with Rex and Moore's Weberian specification of housing classes, as a by-product of their research into the impact of other than white immigration into Birmingham. They recognised that housing was in scarce supply and that in consequence:

> there is a class struggle over the use of houses and ... this class struggle is the central process of the city as a social unit. In saying this we follow Max Weber who saw class struggle was apt to emerge wherever people in a market situation enjoyed differential access to property and such class struggles might therefore arise not merely around the use of the means of industrial production, but around the control of domestic property. (1967: 273–4)

This study reflected the social reality of the city they were investigating. They are writing about individual dwellings, differentiated by tenure (form of ownership and use relation) and amenity, not about areas. Sparkbrook, the neighbourhood they examined, had a high proportion of other than white immigrants, but was and is a multi-racial area, not a ghetto in the US sense. It is impossible to imagine a similar US study in which spatial area was not the key focus of attention.

Rex and Moore's work led to a recognition of the significance of housing tenure in social life. Here we cannot escape the implications of the constitutive role of social policies in relation to everyday life. In the UK a combination of taxation treatment of owner-occupied property and the elimination of general subsidies to social housing[1] which coincided with (and probably was causal to) a massive increase in house prices relative to average earnings, meant that many people have made large, and untaxed capital gains. A collapse in house prices in the late 1980s, especially in London, left many households with 'negative equity' (the mortgage they owed on their dwelling was greater than its resale value) but in the early 80s it looked as if such gains were an absolute and continuing reality. There were always problems with this perception. Capital gains on housing were only realisable when the dwellings were sold, and most sellers had to buy somewhere else to live. However, gains could be the basis of inheritance. The mass spread of owner-occupation in the US and the UK since the 1930s has transformed the pattern of wealth holding and wealth inheritance for middle-income groups in those societies (Murie and Forrest, 1980). Now, most people inherit something from their parents, provided their parents die quickly of uncomplicated conditions and do not incur large health and care bills in the US, and care bills in the UK. It was also true that people could realise capital gains by moving from more expensive to cheaper areas which is a common retirement strategy in the UK.

Saunders attempted to construct a whole new theory of social stratification on this undeniably non-trivial experience. Originally (1986: 156) he proposed that we should replace our understanding of class-based divisions derived from the relations of production, with 'consumption cleavages' based on the command people had over resources in markets, which command was in large part a function of their housing tenure. Subsequently (1990) Saunders took up, with critical reservations, Dunleavy's (1980, 1986) conception of sectoral cleavages, in which production cleavages and relations with the state were understood, in interaction, as the basis of political identity. Saunders asserted that to this we had to add complex material interests based on tenure and on the credit fuelled consumption which was associated with home ownership. This important, if over-simplified point has not been taken up by cultural studies given that the approach characteristically neglects material factors in discussion of consumption and culture.

In considering tenure we must never forget that in the UK where more than 70 per cent of households are owner occupiers, this tenure is now so broad as to be highly internally differentiated (Forrest *et al.* 1990). In other words there are owner-occupied areas which are poor. In Newcastle and Manchester there are areas where a terraced house is worth less than £8000 and others within three miles where exactly the same type of dwelling built from the same nineteenth-century pattern book is worth over £100 000. These differences are the product of simultaneous gentrification and marginalisation, two of the local processes causing urban social polarisation.

Gentrification has played a crucial role in shaping postindustrial cities. Originally this term referred to the transfer of working-class housing to middle-class households. In considering this we should not forget the enormous historical significance of the reverse process of filtration – the movement of housing stock down the class hierarchy, usually with much higher densities of use of it. Microeconomic theories based on notions of a rent-gap (see Smith, 1996) have regularly been employed to explain gentrification. If housing and/or land owners can get more money from their property if it is transferred from being the residences of the poor to the residences of the more affluent, then it will be. Throughout much of the nineteenth century, the reverse was actually true! The best returns from house property were on multi-occupied slums. The Dublin tenements, the locale of O'Casey's plays, were exactly this kind of downwardly filtered property, as was the Notting Hill of Rachmanism based around the need of immigrant households for housing which was the domestic backdrop to the Profumo scandal of the early 1960s (see the film *Scandal*) and the consequent Milner-Holland report on housing rents (see Beirne, 1977). Notting Hill is now an extreme example of gentrification – see the film of that name which is certainly not about a zone of poverty-stricken immigrants and criminals!

Smith has described gentrification as a re-invention of the frontier of settlement in the heart of cities. He identifies the 'revanchist city' (revenge) arguing that:

> Revenge against minorities, the working class, women, environmental legislation, gays and lesbians, immigrants became the increasingly common denominator of public discourse. Attacks on affirmative action and immigration policy, street violence against gays and homeless people, feminist bashing and public campaigns against political correctness and multi-culturalism were the most visible vehicles of this reaction. In short the 1990s have witnessed the emergence of what we can think of as the *revanchist city*. (1996: 44–5, original emphasis)

Smith's story has considerable force in those world cities where the poor and dispossessed confront the rich on a daily basis. The film *The Fisher King* conveys this well for New York in the 1980s. There are two solutions to this issue, both of which may be pursued simultaneously. One is the development of gated fortresses by the rich. The other is the physical expulsion of the poor and disorderly from central urban spaces. Smith's work is primarily concerned with the latter.

Recently much gentrification has taken the form of the changing of use of industrial zones which used to offer employment to the organised working class. The best known example of this is London's docklands which typifies an approach to industrial waterfronts throughout the world. The first such scheme was Baltimore's harbour development. However, important though gentrification is, it is the large-scale processes of deindustrialisation and the creation of postindustrial social order which are the major control parameters of the new urban order and its socio-spatial system.

In a European context, we have to consider the impact of general social changes on social housing areas and the consequent marginalisation of those areas. In the UK, social housing during the Fordist era was predominantly occupied by ordinary working-class households dependent on wages. In much of the industrial UK, council (municipal) housing was the normal tenure and was much sought after. Non-traditional mass housing was generally unpopular, although high-rise blocks in central urban areas have become quite acceptable to households without small children, and many in London have been gentrified. Nonetheless, one of the consequences of deindustrialisation has been the residualisation of social housing. This is a complex process which in part has happened as people grow old in the houses they have always lived in so that in many areas the majority of residents in social housing are pensioners; but it is evident that non-pensioner social-housing residents are not the secure working class of thirty years ago. Marginalisation is a general process across Europe. In Malmo, Sweden's municipal housing built for the Swedish working class now houses refugee immigrants.

An interesting study by Burrows (1999) suggests that selling-off of the better housing stock under 'right to buy' is not now the most important cause of the residualisation of social housing. Those leaving social housing, through death or movement to owner occupation, are generally people with a life history of stable employment. Those entering are the poor and insecure with less stable family forms and work records. Given the significance of housing tenure in shaping contemporary cities, this process is of considerable significance.

Robson's study of the large industrial town of Sunderland was conducted in the Fordist era. Robson concluded that, whereas classical (Chicago) models of urban growth worked well in explaining the nineteenth-century development of the town: 'In the twentieth century, by comparison, the development of council housing and of town planning and the effects of a variety of social changes have had profound effects upon the urban scene and have largely invalidated many of the bases on which the classical models have been built.' (1969: 240) What Robson was describing was the way in which council housing and a town planning system, which was at least to some degree egalitarian in intention, had produced a more equal urban socio-spatial system. Things are not like that now as we move from simple suburbanisation to the development of a new posturban way of living.

Living, shopping and working ex-urban: edge city

We cannot understand the contemporary significance of suburban-isation only in relation to differentiated residence. Garreau puts it like this:

> First we moved our home out past the traditional idea of what constituted a city. This was the suburbanization of America, especially after World War II ... Then we wearied of returning downtown for the necessities of life, so we moved our marketplace out to where we lived. This was the malling of America, especially in the 1960s and 70s ... Today we have moved our means of creating wealth – our jobs – out to where most of us have lived and shopped for two generations. That has led to the rise of Edge City. (1992: 4)

Muller considers that we are seeing the transformation of the American city (and as Garreau emphasises this also applies to UK cities, particularly London) into 'a polycentric metropolis of realms' (1997: 57). The causes derive from the technologies of communication which make globalisation possible. It is perhaps worth questioning whether globalisation is cause rather than effect in relation to sub-urbanisation. The development of the suburbs as locales of residence and consumption and then of employment nodes, particularly office employment nodes, within them might actually be understood as a driving force in globalisation itself. Probably, relationships are recursive – both things cause each other and feed back positively to intensify each other's development.

Angotti has proposed that the trends which have generated the 'edge city' have created a new urban form in the twentieth century – the metropolis:

> The metropolis in the twentieth century is not just a larger city, but a qualitatively new form of human settlement. It is larger, more complex and plays a more commanding role – economic, political and cultural – than the industrial city and town that preceded it. It is not just downtown but more like a collection of towns. The social history of the twentieth century cannot be fully understood without taking into account the emergence of the modern metropolis. Indeed the metropolis is the city of the twentieth century. (Angotti, 1993: 1)

The metropolis is not just a matter of towns growing towards and into each other. Metropolises have a very different character because so much of the activity goes on outside the central area. The very rapidly growing postcolonial city of Dublin – the oldest colonial city of the modern world – demonstrates this very well. The Dublin metropolitan region now has a population of more than one million. Indeed if its westward extensions into Kildare are counted it is substantially more than this. Not only do nearly 60 per cent of these people not live in Dublin, more and more of them do not work there either. They work in industrial parks, office parks and mall areas which exist both as a ring around the core city and scattered through the new postindustrial edge settlements. There is even substantial commuting out of the core city to work in these peripheral zones. The idea of metropolis is important and we will return to it in the conclusion to this book.

The development of suburban employment intensifies social divisions. Spatial segregation and weak transport links between poor people's area of residence and the new employment zones makes access to jobs more difficult. Of course many of the jobs of the edge city, the new urban world without a centre, are low paid and insecure. It is worth noting that in the US, such jobs are more likely to be done by immigrants than by poor native-born citizens. Greene (1997) shows how in Chicago, new immigrants move to where these jobs are, whilst Afro-American native-born citizens are much more likely to remain trapped in central urban ghettos with poor communication connections with the new employment locales. In Cleveland, Ohio where Bogart and Ferry (1999) note the existence of eight edge cities in the greater Cleveland area, Chow and Coulton (1998) demonstrate that during the 1980s and throughout the period of deindustrialisation, there was a markedly increased polarisation and ghettoisation of the urban poor, particularly the black urban poor. Let us turn to issues of urban ethnicity, age cohort and gender.

Ethnicity, age cohort, gender, and the divided city

Garreau considers that the development of the edge city associated with the development of a black middle class with access through equal opportunities legislation to desirable private sector employment is challenging the traditional racial segregation of the urban US. However, Bashi and Hughes (1997), following Massey and Denton (1993), consider that racial segregation of Afro-Americans is so culturally and institutionally engrained in the US that such developments will have little impact on it. Instead we see a limited amount of segregated black suburban housing and some integration among the upper middle class.

There is evidence for both lines of argument in the United States. However, the European evidence is unequivocal. Socio-spatial differentiation in European cities is a function of class, not ethnicity. Wacquant's comparison of 'the Black American Ghetto and the French Urban Periphery' shows this:

> the declining French working-class banlieue and the black American ghetto constitute two *different socio-spatial formations,* produced by different institutional logics of segregation and aggregation and resulting in pronouncedly higher levels of blight, poverty and hardship in the ghetto. To simplify greatly: exclusion operates on the basis of colour reinforced by class and state in the Black Belt, but mainly on the basis of class and mitigated by the state in the Red Belt . . . with the result that the former is a racially and culturally homogenous universe characterized by low organizational density and state penetration, whereas the latter is fundamentally heterogeneous in terms of both class and ethno-national recruitment, with a strong presence of national institutions. (1993: 368, original emphasis)

A range of studies based on detailed analyses of the 1991 small area census data (Byrne, 1998; Coleman and Salt (eds), 1996; Karn (ed.), 1997; Peach (ed.), 1996b) demonstrate that Peach's (1996a) dismissal of the idea that Britain has racially-segregated ghettos is correct. The pattern in the UK, other than in Northern Ireland, is one of different experiences for different groups. Households self-classifying as Indian have locales of concentration but are now dispersing into middle-class suburbia and the developing edge cities. Afro-Caribbeans are a very integrated group with a large proportion of younger men and women living with someone self-classifying as 'white'. The Afro-Caribbean group tends to be poor and working class but to live among the white poor and working class. The most 'segregated' groups in the UK, other than working-class Catholics and Protestants in urban Northern Ireland, are the Muslim minorities from South Asia, with Bangladeshis living in East London social housing being the only group who might be considered to live in constrained ghettos. Pakistanis in the rest of the UK seem to live 'within and apart' (see Byrne, 1998; Rees *et al.*, 1995); there are signs of integration on the pattern identified in France by Wacquant.

There are other principles on which cities can be divided in socio-spatial terms. Perhaps the crucial one is lifestyle as this interacts with age. Sexual orientation is now an important organising principle of local specialisation in consumption, with gay zones in the Castro in San Francisco, the Gay Village in Manchester, and Soho in London. However, only in the Castro is this as much a matter of residence as of retail services and entertainment. Gay zones seem to be a special variant of gentrification and / or cultural consumption.

The same can be said of age as a principle of urban differentiation. With the enormous growth in higher-education participation rates in postindustrial capitalism, a phenomenon which is especially marked in the UK, and given the location of many universities and colleges in urban centres, student zones (both of consumption and of residence) have become a feature of cities in general. Manchester, for example, has more than 100 000 students. Any university teacher can observe the development of the 'youth city', less common in continental Europe where students generally live in their parental homes, but relatively little has as yet been written about it.

Gender is not a general principle of socio-spatial segregation but a gender-related factor is important. This is the effect on the spatial location of a household when it is headed by a single mother. In all advanced industrial countries, but particularly in the UK, such households are differentially concentrated in low-status areas, especially in social housing. There is a dynamic development of the character of single-parent households with many becoming two-parented again during the dependency period of the children, and such a shift in form is often associated with a shift in space (see Byrne, 1999a) but the spatial location and deprivation of such households is important.

What makes cities unequal?

If we are going to understand the socio-spatial structure of our urban areas, we have to take into account the complex interaction of general global processes and specific local factors. First, we must understand that the general effect of the global processes as control parameters is non-linear. The changes they produce are not changes of degree but changes of kind, and these changes happen very rapidly (see Byrne, 1997, for a discussion of the application of complexity theory to an understanding of these changes). Secondly, we have to understand that global processes do not descend mysteriously like Angels of the Lord from somewhere else. Rather they are undertaken by social actors present in the locality, and this is especially the case in relation to the processes of urban planning and land use changes which play such an important role in shaping urban forms. Glocalisation is a good term here. Finally we have to understand local outcomes in relation to specific, and sometimes contingent, local histories.

The processes of cause can be illustrated by looking at any metropolis. We can always see a process of deindustrialisation which reflects global tendencies relating to improved industrial productivity and spatial relocation of employment, interacting in the UK with national macro-economic policy which has seriously disadvantaged manufacturing as against financial services. The effects of these processes are often reinforced by local planning policies which have reinforced the deindustrialising trend.

Planning and gentrification have both played a role in the polarisation of the urban space, but the actual pattern of that polarisation depends on locally contingent factors. We will return to these themes in Chapter 8 when we consider the governance of urban space.

Therborn in the 1980s suggested that the social order of advanced industrial capitalism was likely to undergo a process of Brazilianisation:

> This would produce a society like a richer and somewhat more humane Brazil with increasing trichotomous socio-economic divisions. At the bottom would be the permanently and marginally unemployed with certain welfare entitlements which are almost certain to be reduced over time. Some of these people will make a living in the black economy ... In the middle will be the stably employed, or those with the possibility of re-employment who will probably be increasingly divided according to enterprise, sector and hierarchical position. They will make a fairly decent living, no more, but will be able to congratulate themselves on the widening distance between themselves and the unemployed ... The marginalization of a significant part of the former and the potential working class has already gone hand in hand, in the first half of the 1980s, with increasing wealth and incomes of capitalists and top business managers. They constitute the third layer of mass unemployment societies. (1985: 32–3)

Therborn was wrong about mass unemployment as the basis of these changes but otherwise his account holds. We can see these patterns, with virtually full employment but disempowered trade unions, in the US and increasingly in the UK and as a project in Europe, although there is much more substantial cultural resistance to these tendencies outside the English speaking world.

This seems to be the crucial distinction which distinguishes the urbanised locales of newly industrialising societies from those of the industrialised world. In the cities of the newly industrialising countries, as Schmidt puts it:

> the fastest and most dramatic process of urbanization in human history is taking place in the fringe areas, squatter settlements and slums of the metropolitan areas of the developing countries. Because of globalization and uneven development millions of people are forced to live in physical and social squalor which is reaching the point of ideological disaster. (1998: 133)

Here, there is a process of marginalisation which seems qualitatively different to the processes of the developed world. Auyero has resurrected the concept of 'marginal mass':

The structural historicist perspective on marginality...understood that the functioning of what they called 'the dependent labour market' was generating an excessive amount of unemployment. This 'surplus population' transcends the logic of the marxian concept of the 'industrial reserve army' and led the authors to coin the term 'marginal mass'. The "marginal mass" was neither superfluous nor useless; it was marginal because it had been rejected by the society that created it. (1997: 508–9)

We can identify marginal masses in the mega and other cities of those parts of the world which have not passed through either Fordism or 'socialism' but not in those which have. Contrary to the arguments of Murray (1990), a separated and distinctive cultural group does not seem to be emerging in any advanced industrial society other than the USA where racism is the primary causal factor. Wilson's work (1987, 1992) is much more interesting and important than Murray's polemic. He demonstrates how the interaction of deindustrialisation and racism is creating a black poor, separated not only from whites but from the black middle class, which he now describes as the 'ghetto poor' rather than as an underclass. I originally thought that something similar was happening in the UK but subsequent consideration of the complex trajectories of personal and household lives has persuaded me that whilst we have 'areas' which are different and distinctive, there is so much movement into and out of them that the notion of a permanently separated group does not make sense (see Byrne, 1999a). It certainly does not make logical sense if the poor remain as a reserve army of labour, contra Bauman's (1998) assertion of their economic irrelevance.

It may well be possible that the under-development of the former 'socialist' countries will produce 'marginal masses' but the signs are that this is not happening in those countries which became primarily urban under such regimes. For example, in Poland the forms of urban polarisation seem very similar but not yet as developed as the forms in the industrial countries of Western Europe (see Byrne and Wodz, 1997). China may be different. Although the highly regulated Chinese cities of the 'socialist' era never contained the marginal masses of other East Asian cities, the relaxation of controls over rural migration to urban areas might create that urban form. Certainly the pressures in China are very great.

Concluding remarks and further resources

Polarisation is now taking extreme forms in many cities of the world. The divides which exist within places are almost as great as those which exist on a global basis, certainly if we consider that inequality should be considered in relative terms. Postindustrial capitalism is unequal and the idea that we are experiencing a Brazilianisation of advanced capitalism seems to be pretty well exact as a description of the tendency of the social trajectory of advanced capitalist societies into the twenty-first century. In Latin America and the US (see Davis, 1998; Caldeira, 1996) we see the phenomenon of 'walled enclaves' with the affluent living inside guarded territories which exclude the poor. Films illustrate this well. In *The Big Lebowski* the treatment of 'the Dude', when he intrudes into a gated, locally policed 'beachfront community', illustrates that this division is as much one of class as of any other principle of social segregation. See *East LA* for an account of the Latino experience in that city. The privatisation of public space in malls, and surveillance through real-time CCT of ordinary public spaces is often discussed in relation to polarisation but this is much more a matter of regulation. Malls do exclude but by age rather than anything else in the UK.

There are some good literary treatments. John Updike's experiment in magical realism, *Brazil* (1995), gives a picture of how urban lives are separate but can intersect. The film *La Haine* conveys exactly the implications of Wacquant's account of the nature of the French banlieue. One film which does convey exactly the spatial separation of the lives of the black urban poor in the contemporary US is *Candyman* shot in Cabrini Green in Chicago. Although the film was made in the Fordist era, the spatial relations of rural and suburban affluence and urban squalor (portrayed in *Get Carter*, shot in Gateshead) prefigure the character of the contemporary world. *Central Station* as a literal road movie portrays urban rural relations in Brazil with a particularly shocking, because not at all melodramatic, image of the superfluity of the urban poor, killed for stealing tiny amounts, or treated as the source of body parts for transplants.

6

Culture and the urban: commodity, understanding and resource

This chapter is about 'culture' which means that it is dealing with a word which has many meanings. Moreover we must remember that 'culture' is not simply an object of study. In 'cultural studies' – the territory where the humanities meet the social sciences – the cultural turn does not merely involve an absolutely proper recognition of the significance of 'culture' in all its aspects. It can also imply a commitment to the cultural relativism which generally trades under the name of postmodernism. We have encountered this before. Now we are moving into the major intellectual turf of that approach.

In this chapter we will begin with an examination of the meanings and implications of the word 'culture'. Then we will turn to the classic notions of 'urban culture': Wirth's idea of 'urbanism as a way of life' and Simmel's 'metropolis and mental life'. We will then examine the political economy of cultural production and realisation as this is expressed in the work of Zukin, Garreau and Hannigan. This will be followed by a section addressing the idea of the city as text, of approaches derived from 'cultural studies' which revolve around interpretation. Finally, the chapter will return to a consideration of urban culture as 'ways of life', drawing here particularly on the work of Jenkins, Barth and Wikan and returning to themes we considered in Chapter 3 when we examined 'community'.

The meaning of culture

Any theory of culture must include the concept of the dialectical interaction between culture and something that is not culture. We must suppose

129

the raw material of life – experience, to be at one pole, and all the infinitely complex human disciplines and systems, articulate and inarticulate, formalised in institutions or dispersed in the least formal ways, which 'handle', transmit or distort this raw material to be the other. It is the active *process* – which is at the same time *the process through which men make their history* – that I am insisting on. (E.P. Thompson, 1981: 398)

Thompson was quoting his (in)famous 1961 review of Raymond Williams's *The Long Revolution*, a book considered by many to be crucial in the development of the 'cultural turn' in social sciences and the emergence of a distinctive academic discipline of 'cultural studies'. Williams provides a useful starting point for this chapter because he presents a clear account of the different ways in which culture can be understood, of the different meanings of this slippery word *and* also shows how 'culture' becomes not just an object of understanding but a way of understanding. In other words, we have culture as an aspect, or more properly several interrelated aspects of reality, and cultural method as a way of understanding those aspects, aspects which may be understood as structures, processes, and/or both together. Thompson, the historical materialist's historical materialist, reminds us in his criticism of Williams that there is a reality, however multifaceted, in the social world and that the way people experience that reality through their lived, creative and constitutive engagement with it always matters, always shapes both what is, and how people understand what is, whilst acting on and in relation to what is.

Williams identified three sets of meanings which were attached to the word 'culture'. First, it has a meaning in aesthetics and other contexts, at least in the West where the influence of Plato remains pervasive, as an ideal, the ideal of the real represented in our imperfect world in art (although the idea has extended beyond the domains of art understood in the widest possible sense into politics, especially when the dread word 'pure' is brought into play).

Secondly, it describes representation of the world as it is, rather than attempts to attain some ideal – Williams calls this 'documentary':

Understood in this sense: ...culture is the body of intellectual and imaginative work, in which in a detailed way, human thought and experiences are variously recorded.... The analysis of culture, from such a definition, is the activity of criticism, by which the nature of the thought and experience, the details of the language, form and convention in which these are active, are described and valued. (1965: 57)

Finally there is the social definition of culture as already quoted in Chapter 1 in which culture is identified as a 'way of life'.

Williams notes that this last definition incorporates the approaches of historical criticism, but that from the point of view of the first two traditions it includes things which are not culture at all – the routines of production and reproduction in the conduct of human lives in human societies. The different specifications of culture predicate different ways of understanding it – the methods of interpretative criticism on the one hand and of social science on the other. The methodological tension inherent in this distinction will run through the whole of this chapter.

There is another aspect to culture which we have to consider. Culture constitutes a set of commodities which are produced and consumed as part of the capitalist process of circulation as well as through the processes of 'taste'. This set includes aspects of the urban in the form of the components of the built environment of the city, the town, the suburb and the edge city. These things are both cultural commodities and at the same time the places within which the processes of cultural production and cultural consumption happen. One of the crucial characteristics of the postindustrial urban world is that these commodities, the product of Lash and Urry's 'economies of signs' (1994), form an ever greater part of capitalist production and realisation; and the processes through which they are made, displayed and consumed matter more for lived experience than was the case in industrial capitalism.[1] As Zukin puts it, we have to consider:

> the seductive influence of the arts in political economy. With a continued displacement of manufacturing and development of the financial and non-profit sectors of the economy, cultural production seemed to be more and more what cities were about. (1995: viii)

Here we have a clear link between the themes of this chapter and of Chapter 7 where we will consider the processes of production of the built environment as such.

The classic standards: Wirth and Simmel

Wirth's essay of 1938 'Urbanism as a Way of Life' is an outmoded classic, based on the positivist programme of the Chicago School. Its argument took the form of a causal model in which three independent variables – size, heterogeneity, and density – generated the character of a fourth dependent variable – culture. Culture was seen as a categorical variable: it could take an urban or a rural form according to the values of the causal variables. These independent variables were thought of as continuous or at least ordinal, but they generated a difference of type rather than of degree. Rural areas had small populations which were homogeneous and lived at low densities. In urban areas the reverse held true. In consequence, rural culture was based on full relationships among limited numbers of individuals. Urban culture was based on partial and segmented relations among large numbers of individuals.

Wirth was presenting a mathematical model as a causal account of a distinction which had been made as a commonplace of social theory since the mid-nineteenth century. However, whilst earlier theorists, particularly Toënnies and Simmel, have seen the differences in cultural form as a product of change through time, with the development of urbanisation as part of that historical process, for Wirth the differences were coincident in time but differentiated in space.

Wirth's essay fitted well with the positivist turn in US sociology and was the basis of much work in the 1950s and 60s. However, it is not taken particularly seriously in contemporary urban studies because the account does not correspond to the actual character of social life in an urbanised world. One of the main reasons for this derives from the qualitative work of the Chicago School itself which described communal relationships of identity in urban life. Cities contained many communities with many cultures (as in the immigrant-founded society of the US ethnic cultures) rather than a single all-inclusive culture of place. Nonetheless, people had holistic relationships which existed in the urban world.

Wirth's work is interesting today primarily as an example of the mechanistic form of positivist explanation in the social sciences. Times have changed and the nature of the change is worth thinking about. When Wirth wrote his work, the world as a whole was still predominantly rural. Even within advanced industrial societies like the United States, there were still rural areas within which people led lives which were relatively isolated from national, let alone global processes. Within the contemporary US or Western Europe it would be very hard to find any place which was not part of the general postindustrial world system. Changes happened through time but they did not operate everywhere all at once. Temporal transformation in Wirth's day was represented in large part through spatial differentiation.

Simmel's argument in 'The Metropolis and Mental Life' (1950a) has considerable contemporary significance. Savage and Warde put their finger on why this should be so: 'the importance of Simmel's work lies in his argument that the nature of modernity makes it virtually impossible to pinpoint any coherent way of life at all' (1993: 113). This has been crucial in licensing the assertion that all understanding of the urban must be unique, individual and ideographic, and even idiosyncratic, which runs alongside the separate but related proposition that the proper object of understanding is the formation and enactment of the self. To understand why this should be so, we need to consider the bases of Simmel's general account of the social.

Smith (1980) provides such an account. Simmel worked within a generally dialectical framework. The essence of any dialectical account is that of opposition between two elements. For Simmel these were form and content:

> '[Simmel] posits a fundamental tension between the essential flux of our inner-subjective life and the limitations of the objective forms it can assume. The dynamics of human existence stem from mankind's ceaseless struggle to reconcile this and other paired, interacting polarities that characterize the human condition.... For Simmel, no particular social or political system but the very nature of human existence consists of a dialectical tension between individual creativity – which produces new social roles, social organizations, and forms of human interaction – and the power of these latter forms to become objectified, break loose from their original human purposes, take on a life of their own, and constrain future creativity and innovation. Once institutionalized, social forms, in his view, force life into generalized schemata, thereby robbing the individual personality of its uniqueness. The struggle between life and forms becomes for Simmel, a struggle between individuality and generalization. (Smith, 1980: 89)

Simmel's is a social theory of the self, at sea in a world of things made by people but constraining their freedom, the most important of which constraining forms was money, the subject of his most significant work. His account is psychologistic: it deals not with coherent and mutually self-identifying collectivities, but with the individual self operating under the stresses which have their origins in the complex, chaotic and multiple dynamic processes which constitute modernity as a social system. The urban figures in this as the locus, the place in which modernity is experienced. Simmel's is a very modern theory which appeals to postmodernists because of its relativism.

The political economy of culture – city and suburb in the urban world

There are three stories of culture as commodity in contemporary urban society. One is a story of 'high culture', of aesthetic signs produced and realised in cities, a process which depends in large part on the very high incomes realised by the servants of the global circulation of virtual money. The second is a story, usually but not invariably, of 'mediocre culture', of the commodities which represent the aesthetic of the shopping mall, the world of consumption of the middle masses – the bridge-and-tunnel crowd back in New Jersey as opposed to the sophisticates of rich and bohemian (both at once now) Manhattan; Essex instead of London's Soho / Covent Garden. The third is an idea of the street as the place in which new components of culture are made, from the high aesthetics of jazz as the rural blues met the urban in New Orleans, Chicago and Kansas City, to the contemporary incoherences of Rap. The first two are simple stories of capitalist production and reproduction. The last is a more complicated story of class, culture, ethnicity and gender as all of these interact, and, as the product of that interaction, relates to capitalist production and marketing for the masses of a globalised world in general.

One of the most interesting and coherent writers on the first of these processes is Sharon Zukin who identifies the contemporary significance in postindustrial capitalism of 'the symbolic economy' which:

> features two parallel production systems that are crucial to a city's material life: the *production of space*, with its synergy of capital investment and cultural meanings, and the *production of symbols* which construct both a currency of commercial exchange and a language of social identity. Every effort to rearrange space in the city is also an attempt at visual re-

presentation. Raising property values, which remains a goal of most urban elites, requires imposing a new point of view. But negotiating whose point of view and the costs of imposing it creates problems for public culture. (1995: 23–4, original emphases)

Zukin's *Loft Living* (1988) described how the use, made by artists, of redundant clothing manufacturing lofts in SoHo (South of Houston) New York as simultaneously places of residence and artistic production, became the basis of a combination of realty and art capitalist representation of this area of the city. The object was the enhancement of land values so that the very low and sometimes negative values of old industrial properties could be transformed by a respecification of the social character of the locale. 'Art' as both lifestyle and commodity set was the basis of this transformation. The actual form – the loft

has now become a key component of gentrification in cities across the world.

At the back of Zukin's account is a Marxist theory of rent. Rent is the price which the owners of land can demand in return for the use of that land – the price of a freehold represents the capitalised value of future rental streams. For Zukin the driving dynamic of urban development in all its aspects is the search for enhanced rents. There is a good deal to be said for this argument and we will return to it in Chapter 7. For the moment we should recognise that it describes three different (at least heuristically, although they operate together in real life and are only distinguishable at the level of analysis, which is always a questionable process) strands of 'culture'. One is the aesthetic as commodity, the things artists make and which are sold. Another is the artistic as life-style – the desperate attraction of bohemian, beat, norm challenging lifestyles for those who seek to realise their 'selves' against a world of order and conformity. The last is the actual concretisation of culture in the production and preservation of the built environment both as the new and as heritage.

The story of the city, and in particular of New York, has to be set against the story of the suburb. Although land value enhancement is an important part of the process of mall development, the driving force in this process is the actual mass consumption which goes on through mall outlets. Here we need to think again about the work of Garreau (1992) whose account of *Edge City* is a story not just of spatial reorganisation but of cultural reformation.

The literature on cities often tends to dismiss the edge city as simply the place where those who service the middle levels of the new global-information based capitalism live. However, we need a sense of proportion here. The transactions in global money markets are enormous in abstract size but only become concretised in reality in terms of margins on trades. Trillions of dollars swill around the derivatives trades in the global ether but these only turn into real money when markets cash up on margins which in percentage terms can be tiny. Virtual trillions become mere real billions. This is still a lot of dosh but it is not larger than the products and services of the real economies. Suburban malls in North America and the UK turn over more than the city-centre zones of elite or 'bohemian' consumption in cash terms and do so through the sale of mass goods, even if the mass goods are differentiated and priced accordingly.

Mall culture is Ortega de Gassett's mass society realised in terms of, on the surface at least, a bland globalisation of taste. Performance art is represented only by the multi-screen, showing the same set of current Hollywood blockbusters almost anywhere on the face of the planet at roughly the same time. Cuisine is moderately priced, with the mass chain more common than the 'authentic' ethnic restaurant. The 'street' enters the mall in terms of consumer culture, but not in reality. The surveillance of the privatised marketplace ensures that the authentic 'danger' of the street is rigidly excluded. In the edge city the traditional public spaces of the city are under private control.

We do not have much of a sociology or social anthropology of this middle mass. Garreau's survey gives some fascinating hints which suggest that Whyte's (1957) organisation man (and now, woman as part of the corporation as well being homemaker) is alive and well in something which looks very like Gans's (1968) Levittown, and often of course is exactly that.

UK academics from the Open University (see Charlesworth and Cochrane, 1997) have examined Milton Keynes, the created edge city as new town on the edge of the London metropolis, in which the globalised and virtual world comes to ground. They explored the representation of the US, and in particular Los Angeles, as a 'universal future' towards which all postindustrial capitalism is tending in terms of spatial form and cultural content. There is an undoubted element of 'glocalisation'. In Milton Keynes the planners tried hard to replicate an image of English 'village' as well as of Angeleno 'burb', but the end product could, as Garreau noted in general for the outer metropolitan area surrounding London, as well be almost anywhere in the USA. Despite Dear's (2000) methodological rejection of Los Angeles as the postmodern, although we might say postindustrial, model of urban life, we find that the actual form of that place does seem to serve in exactly that way. In these places we do not find the unique aesthetic sign as commodity or as element of public space. Instead we find the sign becomes mass commodity.

There is an important and interesting argument to be had about social exclusion, about the relationship between polarised socio-spatial systems and the commodities of mass culture. Of particular significance here is the extent to which, through both the industrial and postindustrial phases of Western capitalism in the twentieth century, the uniquely segregated urban world of US blacks has been the basis for the musical and style cultures of the global world. Here jazz stands as the foundation of much of both popular and high musical culture. Other 'world music' forms are often the product of the ethnic slums of the global system. The music industry accesses these excluded spaces in order to generate products for a system which is absolutely tied to the treadmill of constant innovation.

This raises an interesting question about the nature of the 'street' as a locus of authentic culture in postindustrial capitalism. Bohemia has always been the place where high culture met the street and both became commodified as both elite and popular aesthetics. Historically, urban bohemia (bohemia has overwhelmingly been an urban phenomenon) also intersected with the world of the working class – Isherwood's Berlin (see *Mr Norris Changes Trains* and the film *Cabaret*) had the sexual and artistic *demi-mondaine* living among and with a particularly politicised working class. Kerouac's beat culture not only lived among the working class in New York, San Francisco and Los Angeles, but actually used traditional unionised working-class jobs in the merchant marine and on the railways as a means both of sustenance and intellectual stimulation. The black bohemia of Harlem was embedded in a black working class. Now the US working class is largely absent from the spaces which bohemia shares with the rich, or rather, the indigenous politically organised working class is absent from those spaces. It has gone to Edge City. Instead we find immigrant working class and marginalised communities in those spaces, with the degree of assimilation of the

immigrants being signalled, as with Latinos in the US, by their movement out to the edge.

The European situation is different because European (including
British) cities are much less racially differentiated than is the case in
the US. There are contemporary urban bohemias. Kreuzberg in
Berlin is one real example. Of course one connecting strand is
drugs, but the actual consumption of drugs has become highly segmented in terms both of drugs of choice and of their sources. US and
British yuppies using cocaine do not need to seek it on the street.
Actually the last time the worlds of the elite and the immigrant
connected through these things in Britain in urban bohemia seems
to have been in the early 1960s Notting Hill when Christine Keeler's
and Mandy Rice Davies's sexual partners included aristocrats, a
Tory minister, the Russian naval attaché, a notorious Polish immigrant slumlord and a West Indian drugs dealer (see the film *Scandal*).

Radical bohemia as a critical confrontation with the traditional
aesthetics of high art seems to have almost no existence in postindustrial capitalism. Williams offered an explanation as to why this was
so when he suggested that:

> the very conditions which had provoked a genuine modernist art be-
> came the conditions which steadily homogenized event its startling
> images, and diluted its deep forms until they could be made available to
> a universally distributed 'popular' culture . . . It was falsely believed that
> the technologizing 'mass' culture was the enemy of minority modernist
> art, when in fact each was the outcome of much deeper transforming
> forces in the social order as a whole. It was here that the simplicities of
> technological determinism and cultural pessimism forge their unholy alli-
> ance. (1980: 142–3)

There is an elision of two processes in much of the discussion of
culture as commodity in the postindustrial city. Often we are dealing
in a very general sense with consumption as a process, but now
promoted in place of production as the process through which people
establish their identities. As Miles and Paddison put it:

> as consumers we do not simply reproduce our physical existence (in urban
> contexts) but we also reproduce culturally specific, meaningful ways of life.
> Consumption acts as a sort of bridge between the individual and his or her
> experience of the urban environment. (1998: 816)

In the same special issue of the journal *Urban Studies* Zukin asserts that: 'Cities are no longer seen as landscapes of production, but as landscapes of consumption' (1998: 828). We can explore the implications of this by looking at the way in which the actual processes of urban development have become concerned with consumption as the object of that development.

Wynne and O'Connor (1998) identify three aspects of this shift. First, there is a change of land use which typically involves the use of brownfield former industrial sites for consumption related activities. Secondly, this process of simple consumption oriented development is taken a stage further by the use of arts and leisure led regeneration schemes to attract financial and producer-service activity to particular places. Simultaneous with all of this, there is an active effort at the 're-imaging' of the place as postindustrial rather than industrial. These are activities of governance in relation to the production, reproduction and re-presentation of the urban built environment and we will have more to say about them in Chapter 8.

Here what is most interesting is the movement from a set of projects, which presented simple consumption as their objective, towards projects in which high and popular culture, no longer necessarily distinguished, become the means of actual urban regeneration and respecification. This was the basis of Glasgow as 'European City of Culture' in the 1990s. Barcelona seems to be a city which has successfully regenerated on the basis of a combination of global sport, high culture, advanced industrial production and, perhaps crucially, Catalan national identity. The Guggenheim Museum in postindustrial Bilbao; Liverpool's transformation of the Albert Dock into a combination of fun location and high culture art museum; Pittsburgh's reinvention as a city of high culture are simply some examples of what is a global tendency in postindustrial capitalism.

Hannigan's *Fantasy City* drags us back to the world of popular culture as commodity, to 'a new urban economy which has its roots in tourism, sports, culture, and entertainment' (1998: 2). In his survey of developments, not only in North America but now globally, Hannigan identifies six central features of this postindustrial use of urban space:

- Fantasy City is theme-o-centric. Everything is scripted around a story or set of stories which is specific to the space used for

entertainment and disconnected from the spaces around those
separated out as the zone of fantasy.

● Fantasy City is branded. You do not just buy the experience –
you buy the t shirt, the pencils, the electronic organiser – all with
the brand. You went there, and you show you were there.

● Fantasy City is the twenty-four hour experience. Even elements
which on the surface are much more time bounded – sports arenas
which one might think are live only during the game – become
event places to visit and get the brands.

● Fantasy City is modular with many such locales having the global
presence of the same branded experiences – Hard Rock Cafés,
Borders bookstores, Virgin media.

● Fantasy City is solipsistic. It stands separate from that around it.
It may be a literally set off zone like the original Disneyland – a
magic kingdom quite apart from industrial Burbank.

● Fantasy City is postmodern. It depends on simulacra and specta-
cle, not on the experience of the real.

Two rather mild examples in San Diego California illustrate this
quite well. One is the 'Old Town' – an essentially recreated version of
San Diego in the 1840s which is a simulacra of the long-gone real.
This is rather a good simulacra. The elements are San Diego specific
and there is little if any global branding but it is an experience, not a
reality. The other is 'the Gaslight District' – the revived nineteenth-
century city with bars, restaurants, some clubs. Essentially this is a
'safe' alternative to the wild fantasy city of Tijuana, the real Mexico
reached at the end of the San Diego tram ride. Again there has been
some rather careful attention to authenticity, at least in terms of
architectural style, but here we do have the global. At least one of
the bars serves Newcastle Brown Ale on tap, Tyneside's global brand
presented in a form utterly unknown in its place of origin where it is
always a bottled or canned beer!

Fantasy City is an important and useful idea. We might want to
consider how the fantasies addressed to middle-income people intersect with high culture. A connecting strand might be heritage. Certainly the two San Diego examples are heritage heavy, and it would
be wholly wrong if I did not record that I rather enjoyed my visits to
them. Heritage is the middle-brow link between branded fantasy and
elite taste. We are likely to see a great deal more of it in the cities of
the twenty-first century.

The cultural turn: the city as text

What seems to me to be very striking is that nearly all forms of contemporary critical theory are theories of *consumption*. That is to say, they are concerned with understanding an object in such a way that it can be profitably or correctly consumed... Naturally enough, the notion of the work of art as *object*, as *text*, as an isolated artifact became central to all these later consumption theories. It was not only that the practices of *production* were then overlooked ... [t]he real social conditions of production were in any case neglected because they were believed to be at best secondary. The true relationship was seen always as between the taste, the sensibility or the training of the reader and this isolated work. (Williams, 1980: 45–6)

The central theme of the cultural turn in urban study is the description of the city as a text. There are two programmes of 'the text'. The strong programme, often called 'post-structuralism' and associated with the work of Derrida, argues for an autonomy of the text from the processes and actors by which it was produced. Hence, there is no sense in seeking a valid, that is, 'true' account of the text. The text stands unique for each reader. No account can be privileged. Tagg, in the passage quoted in Chapter 1, typifies this approach.

A variant has more to it than the simple turn to the individual interpreter of each text taken anew. This goes by the names of 'post-colonial' and / or 'feminist' and is illustrated by Morris's (1992) 'shocked' encounter with Harvey's *The Condition of Postmodernity* (1989). Morris does not assert an individual, self-founded account of the world. She argues instead that there are different visions, different approaches, which represent cohesive and articulate theories, but which cannot be subordinated to an overweening meta-theory, in Harvey's case an account couched in terms of 'capital and labour' (1992: 255).[2] For Morris there are other stories from other disciplines, other perspectives, other objective positions. We might want to question the notion of a distinctive authority from a discipline base, but the assault on the privilege of economic determinism is serious.

Hall (1981: 235) argues that meanings are encoded in creation and decoded by 'readers', although the approach could be considered to include consumers as well as readers. This approach gels with an emergent realist account: cultural objects and indeed, when we return to 'ways of life', cultures as a whole are not fixed and material. In a social sense the components of the built environment, despite their concreteness, are not fixed and material. Rather they have meaning through the action of interpretation and / or consumption in specific context. This seems to be the approach suggested by Lefbvre when he asserts that urban meaning is socially constructed.

The most prominent English language interpreter of Lefbvre is Shields (1991, 1998) and the relationship between their approaches is neatly summarised by Farrar who remarks:

> If Lefbvre, at his best, ensures that we think of territory not as the physical elements of which it is composed, but as the products of human labour and social meaning, Shields (cued at least in part by Lefbvre) directs us to consider the impact of the discourses which people construct in their effort to make sense of locales. (1997: 108)

Shields examines 'place myths', the ways in which places become constructed and reconstructed as images in social practice. However, as Savage and Warde (1993: 132) note, this account tends to get stuck in cultural geography, to consist of interesting and persuasive accounts of the nature and content of place myths and of the dynamics of transformation of the myths. What is missing is any kind of account of how these myths play a part in social action as such.

Shields argues, in an exposition of the approach of Deleuze and Guattari, that:

> Rather than dissecting an object of analysis which merely renders new objects for further dissection . . . objects must be understood at the ontological level at which they exist as such. They must be understood by their powers, surfaces and effects. We might recognize this as a rejection of depth hermeneutics, for example, realist explanations of urban 'appearances' by deep structures and forces which are permitted to exist but are unproveable as such, only helpful tools for explanation. (1996: 241–2)

I find the conflation of hermeneutics and explanation a little awkward here, but that awkwardness actually helps in understanding what is being said. Explanation is usually thought of in terms of the identification of mechanisms which cause. In a realist account such mechanisms may not be directly accessible to us. We can know them only through their effects in the actual as we notice these effects, thereby making them empirical. However, there is mechanism, however complex and contingent, and hence cause. Interpretation in contrast is about meaning – the essence of hermeneutics is the elucidation of meaning. Usually we speak here of interpretation rather than explanation. Pawson and Tilley's (1997) distinction between Hermeneutics I as interpretation to understand, and Hermeneutics II as interpretation as unique and self-contained act, is very helpful to us here.

If we pursue the actual examples Shields (1996) uses himself, we can get somewhere interesting with this. Shields picks up the way in which cultural forms, expressed in the components of the built environment, are interpreted in causal accounts as the product of political economic processes. The processes are not what we observe. We see the buildings. We see the surface. We live (interact) on the surface expressing desires and selves. Shields argues that we do not need, and cannot get, explanation beyond this level.

To which we might reply: what about emergence? What about understanding relationships in a complex way in which parts, wholes, interiors, surfaces, and the interaction amongst any or all of these are what constitutes the systemic real, with most of that real being the product of social actions. Moreover, we might think of the 'action element' as located along a dimension of fluidity / rigidity with some aspects of the system being the outcomes of continually reconstituted daily, hourly, momentarily fluid recreation and reformulation, and others having much more rigidity as the product of processes which were social and constituted through ongoing action, but have now become solidified. This is an interesting conception because it suggests that historical formations can hold a rigidity, but like all phase shifts from fluid to solid, the solid form is liable to radical fracture and fragmentation.

For me the way out of this dilemma is by turning to the social processes in social construction and a good way of doing that is to think about culture, exactly as a set of ways of life.

Ways of being: the constitution and reconstitution of collective identities

In common American usage, culture is, first of all, 'ethnicity': habits carried through space and time, refined through interaction with church and state, and asserted as a means of differentiation and independence. Culture is also understood to be a legitimate way of carving a niche in society. Now that labor unions and political parties seem powerless to challenge social divisions, culture as 'collective lifestyle' appears as a meaningful and often conflictual, source of representation. (Zukin, 1995: 265)

Notice the active character of 'culture' as 'ethnicity' in Zukin's account here. Culture is something which is actively constructed and actively utilised. It is an inherently collective project, although in this formulation, which in many ways could stand as a modern version of the Chicago School's qualitative account, it is never a single project but a set of multiple, inter-related, and potentially antagonistic projects.

A good starting point for understanding the implication of this is Jenkins's telling statement about identity. He puts it like this:

> The internal and the external dance together in the unfolding of individual and collective identities. And although these identities are imagined, they are not imaginary. (1996: 175)

Jenkins follows the Norwegian social anthropologist Barth. He insists on the processual character of all aspects of the social, and in particular the way in which social interaction in lived experience is the foundation of both collective and individual identities – of self and of culture as a 'way of life'. This approach resonates well with the dynamic foundation of a complexity fixed on culture. Indeed Jenkins's (1996: 96) insistence on the 'generative' character of Barth's approach echoes exactly complexity's account of emergence as the process through which the social becomes real. For Jenkins, it is essential not to see social identity as some 'sub-set of the general symbolic domain of culture' (1996: 113). Instead it provides the foundation of meaning and is fundamental to culture. This is a materialist approach, albeit one which displays the sophistication of historical materialism rather than the crudities of mechanical determination.

Barth's collaborator Wikan has drawn on her long programme of research in Cairo, a mega city of the first order, in order to explore the significance of people's own understanding of the interaction between culture and the dynamics of the life course. She uses Barth's conception of 'cultural competence': 'the arsenal of knowledge, skills, attitudes and institutional practices that people possess and can employ in coping' (1995: 637) to show how:

> a *life cycle* perspective is crucial for assessing development in any popula-
> tion. What may seem insurmountable problems and a clear deterioration
> of a family's situation in the short run, may only be the hardships of a
> typical phase of the life cycle. The hardships may seem unbearable, but
> people know that they will pass. (1995: 636, original emphasis)

This has a great deal in common with Lewis's (1966) original formulation of the idea of a 'culture of poverty' before the New Right
ideologues got their hands on the idea and used it as the basis of a
programme of denunciation of the feckless poor. Harvey and Reed
argue that:

> the virtue of Lewis' thesis lies in the clarity with which it demonstrates that
> poverty's subculture is not a mere 'tangle of pathology', but consists,
> instead, of a set of *positive adaptive mechanisms*. These adaptive mechan-
> isms are socially constructed, that is, collectively fabricated by the poor
> from the substance of their everyday lives, and they allow the poor to
> survive in otherwise impossible material and social conditions ... Unlike
> other explanations of poverty, it concedes that the poor have been
> damaged by the system but insists that this damage does not disqualify
> them from determining their own fate. This last judgement is something
> many social scientists of both the left and right have forgotten. (1996: 466,
> original emphasis)

This is important for any programme of postindustrial urban
politics, and we will return to it in Chapter 8. Here what is most
interesting is that this way of thinking forces us to remember that for
most urban people in the world, whatever the significance of global
consumption (and that significance is very great), there is also a
reality of simple physical survival. E. P. Thompson's Experience I
in its most absolute sense is a daily reality of life.

Concluding remarks and further resources

Culture is a tricky theme in relation to the urban. When we attempt
to grapple with it, we must deal not only with different levels of the

social real, but with arguments about methodology which can go so far as to deny the very existence of any social real outside the process of interpretation. These arguments rely on appeals to a foundational meta-narrative of fragmentation (Jenkins, 1996: 11–12) combined with arguments derived from deductive logic as applied in epistemology. They have to be known about but that is all. What is interesting is the significance in postindustrial globalised capitalism of the multiple and inter-related political economies of cultural production and consumption as the foundation of urban life. This does matter, a lot, and we will return to it when we examine the actual processes of production and realisation of the built environment in Chapter 7. Likewise we do need to think about culture as ways of life and we will return to the implications of that, and of the related idea of 'lifestyle', when we examine the foundations of contemporary urban political consciousness and action in Chapter 8.

The 'postmodern' condition is a cliché of contemporary literature, drama and film and there is a plethora of examples we might consider to illustrate it, most of which describe life under conditions of extreme affluence, or at best the marginalised poverty of the West. Certainly *Bonfire of the Vanities* as both novel and film shows fragmentation and division very clearly. *The Last Days of Disco* illustrates nicely the 'lifestyle' of consumption as it came into being in its modern form. 'Mall' films set in California's 'Valley' world are useful, although most of them are lively teen entertainment with the urban culture as taken for granted context – *Ted and Bill's Awfully Big Adventure* is a good example. Bruce Springsteen's tracks on *The Ghost of Tom Joad* link the history of US capitalism with the way the contemporary migrant experience connects to US working-class culture and experience. In the UK the career of the egregious Damien Hirst, conceptualiser of shark pickling (the technical execution being the work of somebody who knew how to do it) and restaurant proprietor, illustrates the links among 'art', property and consumption. Perhaps the consumption form which best conveys the character of the postindustrial city is the café-bar.

On a global scale we can see the character of postindustrial cultural forms in the footprints of cities on the World Wide Web. A particularly good example is provided by that of the city of Shanghai, which can be contrasted with the perspective provided by the brilliant anthropological film-making of *Shanghai Vice*, in which ordinary lives look very like the lives of globalised modernity rather than postmodernity. There is a fascinating link between the world of the Irish townland and this new global culture in the form of the ersatz Irish bars, most of which have Websites, which are now to be found in all cities with any global pretensions including Shanghai. A corrective is provided by noting that in the townland of Geesala in the far west of County Mayo, the place where Singe set *The Playboy of the Western World*, the local bar is not called 'Scruffy O'Murphy's' or 'Dirty Nelly's', but 'The High Chaparral' in tribute to the global TV culture of Fordist modernity!

7

The production and reproduction of the built environment

> The built environment, despite its solid appearance, is dynamic rather than static. (Ambrose, 1994: 5–6)

This chapter is about the making, remaking and realising of urban space and of the material structures contained in it. It is about planning, building, selling and renting. To use Short *et al.*'s phraseology, it is about how the material form of the urban gets written. Here we are considering the production and reproduction of the built environment. It is helpful to think about the content of the expression 'the built environment'. Environment, in terms of the etymology of the word, is something all around us. Normally environment used without any adjectival qualification means the natural world. Here we qualify with an adjective which identifies the outcome of a specific labour process – building. We are talking about things produced under capitalism as commodities which are bought and sold. However, these things are not the usual commodities which we think of when we consider capitalist production. They are big, expensive and fixed in place. They incorporate materials as brought together and shaped by labour, but they also include land – a specific place in the world.

Moreover, the components of the built environment are not things which we handle or use in an ordinary sense. They are not loaves of bread to be consumed, shirts to be worn, or even lathes to be worked on. Rather than us containing or handling them, the things which make up the built environment, taken separately and taken as a whole, contain us. We enter them, leave them, sleep, eat, wash, watch television, work and play in them. We move around and through them. For most of us for most of our lives we relate to the natural world through them. The built environment for urban people is the locus of the social. We considered this when we examined the cultural meanings of urban space and identified it as a constantly re-interpreted location for the lived and constitutive experience of the social world. Now we have to think about how it came to be, continues to be, and how we change the nature of its being.

In this chapter we are going to consider the production of the built environment in three sorts of urban places. The first is the urban core, the central business district of cities. The second is the edge city, a set of places in which location is not given by the interaction of physical geography and an existing urban system, but is rather a created thing made by developers which then becomes both socially and materially real. The last is the suburb, the place where most people live.

My definition of the suburb is rather different from the general and conventional usage of that term. I include everything which would normally be counted as suburb, but I also want to include all purely residential areas including many which are now centrally located. Of course most of these were originally suburban, built on the fringe of an existing built-up area. The demarcating characteristic for me in identifying the suburb is that the given urban zone is primarily residential. This is never an absolute distinction. In the European and New York tradition people do live in central business districts and in England there is an active programme of getting them to do so. Gentrification can often involve the transformation of industrial land uses into high value residential locales. 'Loft living' is the most fashionable version of this kind of thing. However, whilst detailed location always matters and matters for homes as well as for businesses, the distinction between residential space and commercial space remains useful, particularly when we consider actual processes of land development, construction and the realisation of the built as commodity. It is a sign of the character of postindustrial capitalism that it is not necessary to designate a fourth category of industrial space. We can subsume this into our discussion of 'Edge City'.

The heuristic value of this spatial distinction among urban core, edge city, and the suburb is considerable, but there are crucial aspects of the production and reproduction of the built environment which are common to all of them. We will begin with those common elements using the suburb as an illustration of them and then consider urban core and edge city spaces in turn. Although the primary focus in this chapter will be on urban spaces in the old advanced industrial world, we must note that some of the same processes are global and general. Shanghai and Jakarta illustrate them very well as we shall see. Even in the interior cities of the South and post-communist Asia suburbanisation for the middle masses is beginning to be significant. In *The Guardian* of Saturday 4 March 2000 John Gittings reporting from Hefei in Anhui province, deep in rural China, notes that the senior staff of a car parts company 'live in detached villas with lawns in an upmarket estate. Some even have integral garages – although none yet own cars' (2000: 21).

Land matters: building in space

Peter Ambrose (1986, 1994) outlined the essentials of the processes of production and realisation of the built environment. As with the production of all commodities under capitalism this involves the bringing together of the factors of land, capital and labour. However, in the production of the built environment the land element is incorporated into the product which is fixed in a particular place. This land element has a dynamic development value. In other words, the value of the land changes over time in accordance with changes in the value structure of the overall built environment of which it is a part.

Another unusual characteristic of the commodities of the built environment is that they have two routes to realisation: by sale or through the receipt of a series of rental payments. This is not unique. Some other very expensive goods (buildings are always very expensive in relation to earnings) are leased over a period of time. What is unique about buildings is that they have no simple depreciation period. The turbines of a power station wear out over the period of their design life. Buildings often do not really have a design life and even when they do, the value of the building is so dependent on the potential value of its site in any other feasible use that there is no smooth depreciation curve. The state of a structure can be important in fixing the exchange value of a building, especially of a residential building in the suburb, but it can also be absolutely irrelevant to that value. In general, buildings usually appreciate in real terms rather than depreciate. Edge city malls may turn out to be the exception to this rule but it is almost entirely true for the central city and the suburb, except in very special social circumstances.

Ambrose (1994) identifies five stages in the production of the built environment as commodity, namely:

- Promotion
- Investment
- Construction
- Allocation
- Subsequent management.

I want to illustrate these stages by looking at the production of residential urban space. Here we can see all the elements being brought together. The process operated in nineteenth-century industrial cities where developers acquired land which had a high value because it was located within easy travelling distance of large factories employing highly paid workers. They applied labour and materials to it in laying out streets. The builders brought together land as a plot, materials and labour, and financed their operation by borrowing and selling on to landlords who rented to tenants who paid rent. Large fortunes were made in this business in the UK and the industrial USA. Very similar processes operated in the development of the world's first 'suburban' city, Los Angeles. Boone (1998) demonstrates how real estate promoters attracted people to Southern California between the 1880s and the 1920s and utilised development strategies which continued to be employed in continuing urban development on an even larger scale in the era after the Second World War. The main distinction in this context was that most sales were to owner-occupier purchasers.

If we go back to Ambrose's five stages we can see all of them in operation in nineteenth-century development. The original developers promoted the site, largely by opening it up and using legal covenants to specify the form of housing development. They made considerable initial investments in land purchase and layout. The layout of roads formed part of the construction. The remainder of the construction was carried out by builders using investment finance derived from the permanent building societies in the UK and a mix of banks and Savings and Loans in the US. Allocation and subsequent management in the industrial cities were the function of the private landlords who bought the properties in order to yield streams of investment income, although they often delegated both processes to estate agents who managed their property for them.

After the First World War there was a major shift towards the owner-occupier now being the normal purchaser in developments. The predominant form of building in the suburbs of the modern city has been 'speculative'. Developers/builders, the two roles now amalgamated, have built without an end customer in place. In contracting, the other form of building, the builder builds to order for a customer who owns the land. This has been an important form of construction in the UK for suburban social housing and it is the general form in the central zone and in the non-residential edge city (although there is some speculative construction of small and medium industrial units and office park units). In Europe it has been significant, especially in Sweden, but there is a general tendency in postindustrial capitalist societies for residential development to take the Anglo-American speculative form directed towards sale to owner-occupiers.

Ambrose's five functions remain in place with speculative building for owner occupation but they are differently organised. Promotion, land investment, and construction are all now handled by the developer builder. Allocation is by market purchase. The owner-occupier manages the property themselves. The building societies (US Savings and Loans) and other mortgage lenders provide investment now for a new set of customers – owner-occupiers as opposed to investment landlords.

There are several important distinctions between building on speculation and building to a contract. Ball (1988) reviews these in detail but in summary the speculative builder developer typically owns the land on which the development is undertaken and employs design and quality professionals (architects and surveyors) directly as well as production labour. In contrast, contracts are usually undertaken on land owned by the clients who employ their own architects and surveyors to design, cost and regulate the quality of construction. There are intermediate forms, and the letting of contracts on a design and build basis is becoming much more common, but the customer of a contractor has a good deal of control in relation to the process. The advantage for the contractor is a guaranteed sale and the receipt of interim payments at stages in the process so there is less need for working money capital. The disadvantage is that the contractor cannot make speculative gains on the land and/or building.

To use Ambrose's categories we can see that in the development of social housing the public authority arranges promotion and investment (borrowing through its general powers in the financial markets) and undertakes allocation on a needs basis, and subsequent management. Only construction is handled by the private sector, although if direct labour is used then even this is a public process. Of course the debt interest and repayments mean that there is a substantial private interest in the resulting stock.

The actual capital organisation of building in the two systems of speculation and contract has considerable implications for the labour processes in them, a topic which is ignored by much contemporary writing about the urban. Ball's remark about speculative building can actually be considered to have general application given the cyclical nature of the availability of construction contracts:

> The turnover of capital for a speculative builder...does not depend on steady production rates. Given the volatile market for speculative buildings it is highly unlikely that steady output levels can be achieved, so the production methods have to facilitate variable output levels. (1988: 46)

This is an interesting and persuasive argument. We can recast it in relation to contemporary theoretical debates by saying that the nature of the market for the output of the construction industry means that is has always adopted an inherently flexible production form. Producer services, architecture and surveying, have usually been separated from actual production. Much of the production is done by subcontractors, including workers employed as labour-only subcontractors, often on an individual basis. The employment structure of the industry, other than in the 'Direct Labour Organisations' of the public sector, is highly casualised. This casualisation is extending into professional as well as manual grades and into the public sector with competitive tendering for local authorities and other public bodies which previously have employed large numbers of building professionals.

The ratio of fixed capital to turnover in construction is very low in comparison with manufacturing. It would however be a mistake to think there has been no modernisation of construction methods. Since the mid-nineteenth century there have been innovations in the manufacture of components off site, and recent years have seen the introduction of far more mechanical power on site, the co-ordination of which was an important production innovation of Olympia and York (see Fainstein, 1994). This varies from country to country.

Where labour is very cheap, muscle power still matters, but in most advanced industrial societies manual construction labour is now not labouring as such but in a mix of traditional craft skills and machine operation.

The discussion thus far has focused on the capitalist processes of land development and dwelling production in the suburb. However, the state has played a role in these matters throughout the modern era. This began with the regulation of standards for reasons of public health and continues through a planning system based around the 'expert' knowledge of urban processes and directed under industrial capitalism to the improvement of the social character of the built environment as a whole.

The original form of state intervention was through the regulation of the quality of new construction. In the UK this took the form of local authority regulations, 'by-laws', which specified that housing must be built to at least a specified standard and within a specified densities. These regulated new construction in the latter half of the nineteenth century and were supplemented by powers to clear inadequate older-housing areas, although throughout the nineteenth century in the UK and always in the US, these powers were used more to remove working-class housing on potentially valuable development sites than for any wider social purpose. However, in the 1930s and the 1950s and 60s there was a massive amount of slum clearance in the UK with new social housing being provided to replace that which was demolished.

Evangelistic bureaucrats: experts at work

These regulatory and redevelopment powers are important in relation to what in the 1970s was identified as 'evangelical bureaucracy' (Davies, 1974) and has recently been considered by Rose in terms of expert social governance:

> Social government was expert government. The devices of 'the welfare state' opened up a multitude of new locales for the operation of expert judgements, based on knowledge, training, professional and bureaucratic ethics and specialist skills. (1996: 349)

Davies (1974), Dennis (1970, 1972) and Green (1980) provide empirical accounts of the way this governance was exercised as part of a programme of expertise in the planning based reconstruction of UK cities in the Fordist era, a reconstruction which involved enormous social dislocation and population movement.

There is a convincing sociologically founded critique of planning processes during the reconstruction of the 1960s and the 1970s. The US literature, typified by Gans's *The Urban Villagers* (1962), describes how urban redevelopment displaced existing working-class communities, and in particular black communities, to the benefit of development capital and large social institutions, notably universities.

The UK literature is different, largely it seems because the redevelopment was associated with rehousing, although the logic of it was often central site clearance or the expansion of higher education in the UK as well. Concern is not so much with material interests but rather with, to use a term which has become popular subsequently, the discourses of professional expertise as validation of urban reconstruction. This applied both to clearance decisions and to the form of mass housing which was imposed as a replacement. Here we find an interesting historically based literature (see especially Dunleavy, 1981) which identifies the way in which architectural fashion and the interests of particular civil engineering capitals came to together in the UK to sell non-traditional forms of social housing construction. Much of this construction was an abject failure in both physical and social terms (see Byrne and Parson, 1983, for a discussion of a particularly bad example).

The recent literature on the making of the built environment has neglected the enormously important processes of laying out residential space and building people's homes, although Forsyth's (1999) account of suburban development in Sydney is an important exception. She uses the idea of discourse to describe actual processes through which development is realised, or in her case largely not realised. This is an important recent reassertion of the significance of actors' values in a field largely dominated by concerns with material interest alone. Merrett's two books (1979, 1982) describe the construction process in both the social housing and owner-occupied sectors, and Ball (1988, 1996) describes the construction industry and its relationship to housing production. Most of any urban area today is occupied by residential space. The story of its construction given here has been a very Western-centric one, with the Western here including the urban spaces of former communist states.

However, this is the capitalist norm and there is considerable evidence of global convergence towards it.

Building in the South

This is illustrated in Steinen's (1999) fascinating examination of Medellin in Columbia, a city which she proposes as 'the capital of the 21st century'. Medellin has a history as an industrial city, Columbia's São Paulo, and its development was always a complex mix. The communas in which more than half of the three million population of the conurbation live comprise a mix of planned social housing, often associated with specific industrial enterprises, self-built squatters' housing, and 'pirate' housing built by urban development agencies on both a legal and an illegal basis (Steinen, 1999: 246). It is true that Medellin is exceptional in that since the 1920s it has had an effective urban agency providing very good quality public services, including urban infrastructure, which means that even in the communas there are working sewers, regular garbage disposal, clean drinking water and legal electrical power. However, the city is deeply divided and the narco (drug) capital emerging from the communas has become the determining factor in its constant dynamism as a reconstructed urban space.

Medellin is not a typical case, but the mixture of legal, illegal, semi-legal and formal urban development is characteristic of the cities of the South, other than in China where in the communist period development has been highly regulated. However, the modern tendency, even in this city of narco capitalism, is towards formal construction processes.

Where and how we reside does matter a great deal and the processes of making that residential environment are crucial. The recent emphasis in urban studies has not been on the residential, and still less on the industrial. The focus has been on the mixture of retail and office functions of the urban core and edge city. Let us turn first to the urban core.

Shopping and trading: the postmodern urban core

The old argument for planning had been comprehensiveness and reducing negative externalities – that is preventing development from harming the environment around it...The new claims are competitiveness and efficiency. (Fainstein, 1994: 100)

It is worth beginning with planning, the actual technology of urban studies in application, in our consideration of the urban core as built environment precisely because its nominal objectives have changed so much. Planning has never just been about environmental protection. It has been about comprehensiveness, to use Fainstein's word, about the city seen as a whole: indeed not only seen as whole, but seen as a dynamic system which ought to be moved forward to the 'good' future. Planning is never merely negative feedback: it is about constructing futures.

Here our use of the word 'modern' becomes awkward. Usually modernity is considered to have begun as an intellectual project of the French Revolution and the 'Age of Reason'. However, if we think of 'modern' in terms of the era of the application of expertise to the solution of problems, then the modern urban begins at the turn of the nineteenth to twentieth century. The public health interventions which began in the 1840s are absolutely modern, but the general conception of the city as a whole and the invention of town planning as a discipline and project is a product of the Edwardian era. Before this time, urban development, whilst often comprehensive on a large scale', was about sub-sets of the city and was driven by an accumulation logic.

There is a vivid illustration of this in Newcastle's Graingertown, created by the local state-organised destruction of the medieval, Elizabethan and Georgian city centre of Newcastle and the development of a unified new retail and commercial centre. Its showpiece was Gray Street, often identified as the finest nineteenth-century street in England. Many slum housing areas were cleared, both in the urban development and in bringing the railway into the city centre, but none of this was motivated by a desire to create the general 'good city'. The centre was taken as a zone alone and the objective was profit. Newcastle is a modern city despite its medieval origins. However, its centre was the product of commercial rather than social engineering rationales.

Comprehensive planning at the level of conurbations was attempted in the UK through the abortive county-level structure plans of the 1970s but the UK's 1949 Town and Country Planning legislation did impose comprehensiveness at the level of individual urban authority. Planning was a crucial part of the welfare capitalism of the Fordist era and the nominal and even (rather frequently but by no means always) real objective of the process was the improvement of the quality of life within a generally redistributive framework of public policy.

Fainstein describes the transition of planning regimes from this social programme to the contemporary style in these terms:

> Rather than planning listing an exhaustive and abstractly constructed set of alternatives, planners concerned with maintaining neighbourhoods or bringing new investment into the central business district aim at discerning targets of opportunity. Instead of picking an end state and elaborating means to arrive at it, they establish narrow goals and grab for that mixture of devices which will permit at least some forward progress. (1994: 100)

The idea of a secondary circuit of capital which revolves around accumulation through the production and realisation of the built environment rather than the industrial production and realisation of other commodities was outlined in Chapter 1. It is worth noting that discussions on these lines are almost always discussions of the non-industrial and non-residential aspects of the built environment in the urban core. We do not have to accept the mechanical capital logic of the idea of secondary circuit to recognise that there is something important about capital's relationship with city centre development.

It is impossible to separate any discussion of the redevelopment of urban cores from the general understanding of the character of the globalised postindustrial economy which pervades the mix of academic and policy formation discussion of the future trajectory of capitalism. Haas's useful concept of 'epistemic community' refers to a set of networks of 'professionals with recognized expertise and competence in a particular domain and an authoritative claim to policy-relevant knowledge in that domain or issue area' (1992: 3). Olds (1995) considers that there is an epistemic global community of developers, property professionals and academics[1] who operate in relation to the redevelopment of cities on a transnational basis and has reviewed (1997) the operation of this 'global intelligence corps' in the development of Shanghai, of which more later.

The main concept with which this community works is precisely that of globalised postindustrialism. For them the real economy is the global informational economy. In the extreme form of this representation, the only real economy is the global economy of virtual money. The implications of this for urban development have been profound because the representation is far more than just a matter of assertion in the domain of knowledge. The actual planning processes of urban cores have become dominated by the objective of positioning that urban core in relation to the global process.

Fainstein's (1994) account of London and New York shows how these things worked out in the global core – not well in that the world's largest development company, Olympia and York, collapsed with negative implications for the world banking system which had financed its operations. The same approach has informed planning processes in cities located far further down the global urban hierarchy. There is a nice antipodean comparison to be made between the former heavy industrial cities of Newcastle-upon-Tyne in the UK (see Wilkinson, 1992; Byrne, 1999b) and Newcastle, New South Wales (see McGuirk *et al.*, 1996) which is particularly apposite in that the latter was named for, and developed by capital from, the former. McGuirk *et al.* quote one of the consultants who produced the masterplan for redevelopment in Newcastle, NSW:

> Honeysuckle will not happen if the people of Newcastle place stringent conditions on its development. You must compete with other more prestigious cities nationally and internationally for investment . . . [I]n order to attract investment to Newcastle . . . we have to accept that we must provide an easier, more accommodative investment environment with clearly defined planning objectives. By easier I mean easier than *anywhere else*. I would even go so far as to say that the political process would be taken out of the approval mechanism. (quoted 1996: 1831 – original emphasis)

The Newcastle UK equivalents were not so blunt, at least in public, but their approach showed the same underlying logic. Not only did they make development very easy, they provided a great big pot of public money to subsidise it.

Imrie and Thomas (1993, 1999) review the overall pattern of this kind of development through Urban Development Corporations in the UK. What is particularly interesting is the form of understanding of the causal processes in urban development which underpinned it. Fainstein describes them thus:

> The premise of these types of planning . . . was essentially physically determinist – planners assumed that changes in the physical environment would yield an economic response. Holding a supply-oriented view of urban space, planners expected that private investors would avail themselves of adequately serviced, centrally located land without further incentives. (1994: 99)

It was this sort of process which introduced the expression 'brownfield' into the lexicon of urban regeneration. A brownfield site is a formerly developed site which has been cleared of all existing construction and is available for new development on the same basis as a piece of agricultural land, a greenfield site. In reality there was extra cash over and above site preparation but Fainstein's general account is correct.

This is illustrated by the remarks of the Tyne Wear Development Corporation's expert planning witness at a public enquiry:

> There is, in my opinion, a distinction to be drawn between 'regeneration' and 'redevelopment'. Redevelopment of a site will succeed in bringing land and buildings into whatever use the market determines as the most appropriate for that site at that time. Regeneration on the other hand, aims to create new markets by increasing confidence and attracting inward investment. A regeneration project is needed to rekindle economic and cultural vitality of the site itself and also creates similar betterment to its immediate environs. When combined with other such schemes, it will also be a catalyst for sustained improvement and growth in the whole city and indeed the region. (Jones, 1989: 12, para 3.1.4)

The view was that the task of a public authority was to stimulate a market where otherwise there would be none: as TWDC put it (Jones, 1989: 16, para 3.2.2.4) to act as 'A Catalyst for Regeneration'.

Wilkinson, who described this as postmodern planning, observed that planning in the 1960s:

> was concerned primarily with civic pride and a utopian version of the city as an urban machine fit for living in. It was essentially a modernist vision

with a strong social welfare component, managed by the public sector on Keynesian functional principles. (1992: 178)

In contrast we now find:

the post-modern city ... characterized by a shift away from comprehensive redevelopment projects, characteristic of the 1960s and 1970s, towards the planning of urban fragments, evidenced in the mosaic effect created by the development of the new urban villages, flag-ship schemes, self-contained waterfront developments and cultural quarters. These islands of renewal also act as highly visible symbols of urban regeneration and, as such, they are regarded by public and private-sector agencies as vital ingredients in the place-marketing process. (1992: 177).

We will return to the idea of place marketing when we consider urban governance and politics in Chapter 8.

Building and governance: the exercise of power

Ambrose introduced an interesting method of categorising agencies involved in the urban development process 'in terms of *the way in which their existence and their power to act are legitimated.*' (1994: 43, original emphasis) This dimension of accountability/legitimation crosscuts with that of motivation. We can see the approach clearly when we consider private speculative greenfield builders on the one hand and elected local authorities building social housing on the other. These are straightforward because the motivation of the first is profit, and its legitimacy derives from ownership of resources, whereas the motivation of the other is the meeting of need, and the legitimacy derives from the democratic process – honest markets and honest politics

In the development of the urban core, things are much more complicated. The significance of planning and the complications of land assembly, issues in the US of eminent domain and in the UK of compulsory purchase, mean that the state and the private sector become intimately and inextricably associated. In both countries, there has been a turn to non-elected bodies drawing on powers allocated by central government and working to quasi profit ratio-nales. This period is probably drawing to a close, but its significance for the construction of the urban core has been immense.

In the UK, the US and Australia, such agencies have played a central role in the redesignation of industrial urban sites and, in particular, redundant port land as urban core to be used for post-industrial services, consumption and residence. Olds (1995) shows how a series of Urban Megaprojects in the Pacific rim cities have been initiated on this basis. There is a historical and cultural irony here. The dockland sites which are the location of so many globalised Urban Megaprojects, were exactly the spatial location of key functions of the previous world economy based on international trade in material commodities as opposed to signs. Here we find a literal replacement of the world by the global system.

Edge city: the creation of placeless place

The MetroCentre in Gateshead was, when built in the mid-1980s, the largest out-of-town shopping facility in Europe. It is an excellent illustration of the way in which the edge city represents a new kind of built environment, the creation of which depends absolutely on the new phenomenon of the majority of households owning at least one car. It was the brainchild of Sir John Hall who on a visit to the US observed the development of out-of-town shopping malls and resolved to attempt to do something similar in the UK. His chance came in the early 1980s with the contingent coincidence of a local transport development on Tyneside and an innovation in national urban policy. The transport development was the construction of a 'western bypass' trunk road to take the A1 round the urban core of Newcastle / Gateshead. This meant that there was potentially good road access to a large derelict site, previously a wetland used for dumping ash from two coal fired power stations. Hall acquired the site relatively cheaply.

In the early 1980s the UK's Conservative government designated a series of areas in urban and coalfield localities as 'Enterprise Zones'. This idea had originated with the urban theorist Peter Hall, who had drawn an analogy between successful capitalist development in the UK in the nineteenth century and contemporary capitalist development in the Pacific rim, arguing that both had been greatly facilitated by the absence of burdensome planning regimes. Enterprise Zones did have greatly relaxed planning rules, but even more important were very generous tax breaks for those investing in them. John Hall got his ash dump designated as part of a Tyneside Enterprise Zone which meant that it was exempt from most planning controls and in particular from the structure planning powers of the County Council which was opposed to out-of-town shopping. It also meant that massive subsidy was available, both directly and through tax breaks. Hall did very well out of the MetroCentre and used it as the base for further property development. He subsequently bought Newcastle United football club and has done even better out of that: an excellent illustration of the political economy of 'Fantasy City'.

The MetroCentre is basically a large mall but it is not the only example of an edge city in my locality. In some ways the edge city is not a new thing. Within half a mile of my house is the massive Team Valley Trading Estate, developed from the 1930s onwards on the edge of the Tyneside conurbation in order to facilitate the diversification of the area's industrial base. At its peak this estate had more than 20 000 manufacturing jobs. It now has less than 4 000 in manufacturing but it has at least as many service jobs, many of them in the 5th Avenue Business Park which houses several back-office functions for national financial services companies. There is also a retail park and a massive supermarket. Business parks are the real employment locale of the edge city in the UK. Typical employment on them is in call centres, for example the Newcastle Business Park built on the brown-field site of the enormous Armstrong Armaments works which at its peak employed 30 000 people. There are 25 000 call-centre jobs in the north east of England, all on edge city business parks.

The interesting thing about edge city development is that the space it uses is always contingent. Urban cores are urban cores. They correspond to the central business districts of the classic Chicago model. Edge city developments depend on road patterns but those patterns follow existing local social and physical topography rather than a universal urban development form. Much of the edge cities in the UK is brownfield, especially in the north and Midlands in England, but it is still edge. There are interesting contingent local effects of this. In the north east of England the phenomenon of edge city development has actually sustained populations in wholly redundant colliery villages (and the small former steel-making town of Consett) because people can buy relatively cheap housing in what is reverting to a rural context and easily commute into edge city employment, shopping, and leisure facilities. The only leisure activity which is not available on the edge is live theatre.

There is an interesting question about the edge as built environment. The physical structure of the MetroCentre mall was built with a relatively short design life. It is an integral whole. It must be replaced in toto. Will we see a downward movement of whole malls or even their simple abandonment with new malls opening on new sites? Edge cities privilege no space. Will there be land appreciation returns on these developments?

Garreau (1992) brought the term 'edge city' into the urban lexicon. We have already, in Chapter 5, considered the implications of the edge city for the socio-spatial forms of urban space. Here we must think about its implications as built environment of life. MetroCentre is an extraordinary simulacra. Its mall spaces replicate on a far larger scale the innovative arcade forms of Newcastle's Graingertown, forms that were original in 1840 but are wholly derivative today. We have privatised, globalised 'public' space – the security guards in the MetroCentre are dressed as American cops! MetroCentre is not exclusive – it even has excellent public transport connections! However, it is not the industrial city either.

The development of city centres and peripheries in accordance with the logics of globalised capitalism is a world-wide phenomenon. Shanghai is an extreme case. Yet again we find the old entryport of colonialism into China functioning as the new entryport of globalisation. Olds (1997) has written about the role of 'the global intelligence corps' in the development of that city's new financial district. Olds makes the very important point that not only is foreign direct investment crucial to this process of urban change, but there is a crucial non-material dimension mediated by the design professionals, 'responsible for the flows of images and urban development models that were used in the revise of the masterplan for the Luijiazui Central Finance District in the early 1990s; images and models which then entered subsequent circuits operating at a variety of scales' (1997: 110). This is the human agency component of globalisation. It is worth noting the scale of these operations. Shanghai's authorities are investing more than one billion pounds sterling a year in infrastructure development. Foreign direct investment is often tied to the new consumerism. Wu notes that Japan's giant retail group Yaohan has invested US$100 million in a shopping centre in the new Pudong district (1999: 214), and other international investors include Bell in a joint venture, Eriksson, Philips, Xerox, General Motors, Misubishi and Hitachi, as well as McDonalds and Kentucky Fried Chicken!

There is even more massive investment from the overseas Chinese, many of whom originate from Shanghai.

Pudong is the edge city of Shanghai. At the same time there is massive urban renewal in the old core city of the French Concession and International Settlement. There is extensive clearance of inner-city slum housing, with actually rather generous compensation for residents (see Wu, 1999: 212) in the form of higher-value new housing units. Another example is provided by Jakarta (see Firman, 1998) with direct foreign investment of more than four billion US dollars in 1996 alone. Firman notes how central Jakarta investment is in consumption sectors whilst industrial investment is located in the peripheral parts of the metropolitan region. By 1995 there were more than 25 shopping malls in the Jakarta Metropolitan Area together with international conference hotels and luxury condominium blocks.

Concluding remarks and further resources

We will pick up on the politics of development in Chapter 8. A preliminary conclusion at this stage would be that in postindustrial capitalism, urban development – the production and realisation of the built environment – has become almost as important as the production and consumption of material commodities.

The things to examine in relation to themes of this chapter are the components of the built environment itself, and especially the way in which those components relate to each other in order to form a the material base of urban social systems. Examine your own urban spaces – central zone, suburbs and 'edge'. Look at building forms and try to establish something about development history. Again local histories are enormously useful.

Wolfe has written a novel which moves on from the global masters of the universe dealt with in *Bonfire of the Vanities* to the urban developers of Edge City – *A Man in Full* (1999). The main locus for this piece is Atlanta – the real estate equivalent in the 1990s of global capitalism in finance in the 80s. This book illustrates many of the themes of this chapter in a most lively way. However, in looking at urban development there is no substitute for the Web. The 'global intelligence corps' of building professionals have an intensely graphical sensibility and they love the Web as a way of illustrating both their ideas and the implementation of those ideas. The sites relating to Pudong in greater Shanghai are particularly interesting but you will find Web sites about urban development in virtually any place which has a Web footprint.

In the developed world the suburbs too appear in the virtual sphere. Malls have Web sites. Developer builders promote their schemes on the Web. Again a good trick is to pick a city virtually anywhere in the world and see what you can find. Pace Dear's desire (2000) to resist the idea that Los Angeles is a proto-typical form, you will find it replicated everywhere where people have money to spend or invest. Certainly Katowice now has its malls, its peripheral suburban developments, and the emerging trappings of edge city and you can find them on the Web if you look for them.

8

Politics and governance in urban places

In urban societies, towns and cities are the place of politics: of revolutions as in Paris in 1789 and Petrograd in 1917; of long reformist struggles about 'collective consumption' typified by the urban politics of the UK's industrial cities through the first two-thirds of the twentieth century; of elite-directed urban reconstruction through 'growth coalitions'; and of the new politics of sustainability with its base in 'new social movements'. Of course, the simplest explanation for the urban character of politics in an urbanising world is that politics happen where there are both people and the resources which people can compete for. However, there is something inherently distinctive about the urban as the base of politics. The urban is the locus of the social relations of capitalism. All the great theories of capitalism, and in particular those of Marx and Schumpeter, recognise that capitalism is a system which is constantly in flux. For much of the time this flux does not result in radical change but, with capitalism understood as a globalised, far from equilibric system, the flux constantly tests the boundaries of the system. When those boundaries are breached the system is reconstituted in a new form. So far those new forms have remained essentially capitalist – founded on the wage labour relation and commodity markets. Nonetheless, the changes particularly that from industrial to postindustrial are changes of kind.

The first great social change engendered by emerging capitalism initiated the urban-industrial way of life itself and created an enormous mass of proletarians living in cities, whose lives were and are subject to the constant flux of capitalist development and consequent change and uncertainty. It was precisely this 'Experience I', to use Thompson's terminology (1981), which was the basis of collective class identity and working-class politics in the modern era. The history of urban politics under the conditions of industrial capitalism is a history of class politics. The emergent history of postindustrial politics seems to be about something very different.

In the literature which deals with the governance of cities, we find theories of structure and theories of action. 'Governance' is a term used to describe the set of processes undertaken by both the state at every spatial level, and the institutions, agencies, and interests with which it operates in partnership, in maintaining an existing social order whilst at the same time accommodating the logic of capitalism as a system in constant flux and undergoing continuous development.

Theories of structure are in essence functionalist. They deal with the need for state intervention in order to manage the complex externalities and continuing social and ecological contradictions which are inherent in the dynamics of urban social life. Note the significance of that word 'dynamics': urban places and urban lives are not static. These systems are not close to equilibric. Their natural condition is not a steady state maintained by negative feedback mechanisms. They do change, and change in terms of transformation of form, whilst remaining within the general social relations of capitalism with its foundation of wage labour. The 'task' of the state and associated agents of governance is, in large part, that of handling those changes, whilst at the same time maintaining the social and ecological foundations of the system as a whole. The starting point here is public health: without the maintenance of public health an urban world is not possible. We will find that many of the activities of the state in the urban begin from this point, from the management of human ecologies in an urban system.

At the same time, as we have seen in Chapter 6, the production and realisation of the urban built environment is itself part of the accumulation cycle of capitalism. Capitalism has to have social order but it also has to have processes which facilitate the making of profits. In postindustrial capitalism, it seems as if this second logic is the driving force of governance of urban space and urban systems. There is a serious contradiction between the functions of the state as a maintainer of order, regulator of crises and manager of change on the one hand, and the functions of the state as facilitator of accumulation on the other. This contradiction will be a central theme in this chapter.

The above is all very systemic, functionalist, and mechanistically determinist, although we must always remember that determination is complex and involves the setting of limits rather than the generation of exact occurrences. In a social world these structural processes are expressed through social actions, actions which can be informed by a reflexive understanding of the character of the processes themselves. There are two bodies of theory about agency in the contemporary urban world. One is about the actions of elites in terms of the concept of urban regime. The other is about the potential for urban social movements based around identity politics and / or 'desired futures'. We will try to reconcile the structural understanding with the narrative of agency of both kinds working separately and, increasingly, together.

In this chapter, I want to examine Castells's (1977) notion of collective consumption, review contemporary discussions of urban regimes, and consider the actual and potential character of collective social action in the postindustrial urban world. However, first it is necessary to refer back to the structural idea of locality considered in Chapter 4. We need to grasp what that concept implies for the levels of governance which are necessary in societies where space makes a difference.

The necessity for the local state and for an urban state

Duncan and Goodwin (1988) and Cox and Mair (1987) drew on the realist account of locality in arguing that if localities are real, then there is structural requirement for a level of government which operates at that level. Essentially this is an argument against the possibility of centralised bureaucracy in societies where geographical variation makes a difference. The realist account of both locality and region provided a scientific foundation for this argument but administrative practice had long accepted it. In authoritarian regimes which govern more than a single locality, there has always been a considerable degree of autonomy accorded to local administrators. The French Prefect, with the authority of a general, is the semi-autonomous representative of the French state at the local and regional level. The Satrap of the Persian empire, Procurator of the Roman Empire, Nawab of the Moghul Empire, Mandarin throughout almost all of Chinese history, Viceroy or even District Officer of the British Empire – the existence of these offices and the very considerable extent of their discretionary powers demonstrate that, in the activities of states, geography matters.

However, when we deal with the urban in the modern world we deal with more than the issue of spatial variation, important though that is. We have to deal with the relationship between the urban and democracy. We can see how this works by considering housing in UK towns. Although the powers to deal with housing possessed by UK local authorities derive from national statute, and indeed one of the earliest national interventions of the twentieth century was directed at the problems of housing in rural areas, housing is primarily an urban problem which derives from the management of the problems of human ecology under urban conditions. Public health powers were always local and urban because the trigger for their implementation was the problem of infectious disease under urban conditions.

Once local authorities regulated the minimum standard of new construction under by-laws, they forced up rent levels beyond those which the poorest urban dwellers could afford to pay. This led inevitably to public intervention in the direct provision of housing, although the mass provision of such housing was initially for those who could afford high rents for high quality, the intention being that they would vacate less good but still sanitarily adequate property which would become available to the urban poor at lower rents – the process described as filtration.

What is interesting is the way in which this necessarily local *and* urban process of housing provision intersected with the development of local democracy. In many places, the emergent Labour Party was founded on struggles over the character of urban housing (see Byrne, 1980; 1982). Duncan and Goodwin, drawing on a suggestion by Milliband, make an important point here:

> national representation cannot always deal adequately with local differentiation, and so local electoral politics was clearly a necessary part of representative democracy. But adding a democratic or popular element to some local state institutions also strengthens and legitimizes the role of representing local interests *to* the centre. This may increasingly contradict the role of dealing with local situations *for* the centre . . . local state becomes both obstacle and agent for the national state. (1988: 45–6)

That provides us with a lead to the issues of collective consumption as the foundation of urban politics.

Collective consumption: urban politics and the reproduction of labour power

The term 'collective consumption' was introduced by Castells (1977) to describe the way in which the state, and in particular the local state, was involved in the provision of resources and systems directed at the reproduction of labour power under capitalism. Workers must be adequately fed, clothed and housed. If there is to be a future generation of workers, then resources must be made available to feed, house and clothe children. If trained and educated labour is required, then the production of that also takes resources. In the idealised form of market relationship these resources are paid for by workers from the wage they obtain in return for their labour, for example, by the investment university students make in their own education funded by loans raised against future income.

However, things are not this simple overall. First there are issues of public goods and externalities. Public health represents both. If there is good public health everybody benefits — a public good. If there is not, I might catch a disease from you, even if I have kept myself well in terms of diet and shelter — a negative externality. This is a clear basis for state intervention.

In practice, things have gone far beyond this. States, and in particular local states, provided services both as a means of legitimating the social order of democratic capitalism through the maintenance of what Berlin (1968) called positive liberties, rights to health, education and so on, and in order to handle problems to do with the devalorisation of crucial capitalist activities and responsibilities. Devalorisation happens when a capitalist process which is essential for the maintenance of the system cannot deliver an average rate of return on capital employed. Generally the responsibility for funding such activities is transferred either directly or indirectly to the state. Urban rapid-transit systems are a classic example. Private capital makes its big profits up front from land development on transit routes and the operation of the actual routes always requires public subsidy.

We can see the effects of these processes in the development of welfare states with much of the provision being handled by the democratic local state, especially in the UK and in federal countries like the USA. In the UK since the 1970s many such services have been transferred to appointed QUANGOs such as UDCs. The appointed boards which run such services have been described by Stewart (1995) as 'the new magistracy'. Like the magistrates they are not democratic but are local.

In *The Urban Question* (1977), Castells presented an extremely mechanical account of 'collective consumption' whilst dismissing the Chicago School's claim that 'the Urban' represents a distinctive element in the social order. The focus was on the structural requirements of capitalism as expressed in urban space. In subsequent work (1978) he explicitly dismissed any role for conscious agency. Castells has radically changed his position, but this structuralism was important in its day.

Castells's complicated (not complex!) structuralism was much criticised but it did set an agenda, and the idea of collective consumption remains crucial in our understanding of the urban state, urban governance and urban politics. However, we do have to realise that there is a history to this. Duncan and Goodwin put this well when summarising the implications of a range of studies of the local history of urban political action around issues of housing, health and other aspects of social reproduction:

> Not only does this work succeed in demonstrating empirically the links between economic, social and political change (and thus also the links between these and local government policy making), but it also highlights the importance of social consciousness in creating such change. As these detailed historical studies show, not only do the specificities of local situations influence the actual outcome of general processes, but those general processes are themselves created by conscious, active individuals. In a similar way, political and ideological shifts reflect how people engage actively in social relations, including class relations... To put it simply, neither structures nor events just happen. (1988: 29)

There is an extensive literature describing the pressures against collective consumption in general and urban collective consumption in particular. Cochrane (1993) runs through this in detail but there are three components which are generally identified.

The first is the idea of a 'fiscal crisis' of the welfare state. This concept was formulated in general terms, as opposed to the specific problem of the erosion of the tax bases of US cities, by O'Connor

(1973) who produced a typology of the purposes of public expenditure derived from tax revenues. The crucial distinction he made was between that expenditure which facilitated the accumulation process in capitalism by either reducing the cost or improving the productivity of labour power, and that which was a 'social cost', necessary perhaps for purposes of social legitimation, but not directly facilitating accumulation. O'Connor was writing from the left, but his argument had much in common with a critique mounted from the free market neo-liberal right. At the simplest level, this was an argument to the effect that capitalism could not in the long run afford the bills of the Keynes/Beveridge welfare state. Regulation theory derived accounts of the hollowed-out state, typified by the work of Jessop (1994), are a development of this account. The added gloss is that it is not capitalism in general which cannot afford, but postFordist capitalism in particular which does not need, general high levels of social welfare, for reasons of legitimation and macro-economic management through the smoothing of demand. The system, it is argued, can now function without a universal welfare state.

However, the new right's approach was never merely a matter of technical rationality. It also reflected the significance of neo-liberal ideology, the ideological aspect of globalisation as a general social process. There was a particular gloss placed on this in the UK by Saunders (1984, 1986) whose work on consumption cleavages has already been cited in Chapter 5. Saunders argued that a combination of real increases in middle-level incomes coupled with the gains people had made through the private ownership of assets, and in particular owner-occupied houses, had led to a new social division between those who depended primarily upon the state to meet the costs of their social reproduction and those whose incomes and assets were adequate for them to meet those costs themselves. This introduces an action element into the discussion of fiscal crisis. If we accept Saunders's line we can see that those who can meet the costs of their social reproduction privately will be likely to resent taxation levied on them to meet the costs of the social reproduction of those who depend on state welfare.

Saunders probably made too much of a tenure difference and ignored the general significance of the social provision of health and social care. The tendency for the local state to try to confiscate assets, including owner-occupied dwellings, to pay for the long-term costs of social care, is a source of real resentment in middle England.

However, it is clear that despite the generally social character of health care, social care, social security and education in the UK, there is a force to the line that politics is influenced by a taxpayers' revolt. Certainly New 'Labour' has organised its policies on this basis. The Conservative governments of the 1980s justified the removal of virtually all discretionary tax-raising powers from local authorities (going so far as to introduce a poll tax levied on all adults which was so unpopular that it led to the downfall of Mrs Thatcher as Prime Minister) on the grounds that Labour-controlled urban authorities were elected to office by the urban poor in order to spend money on the urban poor and that this confiscation of the resources of the hard working and non-feckless was not to be tolerated.

In the United States, urban authorities have suffered much more severely because, unlike in the UK and most European industrial countries, there is no general mechanism of redistribution of central resources on a needs basis. US urban areas typically have to rely on local property, sales and even income taxes to fund welfare expenditures and middle class (middle class blacks included) flight to the suburbs has left many US cities with a severely eroded tax base and highly welfare-dependent populations. In some US states, tax-cutting propositions have been passed on state-wide ballots, and local bond issues have been voted down. All this has exacerbated urban fiscal crisis.

If we refer back to the discussion of the transformation of planning as a process in Chapter 7, we can see a change in the objective of local governance with the transition from industrial to postindustrial capitalism. Planning in industrial capitalism, when that capitalism was operating under the Keynes / Beveridge welfare capitalist regime, was at least in formal terms about the development of the good city as the basis of universal collective consumption. We saw that the purpose of planning had changed towards the facilitation of urban accumulation. This leads us to consider the local state as entrepreneur rather than as provider of services.

Entrepreneurial regimes: the policy sciences of the urban state

Regime theory provides a new perspective on the issue of power. It directs attention away from a narrow focus on power as an issue of social control towards an understanding of power expressed through social production. In a complex, fragmented urban world the paradigmatic form of power is that which enables certain interests to blend their capacities to achieve common purposes. Regime analysis directs attention to the conditions under which such effective long-term coalitions emerge in order to accomplish public purposes. (Stoker, 1995: 117)

Regime theory is the latest fashion in debates on urban politics. Imrie and Raco (1999) consider that much of the debate about the new local governance is really identifying things which have always been around – not so much a new city as a city seen anew – and there is much to commend this view, but regime theory is a useful organising framework even if the processes it describes have a long history.

Regime theory is useful because it brings together themes of power which are crucial for political science, and issues of accumulation which are the core of political economy. Mollenkopf (1992) has identified three stages in political science's approach to urban politics and policy. We find a set of pluralist accounts which are basically action theories of reasonably equal competition. We find theories which deal with the power of elites often described as neo-pluralist because such theories do not deny that non-elite groups are active, but recognise that elites, usually economic elites, have especial influence. Finally we find structuralist studies which are essentially economic determinist, but which as Mollenkopf says, have the advantage of being 'factually on target in observing and describing mechanisms that generate systemic, cumulative, political inequality which has a more profound impact on outcomes than the coalition patterns studied by pluralists' (1992: 83).

Regime theory suggests that urban governments must turn to those with control over resources which can be brought to bear on the resolution of urban issues. Stoker puts it like this:

> Regime analysts...do not regard governments as likely to respond to groups on the basis of their electoral power or the intensity of their preferences as some pluralists do. Rather governments are driven to cooperate with those who hold resources central to the achieving of policy goals. (1995: 119)

A simple reading of this passage might lead us to conclude that the policy goals themselves are somehow independent of separate interests. Certainly the claims of urban government in the Fordist era were couched in such universalist terms. This is certainly not the case now. Cox and Mair's (1987) treatment of the significance of locality for governance helps us to clarify this point. They argued that a good deal of capital was tied in space: it was not globally mobile. In particular, capital invested in land is fixed. This meant that there are particular capitalist interests in the development of particular places. This directed attention to the operation of 'growth coalitions' which 'boosted' places as locales for development. Subsequently (see Brotchie *et al.*, eds, 1995) such boosterism has been understood as attempting to locate places within the global hierarchy of cities. Savage and Warde (1993: 168) noted that Cox and Mair's account suggested the revival of the preFordist character of urban politics in the postindustrial phase. We should here recall Imrie and Raco's (1999) demonstration that this sort of approach also characterised much of urban governance in the Fordist era itself.

However, the Fordist era of urban governance was the era of mass democratic control. It was an era in which (in the UK in particular) business interests withdrew from direct engagement with local politics. Clements's (1969) study of Bristol is informative here. The withdrawal happened because local business elites found an unacceptable dissonance between the hierarchical and interest-driven mode of business policy formation and the relatively open world of mass politics with its at least nominal commitment to universal rather than particular goals.

In the US, business interests have always maintained a major role in the control of development. Even in New York, where there was a move towards mass democracy coupled with technocracy as expressed by the role of Robert Moses, fiscal crisis enabled the FIRE (Finance, Insurance and Real Estate) elite to take control of the city's budgets and development processes after the 1970s (see Fitch, 1993). In the UK, the Tory administration in the 1980s abolished the conurbation-wide elected planning authorities, the GLC and Metropolitan County Councils, and transferred significant land and labour planning powers to appointed Urban Development Corporations (UDCs) and Training and Enterprise Councils (TECs).

Since the introduction of 'City Challenge' in the late 1980s, there has been a shift in UK urban policy from simple land development towards projects which are nominally directed at the needs of the people who have suffered most under deindustrialisation. However, closer examination of the City Challenge and its successor Single Regeneration Budget shows that elites dominate in terms of strategic objectives, and elite interests are those which are served. Despite the rhetoric of the role of the 'community' in partnerships, we find that, at very best, community groups have had a role in modifying details of implementation (see Geddes, 1997).

Much of Chapter 7 was concerned with the way in which local governance is now to a considerable extent a matter of collaboration between local states and development capital. As Paddison puts it: 'In the new urban politics the co-production between local state agencies and the private sector of proactive development strategies has become of critical significance' (1997: 321). It is important to realise that this is not simply a matter of money. Although the money resources allocated to QUANGOs by UK central government are now about 60 per cent of the total money resources of elected local authorities, it is not so much a matter of money as of political focus and administrative attention. The Economic Development function of a typical UK urban authority will spend only a very small proportion of that authority's budget, mostly on the salaries of its staff – less than 3 per cent in a typical case. However, the general administrative focus and political priorities of that authority will be on economic development rather than on the routine administration of its central universal welfare services, the collective consumption aspect of its activities.

Deakin and Edwards see this sort of approach as informed by the 'enterprise culture' and define that thus:

'Enterprise' in the political lexicon of the 1980s is a property exclusive to the private sector. The public sector does not possess it, or worse, it is a hindrance to its exercise. But it is also shorthand for a collection of other related values, values which, as Corner and Harvey note are '. . . primarily to do with the economics of neo-liberal "freedom" and the politics of individualism' (1990: 24). Enterprise is having initiative and drive; it is taking opportunities when they arise; it is independence from the state; it is having confidence and being responsible for one's own destiny; it is being driven by the work ethic; and it promotes self-interest. But it is in this last property that its real value as a policy instrument lies. There is no stronger motivating force, so the culture of enterprise tells us, than the pursuit of self interest. This is what gets things done. (1993: 2)

It is true, as Deakin and Edwards point out, that policy makers can only hope to shape enterprise-directed activity in a tangential way. It is hoped that development will yield employment, but it cannot be guaranteed. It is also hoped that development will be achieved at minimum public cost. As we have seen in Chapter 7 that has been an extremely pious hope.

Deakin and Edwards remind us of something which Ambrose (1994) also identified as crucial – the issue of responsibility. In the framework of the new urban governance, who carries the can if development fails or, even worse, succeeds but leaves inner-city people worse off in consequence of that success? This is not at all clear. Deakin and Edwards were reviewing a particular phase in UK urban policy but the election of New 'Labour' into office has not changed the character of the culture of urban governance at all. On the contrary, the establishment of Regional Development Agencies (RDAs) which are 'business led' has put enterprise even more firmly at the heart of the development process.

Panitch (1980) identified these forms as 'authoritarian corporatism' because they brought together the state and capital without organised labour. Organised labour is nominally represented on the RDAs but the signs are that its actual influence on development is likely to be minimal. This has certainly been the case with urban partnerships as Geddes (1997: 123) shows. These examples support the general understanding of regime theory. Whoever is on the bodies of the new governance, only those with control over resources seen as meaningful in relation to policy implementation have any say. In postindustrial capitalism that excludes disorganised labour and dispossessed communities.

There is one further approach to urban governance which we need to consider before we turn to the possibility of mass urban politics through urban social movements. That is the implications for urban governance of the development of the global system through a hierarchy of urban spaces, with those urban spaces being increasingly interconnected directly rather than through national economic systems.

Hollingsworth (1998), Brenner (1999) and Kiel (1998) have all written about what Brenner calls 'the rescaling of governance' as part of the global process of 'reterritorialisation' of space under the new global conditions. Kiel puts it like this:

many of the traditional functions of nation-states are now displaced into lower or upper level state institutions which either did not exist previously or were fundamentally altered in the process. Globalization makes states, but different kinds of states from the ones we've been used to. (1998: 617)

Kiel draws on the work of Magnusson, who argues that the urban locality is the locus of encounter of civil society and the state, and that in the contemporary global system, urban politics, despite the limited powers of local states, is crucial to the governance of that globalisation. This is an important idea. Most of the accounts presented in this book have 'deprivileged' mass collective social action as the source of the character of society. Globalisation is a thesis of disempowerment of everything but global capital. If, however, the urban is a necessary and crucial level of governance in a globalised system, then there is an opening for social action in relation to the issues of everyday life under postindustrial capitalism. We can turn to politics as action.

Civil society, social movements and urban politics

We can begin our consideration of the bases of urban politics by noting Eder's (1993) assertion that whilst the material bases of class formation are as strong as (if not stronger than) ever in postindustrial capitalism, common position in the hierarchy of material inequality and common position in the wage labour relation are no longer adequate bases for collective action. To use Marx's own language, the collective consciousness of class for itself, founded in the politics of production and reproduction conducted within industrial capitalism, has been replaced by classes which are simply aggregates of those in a common condition without the consciousness of that condition, classes in themselves. These are the atomised consumers of postindustrial capitalism.

We might well think that what collectivities lack is not so much a consciousness of common identity as a collective sense of capacity, of the power to make things happen in terms of the interests of that collectivity. Certainly Eder sees this as one aspect of the new politics of class. What then can be the basis of political action in the urban spaces of postindustrial capitalism? To answer that question we have first to consider the meaning of the term 'civil society' and understand the implications of Magnusson's contention that the urban is the context in which civil society and state encounter each other.

The term civil society requires explanation. A useful definition is that given by Urry:

> Broadly speaking the struggles of social classes to reproduce the material conditions of their existence are part of, but not exhaustive of, civil society. Also present within civil society are various other social groupings, particularly those based on gender, race, generation and nation. These groupings are not to be reduced to those of class, although the dominant relations and forces of production fundamentally structure the form that their struggles will take. These groupings derive from how in civil society individual subjectivities are constituted, of gender, race, generation, locality and nationality. The discursive and non-discursive structures within which such constitution occurs, particularly within the family, are in turn related to, but not reduced to, the dominant relations/forces of production. Civil Society is not then to be viewed merely as the world of individual needs, but rather . . . as sets of structured, institutionalized social practices. (1982: 16–17)

This definition is rather showing its age, although it does so by explicit reference to the relations of production which is no bad thing. Bearing in mind Frankel's (1987) pertinent warning that there are in reality no boundaries among economy, state and civil society, the idea still has heuristic value because it identifies a field other than the world of work and outside the world of domestic reproduction but related to both in which social actions make the social real. Urry's definition is particularly valuable because it relates the individual to the collective, the self to the social category. It has another value in that it identifies social classes as one of the sets of collective actors in civil society. However, attention in recent years has tended to dismiss classes and instead focus on 'social movements'.

This shift is exemplified by Castells's radical theoretical shift from the agentless structuralism after Althusser of *The Urban Question* (1977) to the collective agent centred and very historical *The City and the Grassroots* (1983). Castells certainly does not ignore classes, either in that book or in subsequent work, but it is interesting that those who have taken up the idea of 'social movement' in response to his initiative have tended to define the term in a way which explicitly excludes formal political parties and by implication does not include classes as such. For example, Lowe says:

> The term is used here to mean organisations standing outside the formal party system which bring people together to defend or challenge the provision of urban political services and to protect the local environment. The importance of these organisations as 'social movements' is that their objectives are undertaken collectively by the mobilization of a distinct social base and the momentum of their activity is towards changes in policy direction. (1986: 3)

Pickvance has a very similar conception when he defines social movements as 'mobilized groups which advocate ideas and make demands which challenge existing policies and practices, and which make some use of non-institutionalized types of action, but which do not take the form of political parties' (1999: 354). There is a subtle difference because Pickvance explicitly allows for 'ideas' as the basis of a social movement. In other words the linking factor which brings people together may be nothing more than an intellectual commitment to a particular world view. This is implicit in Lowe's definition but it is important that it has now become explicit.

The designation of political parties as outside the set of social movements is interesting. It seems perfectly clear that, in origin, political parties, especially socialist and labour parties, developed exactly as social movements and that an important part of that development was to do with urban politics and disputes around collective consumption. In contemporary Europe, Green parties plainly began as social movements indeed most of the literature on social movements in advanced capitalist societies is about greens – but are now parties.

It is fair to see parties as particular forms of collective organisation which seek election to office, but that leaves us with the problem of distinguishing social movements from pressure groups as understood in traditional pluralist conceptions of the political process. Social movements often function exactly as pressure groups, but the distinguishing characteristic of the social movement is that it involves the mobilisation of people. We might then choose to define social movements as organisations engaged in mass mobilisation for social action but which do not yet seek elective office.

In postindustrial capitalism the generative basis of social movements is often considered to be the politics of identity and, in particular, the politics of gender and of sexual orientation. Certainly there is a gay movement which in particular places, especially in San Franciso (see Castells, 1983), has become a fully-fledged social movement based on mass local mobilisation. However, elsewhere gay groups function much more like traditional pressure groups and seek to influence urban and other policies. Likewise the contemporary 'women's movement' seems to be asserted rather than real. Suffragette movements were plainly social movements with mass and mobilised memberships, but despite the significance of the feminist (in the most general sense of that word) critique of gendered hierarchies, the actual engagement of feminist groups in politics at all levels in postindustrial advanced capitalism generally takes a pressure-group form. There are mobilisations around specific issues and on specific occasions, exemplified by sporadic demonstrations to 'reclaim the night' for women, usually in areas with large bodies of students. Such events are far from trivial and illustrate an important point about the gendered use of urban space. Nonetheless, in general the feminist approach is one of pressure-group representation and a claim, along with ethnically constituted groups, for attention to issues of gender and race in the general direction of urban policy. At the level of the negative liberties of possessive individualism, that is, in terms of outlawing direct or indirect discrimination and going some way to redress historic imbalances in employment and resource allocation, such approaches have had some success. However, they are founded around demands for individual rights rather than for collective interests and are often criticised as having merely advanced the interests of individual, and overwhelmingly middle-class, women without reference to women's interests as a whole. The same criticism is advanced in relation to rights programmes founded around ethnicity.

Contemporary interest in urban social movements seems to derive from a rather desperate effort to identify any kind of coherent collectivities in the globalised/glocalised spaces of the urban world. The hegemony of consumerism, of individualism, of, at best, households as the only unit of collective significance, seems so great that people want to identify some sort of collective level because the absence of agents at that level indicates that there is something wrong with the social order.

In postindustrial capitalism we cannot separate a discussion of urban social movements from the active effort of the state at the level of urban neighbourhood to engage in 'community development'. This process is worth some attention because it indicates how contemporary states, at local, national and block levels, identify the deficiencies of part of civil society as the origins of serious problems in the management of urban social orders.

In the UK the term 'community development' was an example of colonialism brought back home. A good account of its history is given by the Edinburgh–London Weekend Return Group (1980) although subsequent experience suggests that the title they gave to their publication *In and Against the State* was an example of optimism of the will running far too far ahead of pessimism of the intellect. 'In and for the state' would be much more like it. Whilst British colonialism in Africa always ruled through traditional rulers when these were available, as in Northern Nigeria, in other contexts the ruled either had no real history of political elites, as with the Ibo, or had elites with a primarily spiritual function who could not be assimilated to the colonial system, as with the Shona. Sometimes the colonialists had done their best to exterminate the pre-existing elite, a practice originally refined in Ireland. In any event colonial administrators were faced with the need to reorganise so that they could rule in a systematic way and without continuing and inefficient gross coercion. The idea of such 'reconstitution' has influenced UK social programmes for urban areas since the 1930s.

UK practice has also drawn on US approaches, originally developed to assimilate European peasants into US urban society, extended in neo-colonialist forms in Latin America, and developed in a relatively progressive liberal form in the Ford Foundation Gray Area Projects and the Johnson administration's 'War on Poverty' (see Lemann, 1991; Marris and Rein, 1967). The influential UK Home Office civil servant, Derek Morell, saw these projects in action and attempted to emulate them in the UK with establishment of the Community Development Projects (CDPs) in the early 1970s. Although the CDP approach and account proved far too radical for UK national and local states, the significance of deindustrialisation was recognised and the need to intervene in the disorganised neighbourhoods generated by that process remains central to UK urban policy. Indeed given the failure of the trickle-down approach attempted by the Urban Development Corporations, this has assumed even greater significance with the Cabinet Office's Social Exclusion Unit establishing a whole new programme directed at neighbourhood integration.

It is important to realise that the origins of these kinds of initiatives lie in an implicit recognition of the reality of the lived experience described by Wacquant in these terms:

> residents of the French cité and the American ghetto each form an *impossible community* [original emphasis], perpetually divided against themselves, which cannot but refuse to acknowledge the collective nature of their predicament and who are therefore inclined to deploy strategies of distancing and 'exit' that tend to validate negative outside perceptions and feed a deadly self-fulfilling prophecy through which public taint and collective disgrace eventually produce that which they claim merely to record: namely social atomism, community 'disorganization' and cultural anomie. (1993: 374)

Let us turn to a consideration of urban social movements outside the ambit of advanced postindustrial capitalism.

Schuurman and Van Naerssen in their review of *Urban Social Movements in the Third World* (1989) offer us a third specification of the nature of social movements:

> an adequate definition of an urban social movement is the following: a social organization with a territorial identity, which strives for emancipation by way of collective action. (1989: 3)

There are two interesting features to this definition. The first is the emphasis on territorial base, on spatial foundation in something which at least implicitly is identifiable as 'community'. The second is the goal of emancipation. These authors noted with some asperity that Castells's discussion of collective consumption seemed to ignore the reality of repressive states in non-democratic societies which functioned through coercion rather than legitimating social expenditure.

In this context Pickvance's (1999) subsequent survey of the literature on social movements in Eastern Europe, Southern Europe and Latin America is interesting. The societies he surveys have generally undergone a transition from some form of absolutism to some form of democracy and in the process, contrary to what might be expected, social movements have generally become weaker. Pickvance concludes that social movements may well function best and most clearly at times of transition when the absolutist coercion has weakened enough to permit them – although in many absolutist systems such social movements were always tolerated to a degree – but before democratic parties and the hegemony of individual consumerism take over from them. We should not generalise too much on this basis. Whilst Pickvance's account rings true for Poland, what are we to make of Brazil where the Workers' Party is plainly the product of and responsible to a constituency of social movements? It is also true that in India, the world's largest democracy with a fifty year democratic history, social movements are very significant.

Walton has reviewed the literature on social movement related urban conflict in poor countries. His conclusion is interesting:

> When experts reflect on political conflict in third world cities, they typically conclude that it is either endemic or occasional, radical or conservative, tempestuous or quiescent. Depending on their assessment of basic facts, specialists reason further that the evidence confirms either a theory of insurgent class action or opportunistic client cooperation. The masses of urban poor and their occasional allies in organized labour or petty commerce are understood either as autonomous political actors or manipulated clients of elite patronage. The division of opinion is not only diametrical but perennial. (1998. 460)

In summary the urban poor adopt the strategies for action which they anticipate will work. They will go for clientilism if that is seen as fair and effective but mobilise in oppositional ways when it is not. This seems a reasonable account, but it is important to note that most of the references cited in this comprehensive survey are from the mid 1980s or earlier, fairly enough in a survey of perspectives over time. However, the account of globalisation of consumer culture and capitalist forms which underpins much of this text suggests that in contemporary circumstances things may be different.

Certainly Lustagen-Thaler and Schragge's (1998) recent review of the political circumstances of the New Urban Left in Montreal, one of the few large cities in advanced capitalism to have been governed by a political force with its origins in social movements, is pessimistic in the extreme. These authors find that 'with the shift towards the entrepreneurial city, the local state now involves other non-governmental actors in the key role increasing mobilization of local politics in support of economic development.' (1998: 239) This could be taken as just a local illustration of the regime theory, but Lustagen-Thaler and Schragge go further. They show how community-based groups have become involved in the delivery of the collective consumption goods they were established to seek. In this process the constituencies of the community groups are transformed from political base into clients. Funding ties these previously autonomous agencies of civil society to the purposes of the entrepreneurial state. UK and US experience shows that this is a very general tendency. Here we have Piven and Cloward's account of *Poor People's Movements: How They Succeed and Why They Fail* (1979) illustrated yet again. The problem seems to be the lack of universal, comprehensive conceptions of what an alternative future might look like. The only coherent version of that on offer is a derivative of the idea of sustainable city. We will examine that briefly in the next and last chapter of this book.

Concluding remarks and further resources

Politics is about power, and in urban systems power is actually more visible than usual. The political processes are necessarily local and the consequences of it are visible. One of the major contemporary issues of postindustrial capitalism is the reduction in democratic process. One of the big issues is that whilst the consequences of urban political processes are visible the decision-making is less and less visible and less and less accountable. Secrecy and the disproportionate influence of finance capital and developers are not new, but in the postindustrial system they are much more significant than in the Fordist era.

Urban capitalism is the driving mechanism in many *films noirs*, even when the films were made in colour as with *Chinatown* and *The Two Jakes* which complement and inform Davis's account of the development of Los Angeles in *City of Quartz* (1990). Mike Royko's *Boss* (1988) is an account of machine politics in Chicago in the Fordist era. The role of the city as the locus of revolutionary change is conveyed in Eisenstein's *1917*. The long slow processes of social reform do not have the same dramatic character but films of the 1930s, especially dramatisations of the novels of A. J. Cronin, *The*

Citadel (1996) and *The Stars Look Down* (1989) show something of the origins of social concern and the alliance between progressive professionals and the organised working class. Contemporary social movements are not well represented in fictional forms, at least in English language material known to me, although Callenbach's *Ecotopia* (1978) represents a Utopian vision of the 1970s set in a 1999 which has most certainly not come to pass. Kim Stanley Robinson's near future novels of Orange County (1989, 1995) do have a strong political content which describes what is rather well.

Conclusion: the trajectory of complex cities into the 21st century

> just as the central tenets of modernist thought have been undermined, its core evacuated and replaced by a rush of competing epistemologies, so too have the traditional logics of earlier urbanisms evaporated, and in the absence of a single new imperative, multiple urban (ir)rationalities are competing to fill the void. It is the concretization and localization of these effects, global in scope but generated and manifested locally, that are creating the geographies of postmodern society – a new space-time fabric. (Dear and Flusty, 1998: 50)

> it is the absence over time of a singular logic or trajectory to cities which pushes to the fore the many different stories, the many diverse futures, which meet up and coexist within cities. (Allen *et al.*, 1999: 5)

There is something missing from contemporary urban theory – planning. Of course planning is not wholly absent from accounts of the urban but most urban theorists do not see their work as being about the provision of a scientific basis for planning, with planning understood as a process by which human beings, through the production of a built environment in relation to a natural environment, create the basis of their future social world. Urban theory will criticise planning – it will generate critiques until they are coming out of your ears – but it will not inform planning. It will screech like a whole flock of Minerva's owls, but it will not guide. And it will not guide because it has no certainty at its core. It has no general account to offer of how cities work, as a basis for saying how they might be made to work.

Well, so far as positivism is concerned with its mechanical and linear 'certain' prediction, many of us will happily say 'good riddance to bad rubbish' in terms of the application of that approach outside the very limited, but nonetheless important, domain of linearity in the world. That leaves us with a problem, or rather it leaves those of us with a notion that there is an inherent and necessary connection between knowledge and progress with a problem. The contemplative owls can screech to their hearts' content. Can we bring reason to bear on these issues, in a way which does handle the complexity and *consequent* (let me emphasise that emphasis) diversity of the urban world? Has urban theory anything to offer in answer to Wyatt's *cri de coeur*:

> Unlike their academic cousins, planning practitioners have seldom had the luxury of 'retreating from rationality'. They have always had a job to do rationally; in this job they were once comprehensively assisted by researchers into computer aided planning techniques. Yet the intensity of academia's retreat from rationality and the popularity of its rejection of 'rational comprehensiveness' have tended to inhibit such assistance for at least two decades. (1996: 639)

My conception of who are legitimately 'planners' might go somewhat beyond what Wyatt had in mind – we old 'new left' community workers tend to think that the popular masses should have a say, indeed the say, in these things. However, we certainly agree on the need for 'science', science as *nauk*, here.

Wyatt was writing a guest editorial for *Environment and Planning B* (*Planning and Design*). E+P B articles frequently reference the theory debates, but they do something different with them. They set them in the context of making things happen. In order to do this, many of the authors of those articles have taken up the ideas of complexity theory and the implications of its nonlinear conception of the project of science. Prigogine (a Nobel Prize winning physical chemist) summarises these implications in his foreword to a book by Allen, a physicist come to the urban through a concern with the environmental:

> instead of seeing the geographical patterns of economic activity and settlement as being fixed, the models and studies presented here demonstrate that these can be generated by the non-linearities of the interactions between local actors together with their social and cultural preferences, and that they affect in turn the functional organization and effectiveness of the economic system, and the opportunities and pressures that fashion people's preferences. In other words, they show that cities and regions are 'self-organizing' systems, where the interplay of system feedbacks and historical events shape the evolutionary process, and both the overall performance and multiple local experiences that emerge. (in Allen, 1997: x)

Prigogine is perhaps paying too much tribute to micro-economics with this talk of preferences, but the general idea is clear. We have available a systemic account which is exactly about how general principles of organisation produce local variation, but which, and this is the really important thing, do not say that there is an infinite variety of variants available but rather that there are certain possibilities and that action will result in one rather than another of those possibilities becoming real.

Cilliers summarises the explanatory approach of complexity theory thus:

> The most obvious conclusion drawn from this perspective is that there is no over-arching theory of complexity that allows us to ignore the contingent aspects of complex systems. If something really is complex, it cannot be adequately described by means of a simple theory. Engaging with complexity entails engaging with specific complex systems. Despite this we can, at a very basic level, make general remarks concerning the conditions for complex behaviour and the dynamics of complex systems. Furthermore, I suggest that complex systems can be modelled. (1998: ix)

The implications of this passage seem to me to be identical to (a slightly modified version of) Pawson and Tilley's (1997) description of realist causation:

$$\text{Mechanism @ Context} \Rightarrow \text{condition state}$$

Overarching generative mechanism – here globalised informational capitalism in interaction with specific context, here everything contained within the structuralist idea of locality, generates condition state. However, that story is incomplete and needs a further modification:

$$\text{Mechanism @ Context} \Rightarrow \text{the possible set of condition states}$$

In other words, taken globalising informational capitalism as a given, then in any specific local context there is a set of more than one but less than a large number possible outcomes for that place. The task of planning in this framework is to engage in action which will shift a particular place into the 'best possible' (with what is the 'best possible' being a matter of political dispute) attractor trajectory.

Allen puts it like this:

> these models can be used as a basis for planning the development of a region or city towards some desired goal. But of course the models cannot tell us what these goals should be. They can, however, show us what might be possible and how our end might be achieved, and, perhaps more importantly, can show that there are internal contradictions in the system which will prevent the achievement of certain idealized goals. (1997: xv)

These kinds of approaches are only just coming into use in urban science. Garnsey (1998) used Allen's models to explain the genesis of high technology milieu. Her paper illustrates something which Allen addresses explicitly as an issue. We can see this kind of mathematical formalising of non-linear models as very valuable in tracing the path of what Gould (1991) calls the contingent development of history. When we try to get beyond this, we have to bring in human agency. As Allen says, for someone with a background in conventional science: 'It is somewhat disquieting to realize that the model we are going to build will contain the behaviour of actors, which will depend in turn on the models available to them, which will include this one' (1997: 178). Reflexivity indeed!

Allen's suggestions for quantitative model building are fascinating and this kind of approach will certainly be an important part of our approach to understanding the urban in the future. It is important to note that these approaches are possible, only because we have the technology to simulate and model. As Cilliers puts it: 'At the heart of the matter . . . our technologies have become more powerful than our theories . . . We can do with technology what we cannot do with science' (1998: 1–2). Whether we use equations with noise employed to generate perturbations or other iconological approaches, these representational models are extremely important. The underlying account of them is profoundly different from that of traditional reductionist linear science.

I want to equate these local simulations with their quantitative basis with another approach to understanding the urban which on the face of it seems completely different and indeed antithetical – the case study history of particular places. Two examples which will serve are Davis's (1990) account of Los Angeles and Cybriwsky's (1998) account of Tokyo. Both are stories of very specific places with absolutely distinctive local histories. Indeed Davis's later book

(1998) is about history in interaction with both ecology and geomorphology – about Los Angeles as a place with a specific nature as well as a specific history. At the same time these places in their contemporary form are absolutely embedded within the global system. Los Angeles was a product of the world system. Tokyo was one of the last major cities on earth connected to that world system by the forceful persuasion of the US Navy in the mid-nineteenth century. In Davis's and Cybriwsky's books, we find the narrative history of the interactions of these local contexts with the world and then global system, coupled with intense and vivid description of the actual character of the places as they are now and as they are changing in a globalised world. For me, the mathematical models and simulations based around the idea of complex systems, and the text form narrative history / descriptive account individual and ideographic studies, are essentially two sides of the same coin. Note that both approaches allow for something general which matters for the local. The interesting question is whether the local can matter for the general.

Although Dear and Flusty (1998) entitle their article 'Postmodern Urbanism', its postmodern aspect is certainly not its epistemological foundation. With their interesting idea of 'keno capitalism' – based on the character of the Japanese keno game card – they are fully into the grand narrative mode. The spatial organisation of the keno city seems fragmented and disorganised with an almost random distribution of spatial elements. However, beyond the actual space, of the card in the game, there are determinant factors – in the game the rules, in keno capitalism the accumulation logic of flexible capitalism. This approach is absolutely compatible with a complexity founded description. We have mechanism (flexible capitalism) interacting with context (specific locality) and generating form in the way characteristic of urban complex systems.

The elements of keno capitalism have much in common with Castells's account of informational capitalism: in essence we have an account in which there is no coherent oppositional principle. In this sense we are dealing with an end of history, not in the sense that there is an end to change: on the contrary, the perturbations of frenzied capitalism, even more apparent in the keno world than in the world Schumpeter originally described, will drive the system forward. What is absent is a coherent alternative collective political vision.

The necessary localism of the complex account might seem to suggest that there is no space, no possible attractor for the global system, in which the issues which inform local politics and policies can cohere to present a global alternative to the consumption-based consent to capitalism as an economic system which dominates political forms. *There really is no alternative.* So an urban world continues whilst the urban proletarian vision of an alternative future dies.

However, the complexity account is not so pessimistic, precisely because it is not reductionist. Allen (1997: 235) notes that causality is not one way. In other words, actions at the local level can have transformational implications for global level. This matters a great deal. The best way of grasping how this might work is by a consideration of the idea of 'crisis'. The word means 'turning point' (see O'Connor, 1982) and originates in Greek medicine to describe that point in time at which a patient either gets better or dies, an entirely accurate account of the development of an acute infectious disease in which either the patient's immune system overcomes the disease or vice versa. Crisis is not a condition which can be maintained. Things must change.

Since Marx, the idea of crisis has been understood essentially in terms of the character of the economic system of production and reproduction, although the Frankfurt School extended this in a cultural direction with the role of the state in much Frankfurt School derived work being understood as negative feedback to damp down crisis-inducing tendencies. Government acts to keep things within limits. Governors are exactly negative feedback systems in engineering. However, this is all about avoiding crisis. It is not about taking the system through a crisis to a new desired state (understood as an attractor trajectory). The original approach of Keynes, which established the governance mechanisms of Fordism in the aftermath of a global citizen army fought war, was such a shift but we have not seen one since. Indeed the idea of economic crisis as a threat to the survival of capitalism as an economic system seems to have been displaced by a Schumpeterian understanding of crisis as the basis of continuing capitalist reconstruction.

However, if simple economic crises seem no longer negative, then the potential for transformational crisis in the inter-relationships among the social, cultural, economic and natural is quite another matter. In the urban/global world, then the place of such crises must be in the urban system where all these things come together and, to use the form of words we must always employ when thinking dynamically, happen together. Plainly we have something like an urban crisis on our hands. In the UK, in the industrial north of England we seem to be experiencing what Power and Mumford have described as *The Slow Death of Great Cities?* (1999). Note the question mark. Power and Mumford's examination of tendencies in large parts of Newcastle and Manchester, neighbourhoods not of 'new' ethnic minorities but of the amalgam of English, Irish and Scottish (in Manchester, even Welsh) which make up the 'traditional white working class' of the industrial north of England, demonstrates that if things go on as they are, these areas may be abandoned. They are already so dilapidated and disordered that they seem to have no coherent future as they are. These are two of the oldest cities of industrial capitalism. Is this a general future, because in the Manchester and Tyneside regions, no less than in Los Angeles, it is possible to find citadels of the rich as well as ghettos of the poor. The interesting and important thing about the North of England, industrial capitalism's birthplace, is that the crucial crisis is cultural – fragmentation and destruction of industrial and labourist cultures which were the source of oppositional and transformational social democracy. New 'Labour' is not an oppositional or transformational force against globalisation. The discontents of people in these places currently have no voice.

It is interesting that the discontents which are being voiced centre precisely on the ecological implications of unfettered globalisation but have now been extended by those arguing for 'the sustainable city' to include the social implications of 'ubiquitous social polarisation', a key component of the Los Angeles model of the urban future (see Dear and Flusty, 1998: 50). The level at which these arguments are being conducted is important: it is essentially ideological, with ideology understood here in the general sense of different visions of the possible future. The failure of linear-based planning models really matters here. The absence of a coherent frame of understanding of the urban in the 1980s led to the triumphalism of the market, a notion that in a world of indeterminate chaos the only viable decision-making process which would optimise welfare was the free market. In reality, urban regimes used market ideologies as a gloss to cover massive subsidies to development capital, and in any event property-led development has been a disaster, but the ideological hegemony of the assertion of the failure of planning rationality persists. This is the great advantage of the complexity approach: it offers a rational but not deterministic programme and it makes the use of that programme in a political way absolutely explicit.

Bookchin summarises the present situation for those old-fashioned political modernists, like the present author, who see the purpose of knowledge as progress:

> Unless we are to agree that the present competitive, accumulative, and agonistic society, in which each individual is unavoidably embattled with his or her neighbours or co-workers for survival is the 'end of history' – namely, the best social system humanity can achieve over the long course of its history – I submit that we must counterpose public power to realities of oligarchical power. By this I mean that we must counterpose an emerging *political* power, based on a direct popular citizens' democracy, to the *state* power exercised by various parliaments, ministries, and republics, not to speak of overtly authoritarian forms of coercive rule. (1995: 3)

Revolutions mean, to use the language of 1649, that the world gets turned upside down. Things become very different. The important thing about the urban at the end of the twentieth century is that we will only understand it by changing it, and that rationality has a role, provided it is an emergent rationality with due regard for its own social location. Gouldner had something interesting to say about this, even if we need to replace his heroic individual with collective actors and realise that actors have to act as well as live, make as well as exist.

> Reflexive Sociology is and would need to be a radical sociology. Radical because it would recognize that knowledge of the world cannot be advanced apart from the sociologist's knowledge of himself and his position in the social world, or apart from his efforts to change these. Radical, because it seeks to transform as well as to know the alien world outside the sociologist as well as the alien world within him. Radical, because it would accept the fact that the roots of sociology pass through the sociologist as a total man, and that the question he [*sic*] must confront, therefore, is not merely how to *work* but how to *live*. (Gouldner, 1971: 489)

We live in an urban world – it is up to us what we make of it. Complexity offers us a way of systematically understanding the urban so that we can see what we might make of it. If there is to be project of a future different from that of postindustrial capitalism in its present form, then the agents for that project will have to be collective. I have always felt that if we are going to experience a Brazilianisation of advanced capitalism, then we are likely to have something to learn from the Brazilian popular masses. We could go a long way and do worse than imitate the forms of basal social organisation which have created the Workers' Party as a real opponent of globalising postindustrial capitalism.

It is plain that any such social organisation must have a combination of ecological and social objectives and will be based on a fusion of communal organisations concerned with issues of social reproduction, green organisations with environmental goals, and organisations of workers; just like the Workers' Party in fact. Also, just like the Workers' Party, it must draw on the resources of popular urban communal cultures – the devices for surviving transformed into ways of changing. We must use both science and culture constructively here.

Radical progress throughout modernity has used science as a way of informing its actions. Certainly any use of science must be dialogical, must not impose an account on people but should instead be a tool for them to help them choose and make their choices become real. I think we have the prospect of such a science now and we might be able to do something with it. I certainly hope so – mild optimism of both will and intellect.

Notes

Introduction

1. In English, 'science' is usually considered to include observation of what is, for example, in ecology and palaeontology, but the controlled experiment is still privileged as the 'best' method to which other strategies approximate.
2. My *Complexity Theory and the Social Sciences: An Introduction* (Byrne, 1998) provides an elaborated discussion of this approach.
3. There is a substantial 'feminist' literature on the urban but much of this is located within a cultural studies tradition and involves an argument with the gendered character of the idea of *flâneur*. The *flâneur* is not a significant figure in this text. More to the point much of the argument in this book is about the social differentiation which is consequent on the transformation of industrial into postindustrial capitalism. There is certainly a gendered process but not in any simple sense, precisely because most adult women live in households with men, although not necessarily with dependent children. I have addressed these issues more fully in Byrne, 1999a.

Chapter 2

1. This term as used here is due to Gramscii who derived it from military theory. A war of position is one typified by the First World War in which two nearly equal sides grind at each other without much in the way of change in territorial control. The idea is very close to Schumpeter's notion of countervailing power. In a war of position, a blitzkrieg, one side breaks through, disorganises the enemy, gains control of much more territory, and usually (unless the enemy is Russia) wins. The whole strategic picture is transformed.
2. The centrality of the word structure in systemic accounts of the social is a real problem. If systems are dynamic then they change. Structures are either fixed in position or broken down in a complete transformation. There is an analogy between the notion of accumulation of stresses in a structure and processes of transformation, but even that is too static. The proper comparison for the social is a dynamic ecosystem but there is no

simple term for the general category of far from equilibric systems to which both societies and ecosystems belong.

Chapter 5

1. Most importantly these are the abolition of taxation (Schedule A Tax) in 1963 of the imputed income derived from living in your own home whilst retaining the right to charge mortgage interest as an expense against income; and the replacement of general needs subsidies from the central exchequer to council housing revenue accounts with subsidies targeted on low income families through rent rebates. Now rather low income people who are just above the means-test level but live in social housing subsidise the rent rebates of their poorer neighbours to the tune of more than £1 billion a year.

Chapter 6

1. Although we should note that when we examine real history in real places, we find far less of a qualitative break between industrial and postindustrial production and consumption of signs and aesthetic goods than abstract theory suggests. Certainly this is true of the productions of representation in the built environment and it is equally true of many much more epiphenomenal commodities. Glennie (1998: 945) makes this point clearly, noting that for many historians we find merely differences of degree here.
2. For me the problem with Harvey's account is that it leaves labour, or rather class, almost entirely out of the story (see Byrne 1995b). The result is certainly an economic determinism, but it is a determinism devoid of agency. In other words I don't think Harvey is wrong to turn to Marxism as a meta-theory, but instead think that he is using the wrong sort of Marxism! This is not to deny some saliency to the politics of identity and otherness and to ignore their potential and significance, but when push comes to shove it seems to be class that counts.

Chapter 7

1. Including 'radical' academics. Such radicals may not be actively engaged on personal terms with the developers but 'radical' ideas about post-industrial cities actually provide much of the rationale for postindustrial urban development.

Bibliography

Albrow, M. (1997) 'Travelling Beyond Local Cultures: Socioscapes in a Global City', in J. Eade (ed.)

Allen, J., Massey, D. and Pryke, M. (eds) (1999) *Unsettling Cities* (London: Routledge)

Allen, P. (1997) *Cities and Regions as Self-Organizing Systems* (Amsterdam: Gordon and Breach)

Ambrose, P. (1986) *Whatever Happened to Planning?* (London: Methuen)

Ambrose, P. (1994) *Urban Process and Power* (London: Routledge)

Amin, A. (ed.) (1992) *Post-Fordism* (Oxford: Blackwell)

Amin, A. and Thrift, N. (1992) 'Neo-Marshallian Nodes in Global Networks', *International Journal of Urban and Regional Research*, 16(4): 571–87

Anderson, J., Duncan, S. and Hudson, R. (eds) (1983) *Redundant Spaces in Cities and Regions* (London: Academic Press)

Angotti, T. (1993) *Metropolis* (London: Routledge)

Appadurai, A. (1990) 'Disjuncture and Difference in the Global Cultural Economy' in M. Featherstone (ed.) *Cultural Theory and Cultural Change* (London: Sage)

Auyero, J. (1997) 'Wacquant in the Argentine Slums', *International Journal of Urban and Regional Research*, 27(2): 508–11

Bagguley, P., Mark-Lawson, J., Shapiro, D., Urry, J., Walby, S. and Warde, A. (1990) *Restructuring: Place, Class and Gender* (London: Sage)

Ball, M. (1988) *Rebuilding Construction* (Routledge: London)

Ball, M. (1996) *Housing and Construction: A Troubled Relationship* (Bristol: Policy Press)

Banai, R. (1995) 'Critical Realism in Urban and Regional Studies', *Environment and Planning B (Planning and Design)* 22(3): 563–80

Bashi, V. and Hughes, M. (1997) 'Globalization and residential segregation by race', *Annals of the American Academy of Social and Political Science*, 551:105–20

Batty, M. (1995) 'Cities and Complexity: Implications for Modelling Sustainability' in J. Brotchie *et al.* (eds) *Cities in Competition* (Sydney: Longman Australia)

Batty, M. and Xie, Y. (1997) 'Possible Urban Automata', *Environment and Planning B (Planning and Design)* 24: 275–92

Bauman, Z. (1998) *Work, Consumerism and the New Poor* (Buckingham: Open University Press)

Beauregard, R. A. (1995) 'Theorizing the Global-Local Connection', in P. L. Knox and P. J. Taylor (eds) *World Cities in a World System* (Cambridge: Cambridge University Press)

Beaverstock, J. V. (1994) 'Rethinking Skilled International Labour Migration', *Geoforum*, 25(3): 323–38

Beaverstock, J. V., Taylor, P. J. and Smith, R. G. (1999) 'A Roster of World Cities', *Cities*, 16(6): 445–58

Beirne, P. (1977) *Fair Rent and Legal Fiction: Housing Rent Legislation in a Capitalist Society* (London: Macmillan)

Bell, C. (1969) *Middle Class Families* (London: Routledge and Kegan Paul)

Bely, A. (1916, 1983) *Petersburg* (London: Penguin)

Berlin, I. (1968) *Four Essays on Liberty* (London: Oxford University Press)

Bhaskar, R. (1986) *Scientific Realism and Human Emancipation* (London: Verso)

Blasiak, W., Tomasz, N. and Szczepanski, M. (1994) *Upper Silesia 2005: the Restructuring Scenario* (Katowice: Editions AMP)

Boddy, M., Lambert, C. and Snape, D. (1997) *City for the 21st Century* (Bristol: Policy Press)

Bogart, W. T. and Ferry, W. C. (1999) 'Employment Centres in Greater Cleveland: Evidence of Evolution in a Formerly Monocentric City', *Urban Studies*, 36(12): 2099–110

Bookchin, M. (1995) *From Urbanization to Cities* (London: Cassell)

Boone, C. G. (1998) 'Real Estate Promotion and the Shaping of Los Angeles', *Cities*, 15(3): 155–63

Boyle, M., Findlay, A., Lelievre, E. and Paddison, R. (1996) 'World Cities and the Limits to Global', *International Journal of Urban and Regional Research*, 20(3): 498–517

Brenner, N. (1999) 'Globalization as Reterritorialization', *Urban Studies*, 36(3): 431–51

Brody, H. (1986) *Inishkillane* (London: Faber and Faber)

Brotchie, J., Batty, M., Blakely, E., Hall, P. and Newton, P. (eds) (1995) *Cities in Competition* (Sydney: Longman Australia)

Burrows, R. (1999) 'Residential Mobility and Residualisation in Social Housing in England', *Journal of Social Policy*, 28(1): 27–52

Byrne, D. S. (1980) 'The Decline in the Standard of Council Housing in Inter-War North Shields', in J. Melling, (ed.) *Housing, Social Policy and the State* (London: Croom Helm)

Byrne, D. S. (1982) 'Class and the Local State', *International Journal of Urban and Regional Research*, 6(1): 61–82

Byrne, D. S. (1989) *Beyond the Inner City* (Milton Keynes: Open University Press)

Byrne, D. S. (1993) 'Property Development and Petty Markets versus Maritime Industrialism', in R. Imrie and H. Thomas, (eds) *British Urban Policy and the Urban Development Corporations* (London: Paul Chapman)

Byrne, D. S. (1995a) 'Deindustrialization and Dispossession', *Sociology*, 29: 95–116

Byrne, D. S. (1995b) 'Radical Geography as "Mere Political Economy" – The Local Politics of Space', *Capital and Class*, 56: 117–38

Byrne, D. S. (1997) 'Chaotic Places or Complex Places: Cities in a Post-Industrial Era', in S. Westwood and J. Williams (eds) *Imagining Cities* (London: Routledge)

Byrne, D. S. (1998) *Complexity Theory and the Social Sciences* (London: Routledge)

Byrne, D. S. (1999a) *Social Exclusion* (Buckingham: Open University Press)

Byrne, D. S. (1999b) 'Tyne and Wear UDC – Turning the Uses Inside Out: Active Deindustrialization and its Consequences', in R. Imrie and H. Thomas (eds) *British Urban Policy and the Urban Development Corporation* (London: Paul Chapman)

Byrne, D. S. and Parson, D. (1983) 'The State and the Reserve Army', in J. Anderson *et al.* (eds) *Redundant Spaces in Cities and Regions* (London: Academic Press)

Byrne, D. S., and Wodz, K. (1997) 'La Désindustrialization dans les Villes Industrielles en Déclin', in A. Martens and M. Vervaeke (eds) *La Polarisation Sociale des Villes Européannes* (Paris: Anthropos)

Caldeira, T. (1996) 'Building up Walls: The New Pattern of Spatial Segregation in São Paulo' *International Social Science Journal* 48(1): 55–68

Callaghan, G. (1998) '*Deindustrialization, Class and Gender – Young Adults in Sunderland*', unpublished Ph.D. thesis, University of Durham

Callenbach, E. (1978) *Ecotopia* (London: Pluto Press)

Campbell, B. (1993) *Goliath* (London: Methuen)

Castells, M. (1977) *The Urban Question* (London: Edward Arnold)

Castells, M. (1978) *City, Class and Power* (London: Macmillan)

Castells, M. (1983) *The City and the Grassroots* (London: Edward Arnold)

Castells, M. (1996) *The Rise of the Network Society* (Oxford: Blackwell)

Castells, M. (1997) *The Power of Identity* (Oxford: Blackwell)

Castells, M. (1998) *The End of the Millennium* (Oxford: Blackwell)

Charlesworth, J. and Cochrane, A. (1997) 'Anglicising the American Dream', in S. Westwood and J. Williams (eds) *Imagining Cities* (London: Routledge)

Chow, J. and Coulton, C. (1998) 'Was There a Social Transformation of Urban Neighbourhoods in the 1980s? A Decade of Worsening Social Conditions in Cleveland, Ohio, USA', *Urban Studies*, 35(8): 1359–75

Cilliers, P. (1998) *Complexity and Postmodernism* (London: Routledge)

Clark, D. (1996) *Urban World: Global City* (London: Routledge)

Clarke, S. E. and Gaile, G. L. (1997) 'Local Politics in a Global Era: Thinking Locally, Acting Globally', *The Annals of the American Academy of Political and Social Science*, 551: 44–58

Cleaver, H. (1977) 'Malaria, the Politics of Public Health and the International Crisis', *Review of Radical Political Economy* 9: 81–103

Cleaver, H. (1979) *Reading Capital Politically* (Brighton: Harvester Press)

Clements, R. (1969) *Local Notables and the City Council* (London: Macmillan)

Cochrane, A. (1993) *Whatever Happened to Local Government?* (Milton Keynes: Open University Press)

Cohen, A. (1985) *The Symbolic Construction of Community* (London: Tavistock)

Coleman, D. and Salt, J. eds (1996) *Ethnicity in the 1991 Census*, Vol. 1 (London: HMSO)

Cooke, P. (1985) 'Class Practices as Regional Markers', in D. Gregory and J. Urry (eds) *Social Relations and Spatial Structures* (London: Macmillan)

Cooke, P. (ed.) (1989) *Localities* (London: Unwin Hyman)

Cox, K. and Mair, A. (1987) 'Levels of Abstraction in Locality Studies', *Antipode*, 21(1): 121–32

Cronin, A. J. (1989) *The Stars Look Down* (Sevenoaks: New English Library)

Cronin, A. J. (1996) *The Citadel* (London: Vista)

Crowe, G. and Allan, G. (1994) *Community Life* (London: Harvester-Wheatsheaf)

Cybriwsky, R. (1998) *Tokyo* (Chichester: John Wiley)

Dale, A. and Marsh, C. (1993) *The 1991 Census User's Guide* (London: HMSO)

Das, P. K. and Gonsalves, C. (1987) *The Struggle for Housing: A People's Manifesto* (Bombay: Nivarak Hakk Suraksha Samiti)

Davies, J. G. (1974) *The Evangelistic Bureaucrats* (London: Tavistock)

Davis, M. (1990) *City of Quartz* (London: Verso)

Davis, M. (1998) *Ecology of Fear* (New York: Metropolitan Books)

Day, G. and Murdoch, J. (1993) 'Locality and Community: Coming to Terms with Place', *Sociological Review*, 41(1): 82–111

Deakin, N. and Edwards, J. (1993) *The Enterprise Culture and the Inner City* (London: Routledge)

Dear, M. J. (2000) *The Postmodern Urban Condition* (Oxford: Blackwell)

Dear, M. J. and Flusty, S. (1998) 'Postmodern Urbanism', *Annals of the Association of American Geographers*, 88(1): 50–72

Dennis, N. (1970) *People and Planning* (London: Faber)

Dennis, N. (1972) *Public Participation and Planners' Blight* (London: Faber)

Dennis, N., Henriques, F. and Slaughter, C. (1969) *Coal is Our Life* (London: Tavistock)

Dick, H. W. and Rimmer, P. J. (1998) 'Beyond the Third World City', *Urban Studies*, 35(12): 2303–21

Dickens, C. (1995) *Hard Times* (Oxford: Heinemann)

Dickens, P., Duncan, S., Goodwin, M. and Gray, F. (1985) *Housing, States and Localities* (London: Methuen)

Dimonte, D. (1998) 'Redevelopment of Mumbai's Cotton Textile Land: Opportunity Lost', *Economic and Political Weekly*, 33(6): 283–90

Dos Passos, J. (1925, 1987) *Manhattan Transfer* (Penguin: London)

Duncan, O. D. (1964) 'Human Ecology and Population Studies', in Farris, R. E. L. (ed.) *Handbook of Modern Sociology* (Chicago: Rand MacNally)

Duncan, S. (1986) 'What is Locality?', *Working Papers in Urban and Regional Studies*, 51 (Brighton: University of Sussex)

Duncan, S. (1989) 'What is Locality?', in R. Peet and N. Thrif, N. (eds) *New Models in Geography* (London: Edward Arnold)

Duncan, S. and Goodwin, M. (1988) *The Local State and Uneven Development* (Cambridge: Polity)

Dunleavy, P. (1980) 'The Political Implications of Sectoral Cleavages and the Growth of State Employment', *Political Studies*, 28: 364–83

Dunleavy, P. (1981) *The Politics of Mass Housing in Britain 1945–1975* (Oxford: Clarendon Press)

Dunleavy, P. (1986) 'The Growth of State Expenditures and the Stabilization of Sectoral Cleavages', *Environment and Planning D (Society and Space)*, 4: 129–44

Eade, J. (ed.) (1997) *Living the Global City* (London: Routledge)

Eder, K. (1993) *The New Politics of Class* (London: Sage)

Edinburgh–London Weekend Return Group (1980) *In and Against the State* (London: Conference of Socialist Economists)

Ekström, M. (1992) 'Causal Explanation of Social Action', *Acta Sociologica*, 35: 107–22

Emirbayer, M (1997) 'Manifesto for a Relational Sociology', *American Journal of Sociology*, 103(2). 281–317

Fainstein, S. (1994) *The City Builders* (Oxford: Blackwell)

Fainstein, S. and Campbell, S. (eds) (1996) *Readings in Urban Theory* (Oxford: Blackwell)

Fainstein, S., Gordon, I. and Harloe, M. (eds) (1992) *Divided Cities* (Oxford: Blackwell)

Farrar, M. (1997) 'Migrant Spaces and Settlers Time', in S. Westwood and J. Williams (eds) *Imagining Cities* (London: Routledge)

Farris, R. E. L. (ed.) (1964) *Handbook of Modern Sociology* (Chicago: Rand MacNally)

Featherstone, M. (ed.) (1992) *Cultural Theory and Cultural Change* (London: Sage)

Featherstone, M. and Lash, S. 'Globalization, Modernity and the Spatialization of Social Theory', in Featherstone, M. *et al.* (eds) *Global Modernities* (London: Sage)

Featherstone, M., Lash, S. and Robertson, R. (eds) (1995) *Global Modernities* (London: Sage)

Firman, T. (1998) 'The Restructuring of Jakarta Metropolitan Area', *Cities*, 15(4): 229–43

Fitch, R. (1993) *The Assassination of New York* (London: Verso)

Forrest, R., Murie, A. and Williams, P. (1990) *Home Ownership: Differentiation and Fragmentation* (London: Unwin Hyman)

Forsyth, A. (1999) *Constructing Suburbs* (Amsterdam: Gordon and Breach)

Frankel, B. (1987) *The Postindustrial Utopians* (Oxford: Blackwell)

Frankenberg, R. (1966) *Communities in Britain* (London: Penguin)

Friedmann, J. (1986) 'The World City Hypothesis', *Development and Change*, 17: 69–83

Friedmann, J. (1996) 'On the Writing of "The World City Hypothesis"', *Scottish Geographical Magazine*, 112(2): 127–8

Gans, H. (1962) *The Urban Villagers* (New York: Free Press)

Gans, H. (1968) *The Levittowners* (London: Allen Lane)

Garnsey, E. (1998) 'The Genesis of the High Technology Milieu: A Study in Complexity', *International Journal of Urban and Regional Research*, 22(3): 361–77

Garreau, J. (1992) *Edge City* (New York: Doubleday)

Gaskell, E. (1993) *Mary Barton* (Halifax: Ryburn)

Geddes, M. (1997) *Partnership Against Poverty and Exclusion?* (Bristol: Policy Press)

Gibbon, Lewis Grassic (1995) *A Scots Quair* (Edinburgh: Canongate)

Giddens, A. (1984) *The Constitution of Society* (Cambridge: Polity Press)

Glennie, P. (1998) 'Consumption, Consumerism and Urban Form: Historical Perspectives' *Urban Studies* 35: 5–6 927–51

Gorz, A. (1982) *Farewell to the Working Class* (London: Pluto Press)

Gorzelak, G. (1996) *The Regional Dimension of Transformation in Central Europe* (London: Jessica Kingsley)

Gould, B. and Smith, D. (1998) 'Introduction to Special Issue on Labour, Society and Sustainable Urbanization in South-East Asia', *Third World Planning Review*, 20(2): i–x

Gould, S. J. (1991) *Wonderful Life: The Burgess Shale and the Nature of History* (London: Penguin)

Gouldner, A. W. (1971) *The Coming Crisis of Western Sociology* (London: Heinemann)

Graham, J. (1992) 'Post-Fordism as Politics', *Society and Space* (*Environment and Planning D*), 10(2): 393–410

Green, D. G. (1980) *Power and Party in an English City* (London: Allen and Unwin)

Greene, R. P. (1997) 'Chicago's New Immigrants, Indigenous Poor, and Edge Cities', *The Annals of the American Academy of Political and Social Science*, 551: 178–90

Gregory, D. and Urry, J. (eds) (1985) *Social Relations and Spatial Structures* (London: Macmillan)

Haas, P. (1992) 'Introduction: Epistemic Communities and International Policy Coordination', *International Organization*, 46(1): 1–36

Hall, P. (1966) *The World Cities* (London: Weidenfeld and Nicolson)

Hall, S. (1981) 'Notes on Deconstructing the Popular', in R. Samuel (ed.) *People's History and Socialist Theory* (London: Routledge and Kegan Paul)

Halliwell's Film and Video Guide (London: HarperCollins)

Hamnett, C. (1996) 'Social Polarization, Economic Restructuring, and Welfare State Regimes', *Urban Studies*, 33(8): 1407–30

Hannigan, J. (1998) *Fantasy City* (London: Routledge)

Hardy, T. (1994) *Far From the Madding Crowd* (London: Penguin)

Harris, N. (1995) 'Bombay in a Global Economy', *Cities*, 12(3): 175–84

Harvey, D. (1985) *The Urbanization of Capital* (Oxford: Blackwell)

Harvey, D. (1989) *The Condition of Postmodernity* (Oxford: Blackwell)

Harvey, D. L. and Reed, M. H. (1996) 'The Culture of Poverty: An Ideological Analysis', *Sociological Perspectives*, 39(4). 465–95

Healey, P., Davoudi, S., O'Toole, M., Tavsanoglu, S. and Usher, D. (eds) (1992) *Rebuilding the City* (London: E. and F. N. Spon.)

Hewett, D. (1959, 1989) *Bobbin Up* (London: Virago)

Hollingsworth, J. R. (1998) 'New Perspectives on the Spatial Dimensions of Economic Coordination', *Review of International Political Economy*, 5(3): 482–501

Hudson, M. (1994) *Coming Back Brockens: A Year in a Mining Village* (London: Cape)

Imrie, R. (1997) 'National Economic Policy in the United Kingdom', in M. Paccione (ed.) *Britain's Cities* (London: Routledge)

Imrie, R. and Raco, M. (1999) 'How New Is the New Local Government? Lessons From the UK', *Transactions of the Institute of British Geographers*, 24(1): 45–63

Imrie, R. and Thomas, H. (eds) (1993) *British Urban Policy and the Urban Development Corporations* (London: Paul Chapman)

Imrie, R. and Thomas, H. (eds) (1999) *British Urban Policy* (London: Paul Chapman)

INURA (1999) *Possible Urban Worlds: Urban Strategies at the End of the 20th Century* (Basel: Birkhausen Verlag)

Isherwood, C. (1996) *Mr Norris Changes Trains* (London: Minerva)

Jacobs, J. (1994) 'The City Unbound: Qualitative Approaches to the City', in R. Paddison *et al.* (eds) *International Perspectives in Urban Studies* (London: Jessica Kingsley)

Jameson, F. (1984) 'Postmodernism, or the Cultural Logic of Late Capitalism', *New Left Review*, 146: 53–92

Jenkins, R. (1996) *Social Identity* (London: Routledge)

Jessop, B. (1991) 'Thatcherism and Flexibility', in Jessop, B. *et al* (eds.) *The Politics of Flexibility* (Aldershot: Edward Elgar)

Jessop, B. (1994) 'Post-Fordism and the State', in A. Amin (ed.) *Post-Fordism* (Oxford: Blackwell)

Jessop, B., Kastendiek, K., Nielsen, K. and Pedersen, O. (eds) (1991) *The Politics of Flexibility* (Aldershot: Edward Elgar)

Jones, P. W. (1989) 'Proof of Evidence of P.W. Jones – Debenham, Tewson and Chinnock Ltd – East Quayside Compulsory Purchase Order Inquiry', DOE Reference N/5038/12P/9 – 6th November 1989

Judge, D., Stoker, G. and Wolman, H. (eds) (1995) *Theories of Urban Politics* (London: Sage)

Kamdar, M. (1997) 'Bombay/Mumbai – The Postmodern City', *World Policy Journal*, 14(2): 75–88

Karn, V. (ed.) (1997) *Ethnicity in the 1991 Census: Volume 4* (London: HMSO)

Kiel, R. (1998) 'Globalization Makes States', *Review of International Political Economy*, 5(4): 616–46

King, A. D. (1990) *Global Cities: Post-Imperialism and the Internationalization of London* (London: Routledge)

King, A. D. (ed.) (1996) *Re-Presenting the City* (London: Macmillan)

Kleinberg, B. (1995) *Urban America in Transformation* (London: Sage)

Knox, P. L. (1996) 'Globalization and the World City Hypothesis', *Scottish Geographical Magazine*, 112(2): 124–6

Knox, P. L. (1997) 'Globalization and Urban Economic Change', *Annals of the American Academy of Political and Social Science*, 551: 17–27

Knox, P. L. and Taylor, P. J. (eds) (1995) *World Cities in a World System* (Cambridge: Cambridge University Press)

Lane, T. (1987) *Liverpool: Gateway of Empire* (London: Lawrence and Wishart)

Lash, S. and Urry, J. (1994) *Economies of Signs and Space* (London: Sage)

Lawless, P., Martin, R. and Hardy, S. (eds) (1998) *Unemployment and Social Exclusion* (London: Jessica Kingsley)

Lemann, N. (1991) *The Promised Land* (London: Macmillan)

Lever, W. F. (1991) 'Deindustrialisation and the Reality of the Postindustrial City', *Urban Studies*, 28: 938–69

Lewis, O. (1966) *La Vida* (New York: Random House)

Lipietz, A. (1988) 'Accumulation Crises and the Ways Out', *International Journal of Political Economy*, 18(2): 10–43

Lipietz, A. (1994) 'Post-Fordism and Democracy', in A. Amin (ed.) *Post-Fordism* (Oxford: Blackwell)

London, J. (1998) *The People of the Abyss* (London: Pluto Press)

Lovering, J. (1997) 'Global Restructuring and Local Impact', in M. Paccione (ed.) *Britain's Cities* (London: Routledge)

Lowe, S. (1986) *Global Social Movements: The City After Castells* (London: Macmillan)

Lustager-Thaler, H. and Schragge, E. (1998) 'The New Urban Left: Politics Without Actors', *International Journal of Urban and Regional Research* 22(2): 233–44

Lynd, R. S. (1959) *Middletown* (New York: Harvest Books)

Marris, R. and Rein, M. (1967) *Dilemmas of Social Reform* (London: Routledge and Kegan Paul)

Martens, A. and Vervaeke, M. (eds) (1997) *La Polarisation Sociale des Villes Européannes* (Paris: Anthropos)

Martin, R. and Rowthorn, R. (eds) (1986) *The Geography of Deindustrialization* (London: Macmillan)

Massey, D. (1984) *Spatial Divisions of Labour* (London: Edward Arnold)

Massey, D. (1991) 'The Political Place of Locality Studies', *Environment and Planning A*, 23(2): 267–81

Massey, D. S. and Denton, N. A. (1993) *American Apartheid* (Cambridge, MA: Harvard University Press)

McGuirk, P. M., Winchester, H. P. M. and Dunn, K. M. (1996) 'Entrepreneurial Approaches to Urban Decline', *Environment and Planning A*, 28(6): 1815–41

McInerney, J. (1994) *Bright Lights: Big City* (London: Penguin)

Melling, J. (ed.) (1980) *Housing, Social Policy and the State* (London: Croom Helm)

Merrett, S. (1979) *State Housing in Britain* (London: Heinmann)

Merrett, S. (1982) *Owner-Occupation in Britain* (London: Routledge and Kegan Paul)

Merrifield, A. (1993) 'The Canary Wharf Debacle: From TINA to THEMPA', *Environment and Planning A*, 25(6): 1247–65

Miles, S. and Paddison, R. (1998) 'Urban Consumption: A Historiographic Note', *Urban Studies*, 35(5/6): 815–23

Mingione, E. (ed.) (1996) *Urban Poverty and the Underclass* (Oxford: Blackwell)

Mollenkopf, J. (1992) *A Phoenix in the Ashes: The Rise and Fall of the Koch Coalition in New York City Politics* (Princeton: Princeton University Press)

Morenoff, J. D. and Tienda, M. (1997) 'Underclass Neighbourhoods in Temporal and Ecological Perspective', *Annals of the American Academy of Political and Social Science*, 551: 59–72

Morgan, G. (1993) 'Frustrated Respectability: Local Culture and Politics in London's Docklands', *Society and Space (Environment and Planning D)*, 11(3): 523–41

Morris, L. (1995) *Social Divisions* (London: UCL Press)

Morris, M. (1992) 'The Man in the Mirror: David Harvey's "Condition of Postmoderity"' in M. Featherstone (ed.) *Cultural Theory and Cultural Change* (London: Sage)

Mouzelis, N. (1995) *Sociological Theory: What went Wrong?* (London: Routledge)

Muller, P. O. (1997) 'The Suburban Transformation of the Globalizing American City', *Annals of the American Academy of Political and Social Science*, 551: 44–58

Murdoch, J. (1997) 'The Shifting Territory of Government', *Area*, 29(2): 109–18

Murie, A. and Forrest, R. (1980) 'Wealth Inheritance and Housing Policy', *Policy and Politics*, 8(1): 1–19

Murray, C. (1990) *The Emerging British Underclass* (London: IEA)

Myrdal, J. (1963) *Report from a Chinese Village* (London: Penguin)

Nelson, J. I. (1995) *Post-Industrial Capitalism* (London: Sage)

Newby, E. (1956) *The Last Grain Race* (London: Secker and Warburg)

O'Byrne, D. (1997) 'Working-Class Culture: Local Community and Global Conditions', in J. Eade (ed.) *Living the Global City* (London: Routledge)

O'Connor, J. (1973) *The Fiscal Crisis of the State* (New York: St Martin's Press)

O'Connor, J. (1982) 'The Meaning of Crisis', *International Journal of Urban and Regional Research* 5: 301–28

O'Hare, G., Abbott, D. and Barke, M. (1998) 'A Review of Slum Housing Problems in Mumbai', *Cities*, 15(4): 269–83

Olds, K. (1995) 'Globalization and the Production of New Urban Spaces: Pacific Rim Megapolises in the Late Twentieth Century', *Environment and Planning A*, 27(6): 1713–43

Olds, K. (1997) 'Globalizing Shanghai: The "Global Intelligence Corps" and the Building of Pudong', *Cities*, 14(2): 109–23

Paccione, M. (ed.) (1997) *Britain's Cities* (London: Routledge)

Paddison, R. (1997) 'Politics and Governance', in M. Paccionne (ed.) *Britain's Cities* (London: Routledge)

Paddison, R., Money, J. and Lever, B. (eds) (1994) *International Perspectives in Urban Studies* (London: Jessica Kingsley)

Pahl, R. (1968) 'Class and Community in an English Commuter Village', in R. Pahl (ed.) *Readings in Urban Sociology* (Oxford: Pergamon)

Pahl, R. (ed.) (1968) *Readings in Urban Sociology* (Oxford: Pergamon)

Panitch, L. (1980) 'Recent Theorisations of Corporatism', *British Journal of Sociology*, 31(1): 159–87

Park, R. E. (1952) *Human Communities* (New York: Free Press)

Park, R. E. and Burgess, E. W. (eds) (1925) *The City* (Chicago: University of Chicago Press)

Parnwell, M. and Turner, S. (1998) 'Sustaining the Unsustainable: City and Soceity in Indonesia', *Third World Planning Review*, 20(2): 147–63

Pawson, R. and Tilley, N. (1997) *Realistic Evaluation* (London: Sage)

Peach, C. (1996a) 'Does Britain Have Ghettoes?', *Trans. Inst. of Brit. Geographers*, NS **21**: 216–35

Peach, C. (ed.) (1996b) *Ethnicity in the 1991 Census, Vol 2* (London: HMSO)

Peet, R. and Thrift, N. (eds) (1989) *New Models in Geography* (London: Edward Arnold)

Pickvance, C. J. (1999) 'Democratization and the Decline of Social Movements', *Sociology*, 33(2): 353–72

Piercey, M. (1978) *The High Cost of Living* (London: Women's Press)

Piercey, M. (1998) *Small Changes* (London: Fawcett Press)

Piven, F. F. and Cloward, R. (1979) *Poor People's Movements: How They Succeed and Why They Fail* (New York: Vintage)

Power, A. and Mumford, K. (1999) *The Slow Death of Great Cities?* (York: Joseph Rowntree Foundation)

Prigogine, I. and Stengers, I. (1984) *Order out of Chaos* (New York: Bantam)

Rawlinson, R. (1850) *Report to the Board of Health on the Borough of Gateshead* (London: HMSO)

Reed, M. and Harvey, D. L. (1992) 'The New Science and the Old: Complexity and Realism in the Social Sciences', *Journal for the Theory of Social Behaviour*, 22: 356–79

Rees, P., Phillips, D. and Medway, D. (1995) 'The Socioeconomic Geography of Ethnic Groups in Two Northern British Cities', *Environment and Planning A*, 27: 557–91

Rex, J. and Moore, R. (1967) *Race, Community and Conflict* (Oxford: Oxford University Press)

Robertson, R. (1995) 'Glocalization: Time-space and Homogeneity-heterogeneity', in M. Featherstone *et al.* (eds) *Global Modernities* (London: Sage)

Robinson, K. S. (1989) *The Gold Coast* (London: Futura)

Robinson, K. S. (1995) *Pacific Edge* (London: HarperCollins)

Robson, B. (1969) *Urban Analysis* (Cambridge: Cambridge University Press)

Rose, N. (1996) 'The Death of the Social? Refiguring the Territory of Government', *Economy and Society*, 25: 327–56

Rowthorn, B. (1986) 'De-industrialization in Britain' in R. Martin and B. Rowthorn (eds) *The Geography of Deindustrialisation* (London: Macmillan)

Rowthorn, R. and Ramaswamy, R. (1997) *Deindustrialization – Its Causes and Implications* (Washington: International Monetary Fund)

Royko, M. (1988) *Boss* (New York: New American Library)

Samuel, R. (ed.) (1981) *People's History and Socialist Theory* (London: Routledge and Kegan Paul)

Sassen, S. (1994) *Cities in a World Economy* (Thousand Oaks, CA: Pine Forge Press)

Sassen, S. (1996a) 'Analytic Borderland: Race, Gender and Representation in the New City', in A. D. King (ed.) *Re-Presenting the City* (London: Macmillan)

Sassen, S. (1996b) 'Rebuilding the Global City: Economy, Ethnicity and Space', in A.D. King (ed.) *Re-Presenting the City* (London: Macmillan)

Sassen, S. (1998) 'The City: Strategic Site / New Frontiers', in INURA (1999) *Possible Urban Worlds* (Basel: Birkhausen Verlag)

Saunders, P. (1984) 'Beyond Housing Classes', *International Journal of Urban and Regional Research*, 8(2): 202–27

Saunders, P. (1986) 'Comment on Dunleavy and Pretceille', *Society and Space* (*Environment and Planning D*), 4(1): 155–63

Saunders, P. (1990) *A Nation of Home Owners* (London: Unwin Hyman)

Savage, M. and Warde, A. (1993) *Urban Sociology, Capitalism and Modernity* (London: Macmillan)

Sayer, A. (2000) *Realism and Social Science* (London: Sage)

Schachar, A. (1994) 'Randstaad Holland: A World City', *Urban Studies*, 31(3): 381–400

Schmidt, J. D. (1998) 'Globalization and Inequality in Urban South East Asia', *Third World Planning Review*, 20(2): 127–45

Schuurman, F. and Naerssen, T.V. (1989) *Urban Social Movements in the Third World* (London: Routledge)

See, L. (1999) *The Interior* (London: Century)

Serge, V. (1932, 1975) *Conquered City* (London: Readers and Writers Cooperative)

Shields, R. (1991) *Places on the Margin* (London: Routledge)

Shields, R. (1996) 'A Guide to Urban Representation and What to Do About It', in King, A. D. (ed.) *Re-Presenting the City* (London: Macmillan)

Shields, R. (1998) *Lefbvre: Love and Struggle* (London: Routledge)

Short, J., Benton, L., Luce, W. and Walton, J. (1993) 'Reconstructing the Image of an Industrial City', *Annals of the Association of American Geographers*, 83(2): 207–24

Short, J. R. (1996) *The Urban Order* (Oxford: Blackwell)

Short, J. R., Kim, Y., Klaus, M. and Wells, H. (1996) 'The Dirty Little Secret of World Cities Research', *International Journal of Urban and Regional Research*, 20(4): 696–717

Simmel, G. (1950a) 'The Metropolis and Mental Life' in G. Simmel *The Sociology of George Simmel* (New York: Free Press)

Simmel, G. (1950b) *The Sociology of Georg Simmel* (ed. K. Wolff) (New York: Free Press)

Sinclair, U. (1985) *The Jungle* (London: Penguin)

Smith, D. A. and Timberlake, M. (1995) 'Conceptualizing and Mapping the Structure of the World Systems City System', *International Journal of Urban and Regional Research*, 32(2): 287–302

Smith, M. P. (1980) *The City and Social Theory* (Oxford: Blackwell)

Smith, N. C. (1996) *The New Urban Frontier* (London: Routledge)

Stacey, M. (1969) 'The Myth of Community Studies', *British Journal of Sociology*, 20(2): 134–47

Steinen, A. (1999) 'Welcome to Medellin – Capital of the 21st Century', in INURRA *Possible Urban Worlds* (Basel: Birkhausen Verlag)

Stewart, J., Greer, A. and Hogget, P. (1995) *The Quango State: An Alternative Approach,* CLD Research Report 10 (London: Council for Local Democracy)

Stoker, G. (1995) 'Regime Theory and Urban Politics', in D. Judge, *et al.* (eds) *Theories of Urban Politics* (London. Sage)

Tagg, J. (1996) 'This City Which Is Not One', in A. D. King (ed.) *Re-Presenting the City* (London: Macmillan)

Taylor, I., Evans, K. and Fraser, P. (1996) *A Tale of Two Cities* (London: Routledge)

Therborn, G. (1985) *Why Some Peoples are More Unemployed than Others* (London: Verso)

Theroux, P. (1989) *Riding the Iron Rooster* (London: Penguin)

Thompson, E. P. (1981) 'The Politics of Theory' in R. Samuel (ed.) *People's History and Socialist Theory* (London: Routledge and Kegan Paul)

United Nations (1996) *Demographic Yearbook* (New York: United Nations)

Updike, J. (1995) *Brazil* (London: Penguin)

Urry, J. (1982) 'Some Theories in the Analysis of Contemporary Capitalist Societies', *Acta Sociologica*, 25(1): 28–48

Wacquant, L. D. (1993) 'Urban Outcasts: Stigma and Division in the Black American Ghetto and the French Urban Periphery', *International Journal of Urban and Regional Research*, 17(3): 366–83

Wacquant, L. D. (1995) 'Red Belt, Black Belt: Racial Division, Class Inequality and the State in the French Urban Periphery and the American Ghetto', in E. Mingione, (ed.) *Urban Poverty and the Underclose* (Oxford: Blackwell)

Wallerstein, I. (1974) *The Modern World System* (London: Academic Press)

Wallerstein, I. (1996) *Report of the Gulbenkian Commission on Restructuring the Social Sciences: Open the Social Sciences* (Stanford, CA. Stanford University Press)

Walton, J. (1998) 'Urban Conflict and Social Movements in Poor Countries: Theory and Evidence of Collective Action', *International Journal of Urban and Regional Research*, 22(3): 460–81

Warf, B. and Holly, B. (1997) 'The Rise and Fall and Rise of Cleveland', *The Annals of the American Academy of Political and Social Science*, 551: 208–21

Westwood, S. and Williams, J. (eds) (1997) *Imagining Cities* (London: Routledge)

Whyte, W. J. (1957) *The Organization Man* (London: Penguin)

Wikan, U. (1995) 'Sustainable Development in the Mega City', *Current Anthropology*, 36(4): 635–55

Wilkinson, S. (1992) 'Towards a New City', in P. Healey, *et al.* (eds) *Rebuilding the City* (London: E. and F. N. Spon.)

Williams, M. (1999) *Science and Social Science* (London: Routledge)

Williams, R. (1965) *The Long Revolution* (London: Penguin)

Williams, R. (1979) *Politics and Letters* (London: Verso)

Williams, R. (1980) *Problems in Materialism and Culture* (London: Verso)

Williams, R. (1983) *Towards 2000* (London: Chatto and Windus)

Williamson, W. (1982) *Class, Culture and Community* (London: Routledge and Kegan Paul)

Willmott, P. and Young, M. (1957) *Familey and Kinship in East London* (London: Routledge and Kegan Paul)

Wilson, D. (1997) 'Preface', *Annals of the American Academy of Social and Political Science*, 551: 1–17

Wilson, W. J. (1987) *The Truly Disadvantaged* (Chicago: University of Chicago Press)

Wilson, W. J. (1992) 'Another Look at "The Truly Disadvantaged"', *Political Science Quarterly*, 106: 639–56

Wirth, L. (1938) 'Urbanism as a Way of Life', *American Journal of Sociology*, 44(1): 1–24

Wodz, K. (1994) *Transformation of Old Industrial Regions as a Sociological Problem* (Katowice: Silesian University Press)

Wodz, K. (ed.) (1995) *Regional Identity: Regional Consciousness* (Katowice: Silesian University Press)

Wolfe, T. (1990) *Bonfire of the Vanities* (London: Picador)

Wolfe, T. (1999) *A Man in Full* (London: Picador)

Wu, W. (1999) 'City Profile: Shanghai', *Cities*, 16(3): 207–16

Wyatt, R. (1996) 'Guest Editorial', *Environment and Planning B* (*Planning and Design*), 23: 639–54

Wynne, D. and O'Connor, J. (1998) 'Consumption and the Postmodern City', *Urban Studies*, 35(5/6): 841–64

Zukin, S. (1988) *Loft Living* (New York: Radius)

Zukin, S. (1995) *The Culture of Cities* (Oxford: Blackwell)

Zukin, S. (1996) 'Space and Symbols in an Age of Decline', in A. D. King (ed.) *Global Cities* (London Routledge)

Zukin, S. (1998) 'Urban Lifestyles: Diversity and Standardization in Spaces of Consumption', *Urban Studies*, 35(5/6): 825–39

Index